THE ECONOMIC HISTORY OF COLONIALISM

Leigh Gardner and Tirthankar Roy

BRISTOL
UNIVERSITY
PRESS

First published in Great Britain in 2020 by

Bristol University Press
1-9 Old Park Hill
Bristol
BS2 8BB
UK
t: +44 (0)117 954 5940
www.bristoluniversitypress.co.uk

British Library Cataloguing in Publication Data
A catalogue record for this book is available from the British Library

ISBN 978-1-5292-0763-7 (hardback)
ISBN 978-1-5292-0764-4 (paperback)
ISBN 978-1-5292-0765-1 (ePDF)
ISBN 978-1-5292-0766-8 (ePub)

Cover design by blu inc
Front cover image: Alamy/Granger Historical Picture Archive

Printed and bound by CPI Group (UK) Ltd, Croydon, CR0 4YY

Map 1: Asia, 1914

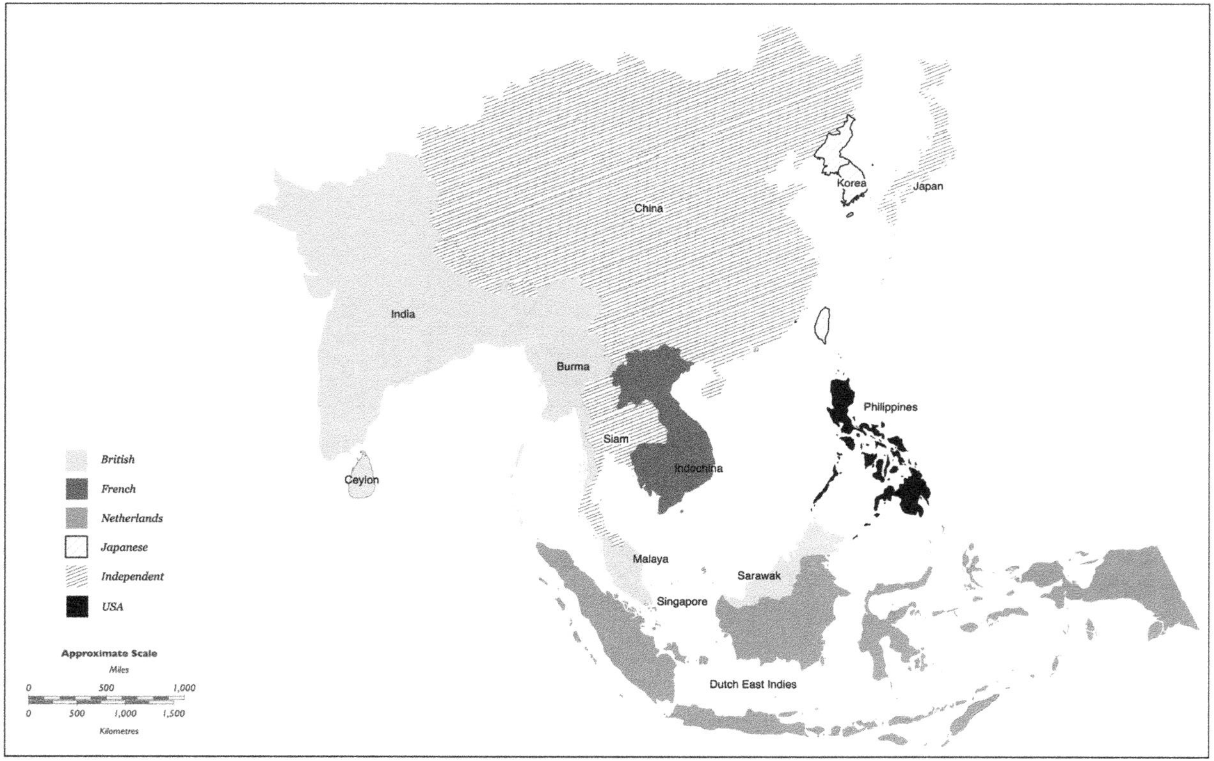

British	
French	
Netherlands	
Japanese	
Independent	
USA	

Japan

Korea

China

India

Ceylon

Burma

Siam

Indochina

Malaya

Singapore

Sarawak

Dutch East Indies

Philippines

Approximate Scale

Miles

0   500   1,000

0   500   1,000   1,500

Kilometres

Map 2: India, 1939

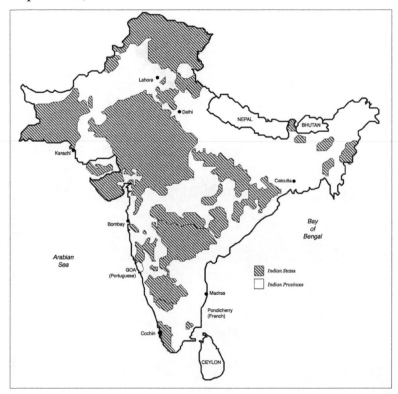

Map 3: Africa, 1914

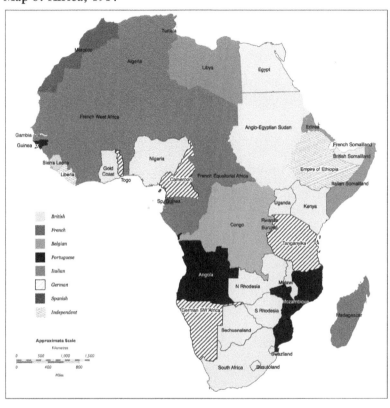

Map 3: Africa, 1914

Contents

List of Figures, Tables and Boxes

Figures

Tables

Boxes

Glossary

People, events and places

Alexandre de Rhodes (1591–1660) Jesuit missionary in Vietnam, Macau and Persia. Building on efforts by his predecessors, de Rhodes established a church in Vietnam. A linguist and a lexicographer, his work created a knowledge base on Southeast Asia for the Europeans and also influenced Vietnamese culture.

Atlantic Slave Trade (c.1500–c.1870) Refers to the export of enslaved Africans from the Atlantic coast of West Africa. The trade began slowly during the 16th century after the arrival of Portuguese merchants on the coast. They were soon joined by merchants and firms from other European countries, who traded a variety of goods for enslaved men and women. The volume of the trade reached its peak in the 18th century, and declined gradually after a number of European countries abolished the trade in the early 19th century.

Berlin Conference (1884–85) Called by the first Chancellor of Germany, Otto von Bismarck, the conference in Berlin became an occasion to discuss division of territories in West Africa. Fourteen countries, which had a presence in the coastal areas and little presence in the interior, took part in it.

Cecil Rhodes (1853–1902) British businessman in southern Africa, and prime minister of the Cape Colony (1890–96). Although successful and far-sighted in his mining enterprises, Rhodes' political legacy is controversial for a variety of reasons, including for his role as a facilitator of settler rule in southern Africa.

Central African Federation (1953–63)   Also known as the Federation of Rhodesia and Nyasaland. Short-lived union of Northern Rhodesia (now Zambia), Southern Rhodesia (now Zimbabwe) and Nyasaland (now Malawi). It was controversial, particularly among the African majority who believed it would extend racially discriminatory policies from Southern Rhodesia to the other two territories. After its collapse, Northern Rhodesia and Nyasaland became independent from Britain. Southern Rhodesia issued a unilateral declaration of independence in 1965, and remained under white minority rule until 1979.

CFA franc   French colonial currency created in 1945, and retained by many (though not all) formerly French colonies in Africa after independence, when the name was changed from Colonies Françaises d'Afrique to Communauté Financière Africaine. The CFA franc zone comprises two currency unions in West Africa and Central Africa. The CFA franc was initially issued at a fixed rate with the French franc, and is now fixed to the euro.

David Livingstone (1813–73)   Scottish missionary, doctor and anti-slavery campaigner; his explorations in Central Africa facilitated further European expeditions in the region.

East India Company, British   Founded in 1600 by London merchants, bankers and shipping magnates, and with a Crown monopoly to trade in the Indian Ocean region, the Company was among the richest business firms in the world during much of its career. From the mid-17th century, its field of operation moved mainly towards India. The Company began to politically control a part of India from 1757–65, and was in possession of an empire by 1858, when the Crown took over the rule of India. The Company formally continued for a few more years, without business to conduct.

East India Company, Dutch	Started in 1602 by the amalgamation of several trading firms to trade in Asia. In the 17th century, the Company was the largest among the European trading firms in Asia, especially in Coromandel and Malabar (India), Java, Japan, Taiwan, Malacca (Malaya) and Ceylon. In the mid-18th century, the Company concentrated mainly on Southeast Asia. In 1800, the Batavian Republic created after the French Revolution took over the bankrupt Company's assets and debts.
East India Company, French	Created in 1660 with the amalgamation of three trading firms and a royal charter, the Company was taken over by the king in 1769 and liquidated in 1794. In the 18th century, the Company had established ports in the Indian Ocean islands and the Indian seaboard, and fought wars with the British in India.
H.M. Stanley (1841–1904)	Welsh journalist and explorer in equatorial Africa. Stanley's knowledge of the region facilitated organized attempts to control and exploit territories, most famously Leopold II's enterprise in the Congo.
Henri Duveyrier (1840–92)	French explorer whose accounts of the Sahara contained valuable geographical information that helped later visitors in the region.
Indian Mutiny (1857–58)	A mutiny by infantry soldiers of the East India Company army, which later turned into a civilian rebellion against British rule in India. It was confined to a few districts in northern and central India, but threatened to engulf all of British India. The rebellion failed, among other reasons because the rebels could not form a viable government in the areas it gained control over, and many Indian business interests did not join the rebels, so that the port cities remained peaceful.
J.A. Hobson (1858–1940)	English economist best known for publishing *Imperialism: A Study* in 1902. The book argued that imperialism was the result of capitalist elites seeking

profitable outlets for investment abroad when productive capacity increased faster than demand for the goods they produced. Imperial expansion served their interests, and not those of the majority.

Kwame Nkrumah (1912–72)   Nationalist leader in the Gold Coast, Nkrumah founded the Convention People's Party in 1949 and went on to become first prime minister and then president of independent Ghana. As president, he was a strong proponent of both socialist-inspired state-led development and pan-Africanism. He was ousted from power in 1966.

Leopold II, King (1835–1909, reign 1865–1909)   King of Belgium, founded and controlled the Congo Free State from 1885 until the Belgian state's takeover of Congo in 1908. The Congo Free State was mainly a business enterprise for Leopold II, one that became controversial for the brutal methods applied to procure resources.

Mau Mau Uprising (1952–60)   A conflict between members of a secret society known as Mau Mau and British colonial authorities in Kenya. It was triggered by both growing nationalist pressure as well as tensions within Kikuyu communities over the distribution of land and other resources. British counter-insurgency campaigns involved the widespread imprisonment and sometimes torture of those suspected of being Mau Mau.

Ottoman Empire   Begun as a small frontier state in the 14th century, the empire emerged in the 16th century with territorial expansion in Anatolia, the Balkans and the Arab lands. When the Europeans started trading in the Indian Ocean, the empire controlled the overland trading routes between Europe and Asia. Wars in the 17th and 18th centuries weakened the state. European inroads into North Africa and West Asia in the 19th century derived partly from the challenges the Ottoman Empire faced.

Robert Clive (1725–74) — East India Company officer turned statesman, Clive played a leading role in two episodes that consolidated the Company's political power in India: the Carnatic Wars (1746–63), and the wars with the Nawab of Bengal (1757–64). Clive's victory on these occasions put an end to French territorial ambitions in India.

Savorgnan de Brazza (1852–1905) — Italian-French explorer and anti-slavery campaigner. Brazza's travels and diplomacy facilitated a French colonial empire in equatorial Africa.

Scramble for Africa — Term used to describe the rapid acquisition of territory in sub-Saharan Africa by European colonizers in the late 19th century. Explanations for why European claims of territory expanded so quickly vary, but it was likely linked to both competition between European powers and political instability in much of 19th-century Africa. In popular histories, this is often associated with the Berlin Conference (1884–85), but this association is somewhat misleading.

Settlers — Often used to refer to Europeans from colonizing countries who relocated to colonies on a permanent basis, and distinguished from government officials or businessmen whose residence was often temporary. However, large numbers of people relocating within empires were not necessarily of European origin, and the term can be defined more broadly to reflect these movements.

Suez Canal — Waterway connecting the Mediterranean and Red Seas through the Isthmus of Suez in Egypt. The Canal opened in 1869 after ten years of construction work which relied on forced labour. It dramatically decreased the distance between Europe and Asia.

Thomas Baines (1820–75) — Artist and explorer in Southern Africa. Baines' paintings, sketches and writings provide insight into the region in the mid-19th century.

| **Western Design Plan (1655–66)** | English design to attack the Spanish West Indies, ending up with much loss of life, and the emergence of small English settlements, especially in Jamaica. |

Concepts

Cash crop	Term used to refer to agricultural produce intended for commercial sale rather than subsistence (home) consumption. Certain crops (for example, maize, groundnuts and palm oil) could be both consumed by the producer and marketed, while others (cocoa, coffee and tea) were primarily produced for export.
Columbian exchange	Alfred Crosby's term referring to transactions in flora, fauna, disease organisms, people, culture and knowledge between Europe and the New World in the two centuries after Columbus' arrival in the Americas.
Concession companies	A company granted exclusive rights over territory or some other resource in return for investment. In colonial contexts, concession companies were often expected to perform some government services in concession areas, including the collection of taxes and the creation of military and police forces. The granting of such concessions was a common method for imperial governments to extend their control or influence over a territory while reducing the costs of direct administration.
Conservation	Broadly defined efforts to preserve and protect environmental systems. The colonial period saw a considerable expansion of conservation efforts in response to the rapid expansion of agricultural production and other resource exploitation during the era of globalization in the late 19th and early 20th centuries. However, colonial conservation efforts were often influenced by unequal distributions of power and faced resistance when clashed with indigenous systems of resource management.

Currency unions   In most cases, a colony's currency would be firmly linked to the currency of the ruling country, to eliminate exchange rate risks and thus stabilize trade and remittances between the two. The practice in effect created a currency union among all countries within an empire. The union came under pressure when the pegged exchange rate had to change, which happened when the international gold standard ended. After formal rule ended in the mid-20th century, some unions survived for a while (see entry for CFA franc zone).

Drain theory   A term the Indian nationalists introduced (around 1900) to the vocabulary of anti-colonial movements, to refer to a systematic net outflow of money made by British India to Britain. Technically India's payment for services purchased in Britain, the outflow, the drain theorists claimed, represented a one-sided tribute without compensation.

Globalization   Economic history uses the term in two senses: an unprecedented rise in the measurable scale of trade, migration and cross-border investment; and a phase of relatively rapid growth in transactions between cultures including exchange of ideas, technologies, products and pathogens, commodities, capital and labour. The former process can be dated around 1850. The latter process began at least a century or more earlier.

Gold standard   Currency regime which dominated during the late 19th and early 20th centuries in which the value of currencies was backed by gold or other gold-backed currencies (known as the gold-exchange standard). The gold standard era was characterized by unprecedented growth in foreign investment. One effect of colonial currency regimes was to integrate colonized territories into the gold standard system.

Gross Domestic Product (GDP)   A measure of economic output widely used since the Second World War to measure and compare economic performance in countries. Commonly expressed in per capita terms (GDP per person) as a composite measure of living standards.

Human Development Index (HDI) Created by the United Nations Development Programme (UNDP) in 1990 to provide a broader measure of wellbeing than GDP per capita, HDI incorporates measures of health and education with measures of income. While the precise measures used vary by context, historical HDI data often includes measures of life expectancy (health) and literacy (education).

Indentured servitude A common method of facilitating the migration of labour from the early modern period, indentured workers bound themselves to particular employers for a limited period of time in exchange for the cost of passage. This included thousands of European migrants to the Americas, as well as Indian and Chinese labourers who migrated to various parts of the world under indenture contracts.

Indirect rule Refers to the practice of granting autonomy to territories within an empire. Universally, indirect rule involved conditions restricting the possession and use of arms, juridical autonomy and restrictions on movements of traded goods. However, the unit in question was sometimes a recreated political unit, and sometimes an existing kingdom, as in India.

Inequality Refers to the unequal distribution of resources, either between individuals in the same community or between communities. The colonial period saw rising inequality both within colonies, between, for example, individuals or regions which had better access to markets or education, and often also between colonized countries and their colonizers.

Imperial preference Preferential trade agreements between countries in the British Empire. The idea grew in popularity in Britain at the turn of the 20th century, and was widely applied in the 1920s.

Legal pluralism Refers to the operation of more than one legal system in a single country. This was a common feature of colonial governance, for two reasons. One was that as some colonies shifted from one colonizer to another, some laws were retained from the previous colonizer. A second, more common, reason was the codification of 'traditional' laws within systems of indirect rule.

Legitimate trade Phrase used in the 19th century and in subsequent historical research to refer to the transition in West Africa from the export of enslaved people to the export of forest products and agricultural produce (cash crops) over the course of that century. This marked a dramatic shift in the organization of West African economies, but there remain debates about the extent of social and political change.

Market integration The integration of two (or multiple) markets increases with the volume and frequency of trade between them. It is often measured through the convergence of prices; in integrated markets, prices for comparable goods will move together. The era of rapid globalization in the 19th and early 20th centuries saw the increasing integration of a diverse range of markets around the world.

New Institutional Economics (NIE) An area of economic thinking which emphasizes the importance of institutions in resolving potential market failures not addressed by standard neoclassical theory. Institutions can include both formal laws and more informal norms that reduce the potential for opportunism and facilitate economic exchange.

Opium In the 19th century, traded opium mainly came from British India, where the government collected a revenue from licensing its production. Opium went to China or ports (like Singapore and Hong Kong) controlled by the British on its way to China. In these ports, the authority collected a revenue by monopolizing the retail sale. In this way, opium sustained early-colonial British states in Asia, free trade and increased Britain's stake in China.

Plantation A large estate specialized in the production of cash crops. These were often owned by foreign companies and individuals, though colonies in both Asia and Africa also had substantial indigenous plantations. In histories of cash crop production in colonial contexts, systems of production plantation are often contrasted with those in which cash crops were produced mainly by smallholders.

Tariffs Taxes on goods imported or exported from a given country. In many countries (both colonized and independent), tariffs were an important source of government revenue during the 19th and early 20th centuries. During the interwar period, they were increasingly used to increase the relative price of goods from some places in order to give an advantage to others. Imperial preference, discussed in a previous Glossary entry, was one example.

World Systems Theory Created by sociologist Immanuel Wallerstein, this approach to historical study proposes the existence of a global economic system which favours the interest of some countries at the expense of others, building on the dependency theories of the 1970s. It has been criticized for leaving little room for individual agency in less-favoured regions.

Colonial and Indigenous Origins of Comparative Development

By the early 20th century, a small number of European states ruled not only the territory and people within their own boundaries but also a large share of the rest of the world. According to one calculation, Europeans conquered some 84 per cent of the world between 1492 and 1914, before losing the vast majority of these territories by 1960 (Hoffman 2015: 2). That same period saw a rapid and substantial divergence in per capita incomes between the poorest and wealthiest countries, with trade and industrialization bringing previously unknown levels of prosperity to some regions while others saw little sustained growth. Together, these two transformations have shaped the world today.

In broad terms, this book explores the link between them. The conquest and rule of so large a share of the world reflected imbalances in political, technological and military capacities which grew during the period of industrialization. It remains the subject of debates whether resources gained by European powers may have aided them in the process of industrialization, or whether empires diverted resources that might have been more profitably invested at home. For the colonies themselves, the impact of colonial interventions varied widely across space and time, which makes it difficult to sustain simplified narratives of resource extraction.

Discussions of the economic impact of colonial rule using a variety of theories and methods are now more than a century old, and can be roughly divided into three groups. In one, the range of different colonial experiences came as a result of European decisions and policies, which provided a solid foundation for economic development in some colonies but not in others. In the second, it was indigenous responses to European intervention which shaped colonial economies and the legacies of imperial rule. A third group might be described as a hybrid of these two, in which local geographic, economic and political circumstances determined both European policies and indigenous responses.

This chapter reviews these debates. It aims to provide a foundation for questions about the origins, experience and legacies of colonial rule, which are the focus of the rest of the book. It begins with a brief review of the historiography of empires and how it has changed over time, before presenting some broad evidence on the economic performance of colonies and empires. It then examines these three groups of scholarship in greater detail, and concludes by posing a further set of questions for understanding the economic history of colonialism and its legacies for the global economy which inform subsequent chapters.

Writing the history of empires

The study of colonialism has come in and out of fashion since the end of imperialism as an ongoing political system made it a subject of historical rather than contemporary study. In the middle of the 20th century, as empires were ending, the topic became rather unfashionable among a group of scholars determined to look either forward, to a modern world of nation states, or back, to the longer histories of Africa and Asia (Cooper 2005). Nigerian historian Jacob Ajayi (1968) observed that 'in any long-term historical view of African history, European rule becomes just another episode'. However, the failure of many (though not all) former colonies to converge on the levels of income and development enjoyed by the former colonizers has prompted a renewed turn towards colonialism as part of the explanation.

The first debates about the economics of imperialism were contemporary rather than historical. Colonial expansion was controversial, particularly in the era of 'modern' imperialism during the 19th and 20th centuries. This period can be distinguished from the imperialism of the early modern by the nature of the relationship between colonizer and colonized. In the earlier period, both the great land-based empires of Asia, as well as the initial overseas extensions of European countries, were primarily relations of tax and tribute. By the 19th century, however, the economic relationships between the industrialized or industrializing 'core' and a 'periphery' specializing in the production of primary exports had changed, and modern empires reflected the need to protect business interests (Tomlinson 1999).

At the same time, the rapid acquisition of territory in the 19th and 20th centuries coincided with the expansion of the franchise, which created new groups of stakeholders in the national budget. In this context, contestation over the distribution of state resources generated lively discussions about whether colonial expansion was likely to repay its costs to imperial treasuries. An editorial published in *The Economist* in response to the Ashanti uprising in 1900 claimed that

> Empire cannot be run 'on the cheap'. It entails to the country which enters on the path of imperial expansion a very large and increasing expenditure. Whether that expenditure is worth incurring for the sake of prospective gains is a question which the Government and the country ought to consider carefully before determining on an expansionist policy.[1]

Others went beyond the purely 'pounds and pence' approach adopted by *The Economist* to consider the ways in which empire both reflected and shaped the economic structures of the day. In Britain, critics like Richard Cobden and J.A. Hobson argued that empire actively undermined the growth prospects of colonizing countries to serve the narrower interests of political and financial elites by interfering with the distribution of resources. Others argued, to the contrary, that empire provided markets for imperial exports and that if Britain did not retain imperial rule, others would capture those markets instead (Cain 2010: 352–3). This was countered by the claim that Britain's economic and military supremacy was such that it did not need an empire to dominate overseas markets.

Colonial powers which lacked the same status could not make this same argument, and the need to compete against Britain played an important role in the same discussions happening in Paris, Brussels and Berlin. However, this should not suggest that empires enjoyed popular support. One account of French colonial expansion argued that 'from 1880 to 1930 a minority of die-hard colonialists acquired and occupied a large colonial empire on behalf of a non-committed majority of the French people' (Marseille 1984, quoted in Dormois and Crouzet 1998: 324). In Brussels, King Leopold II's colonization of what became the Congo Free State was sufficiently unpopular with Belgian politicians that Leopold initially took on the colony as a personal project, pledging to use only his own funds. The Belgian state was forced to take over governance of the Congo in 1908 only after Leopold's underestimate of the costs involved resulted in several loans from the Belgian governments and local atrocities in tax collection which drew international condemnation (Gardner 2013).

At the time, with the exception of notorious cases like that of the Belgian Congo, metropolitan discussions focused primarily on the interests of imperial states rather than on the colonies. As *The Economist* article put it, 'under ordinary circumstances we should probably pay little heed to the Ashanti difficulties; for, outside a limited commercial circle, few persons can be reasonably expected to pay much attention to that swampy and savage region.' However, some did consider the impact of colonial rule on the colonies themselves. Editorials published by Karl Marx in the *New York Daily Tribune*, for example, argued that British rule in India had undermined local industry. His conclusions did not necessarily reflect a consensus view, and others argued just as forcefully that colonialism had contributed to economic growth in the colonies. Allan McPhee, often credited as one of the pioneers of African economic history, argued in his *Economic Revolution in British West Africa* (1926) that European intervention was the source of economic growth in the region.

Voices from the colonies contributed to this debate in increasing numbers during the 20th century, often though not always as critics. In 1901, Dadabhai Naoroji began his *Poverty and Un-British Rule in India* by pointing out the benefits – potential and actual – to India of British rule before arguing that the form of colonial government at that time was undermining economic development in the sub-continent. Naoroji was one of the co-founders of the Indian National Congress, which would ultimately lead the fight for Indian independence in 1947. However, in his 1901 book, he imagined ways in which British rule could benefit both India and Britain. In fact, many of the groups initially formed to pressure the colonial state often did so with a view to addressing specific grievances or achieving greater recognition within the colonial system, without necessarily fighting initially for national independence (Gardner 2012: 224–5).

The gradual inclusion of the perspective of the colonized in imperial histories has been an important shift over time. In his survey of the historiography of the British Empire, A.P. Thornton (1999: 615) writes that

> imperial historians have a particular problem: whether to camp in comfort inside officialdom's lighted circle or go out into the areas of darkness – bush, outback, jungle, suburb – there to mix with the locals and rummage among what C. A. Bayly calls the records of Dustypore, if the termites

haven't got to them first. The decisions reached shape the history we have.

Those decisions, and consequently that history, have changed over time, such that as early as the 1960s and 1970s it was becoming less acceptable for researchers to complete work on imperial history solely using records produced in imperial capitals. Local archives painted a different picture of how colonial states worked than the formal policy pronouncements found in imperial archives. Instead, they highlighted what was often a messy system of colonial governance in which the actions of indigenous people as well as a range of others, including merchants and missionaries, became more important.

These records have also allowed for the study of a range of related questions on economic development over time which a lack of accessible written records made it difficult to answer (Fourie 2016). In particular, they have facilitated more quantitative approaches to longstanding questions about the link between colonialism and growth, for both colonizer and colonized. The next section uses this evidence to present an overview of long-run economic performance in both groups during the era of colonial rule. These data show the heterogeneous experiences of colonizer and colonized and suggest there is no neat narrative connecting colonial rule and economic growth.

Many colonies, many stories

One challenge in understanding the economic history of colonialism is understanding the variety of experiences of both colonizer and colonized over a period of nearly 500 years from 1492 until the collapse of the European empires in the 1960s. Stanley Engerman and Kenneth Sokoloff (2013: 75) write that 'one cannot fail to be impressed with how much of the globe – both in land area and population – had direct experience of being a colony'. Former colonies include a range of countries from Canada to the Democratic Republic of the Congo, from South Korea to Jamaica. The United States went from its own colonial beginnings to becoming a colonial power in its own right. Each had its own complex history of foreign rule, which took different shapes and influenced its development in various ways. Heldring and Robinson (2012: 2) put the problem as follows:

> it seems difficult to believe that in any plausible counter-factual Australia or the United States would today have

higher GDP per capita if they had not been colonized. At the same time, … it is difficult to believe that the income per capita of Botswana or Ghana would not be higher today had it not been colonized.

Complicating such counterfactuals is the fact that this was a period of rapid and substantial economic and technical change which transformed the lives and livelihoods of people in virtually every region of the world. Figure 1.1 gives long-run GDP data for a number

Figure 1.1: GDP per capita over the long run, 1500–1900

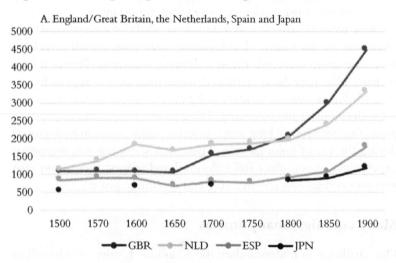

A. England/Great Britain, the Netherlands, Spain and Japan

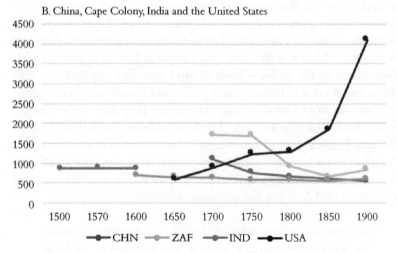

B. China, Cape Colony, India and the United States

Sources: Broadberry et al (2018); Fourie and van Zanden (2013); Bolt and van Zanden (2014).

of different countries, which include at various times both colonies and colonizers.

The first figure shows three European colonizers plus Japan, which was the first nation outside Europe or North America to industrialize and build its own empire in Asia during the interwar period. The second shows four countries that were colonized, either formally or informally, at some stage in the colonial period considered here. First, it shows that in 1500, the countries for which data are available were well above subsistence levels of income, in this metric defined as $400 a year (reflecting the World Bank's 1990 definition of poverty as $1 a day plus a small elite). In the 16th century, Chinese GDP per capita was similar in level to that of European countries, as was that of India and, to a lesser extent, Japan (Broadberry et al 2015; Broadberry et al 2018). The early modern period saw 'revolutions of imagination, taste and consumption' in many parts of the world (Bayly 2008: 5). England and the Netherlands broke away from the others during the 17th century while Spain, one of the earliest colonizers, saw its income stagnate until the late 19th century. Meanwhile, the Cape Colony, which was comprised of a comparatively affluent community of Dutch settlers in the early 18th century, suffered a decline through the late 18th and early 19th centuries. The same was true of China and India. The United States, another settler colony, had low levels of GDP per capita in the 17th century but this increased rapidly such that by 1900 it had eclipsed that of Great Britain.

Even this relatively basic overview challenges any simple narratives about colonization and economic development. Not all countries that were wealthy in the early modern period acquired overseas colonies – though China did expand its existing boundaries by conquering neighbouring regions. Further, not all colonizers industrialized early. Some colonies and former colonies were able to achieve high levels of income, suggesting that colonial rule in itself was not necessarily antithetical to growth, either in the first era of empires or the second. Arroyo Abad and van Zanden (2016) find that at least some Spanish colonies in Latin America enjoyed impressive rates of growth during the colonial period, with a few, like Mexico, achieving parity with Spain. The same is true for colonies in Asia and Africa in the 19th and 20th centuries.

For more recent periods it is possible to use measures which take a wider definition of living standards than GDP per capita. Figure 1.2 presents human development index (HDI) measures for countries in Africa and Asia through the colonial period.

Figure 1.2: Human Development Index in Asia and Africa, 1870–1960

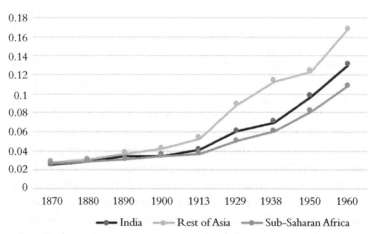

Source: Prados de la Escosura (2015).

HDI incorporates measures of education and life expectancy in addition to income to provide a more holistic view of people's standards of living. The figure shows that even under colonial rule, improvements in HDI were possible. This was partly linked to expansion in trade and export production. As Chapter 6 discusses in greater detail, encouraging such expansion was in the interests of both the colonial state as well as many indigenous producers. There were also at least some improvements in education and life expectancy, the latter through technological advances in medical care.

This does not, of course, mean that colonialism was not a violent and disruptive process. Broad measures like GDP per capita and HDI leave many questions unanswered about the distribution of any gains in income or education, and thus the significance of growth for most of the population. Despite the increased availability of data in recent decades, it remains difficult to construct detailed measures of living standards which take into account patterns of potentially unequal distribution. Measures of inequality under colonial rule remain restricted to a small number of countries, but virtually all show an increase. In their study of Botswana, Bolt and Hillbom (2016) find that inequality rose along with the growth of commercial cattle and beef exports from the 1920s. Using data on heights as a proxy for living standards, Alexander Moradi (2008) shows that while there were improvements in height in Kenya and Ghana during the colonial period, only some regions and ethnic groups seemed to benefit. Roy (2014) finds that regional inequality in India rose during parts of the colonial period. Inequality, whether between regions or individuals, had in some cases serious political consequences after independence, contributing to conflict between regions or groups perceived as having benefitted to different degrees from colonial governance.

The story of economic growth and development during the era of modern imperialism in the 19th and 20th centuries is thus a complex one, and how the two connect to one another has been debated since colonial rule was in place. But how can we explain the differences? Can the impact of colonial policies be distinguished from, for example, geographical features of the countries and regions being studied? How did these two interact? The answers to these questions are often linked to the issues of agency and power raised earlier. The next three sections review different approaches to this question, beginning with what might be called a 'Eurocentric' approach, which emphasizes the importance of Europeans and European policies in determining economic outcomes in the colonies.

European origins of comparative development

A focus on the importance of European governments and administrators in shaping the economies of their colonies characterized much early writing on empire. This was one of the reasons why the study of the history of empires languished in the decades after decolonization. Frederick Cooper (2005: 5) writes that 'in African history, my generation avoided colonial history for fear of being thought to do "white history"'.

This approach experienced a revival in the 2000s through new quantitative research investigating links between historical events and current gaps between wealthy and poor countries. Initially, this was a response to research in the 1980s and 1990s which placed the burden of explanation for the poverty of many former colonies on the bad policies adopted by post-independence governments. One example was what is often referred to as the 'Africa dummy' debate. In a landmark paper using a global sample of countries to identify the causes of growth, Barro (1991) observed that a dummy variable indicating whether a country was in Africa remained negative and significant even controlling for other factors thought to influence the rate of economic growth. In layman's terms, something about being in Africa seemed to be bad for growth even accounting for other known contributors to economic growth. Attempts to explain this result zeroed in on various policies adopted by African governments since independence, often linked to rent-seeking and protectionism

(Ndulu 2008). However, this left open the question of why so many African governments, which had a range of political systems and histories, adopted poor policies in the 30 years since independence (Englebert 2000b). Further, why had many Asian countries, which at independence had comparable levels of per capita income to much of Africa, adopted policies seemingly better able to promote economic development?

In response to these debates, economists turned to deeper historical causes for the wealth and poverty of different countries. In particular, they focused on differences not just in particular policies but to more fundamental issues of institutional structure, drawing inspiration from the New Institutional Economics (NIE) theories pioneered by Douglass North (1990), among others, which argued that economic behaviour is shaped by the 'rules of the game' in the societies in which people operate. The history of colonialism became part of this discussion by providing something like a natural experiment in which inherited institutions influenced the economic behaviour of people in each country and thus explain differences between them in levels of income even decades after the end of colonial rule. Perhaps the broadest statement of this argument appeared in the widely cited papers by Acemoglu et al (2001, 2002). Their aim was to identify 'the fundamental causes of the large differences in income per capita across countries' (Acemoglu et al 2001, 1369–70). They argue that 'different types of colonization policies … created different sets of institutions'. These they divide into two categories: 'extractive states', which provided little protection of property rights or checks and balances; and 'neo-Europes', which replicated European institutions.

In their theory, what determined the adoption of one set of institutions or the other was the mortality rate of settlers. Where settlers were likely to survive, they created institutions which resembled those they had left behind. Where mortality rates were high, however, it was more likely that colonial governments would create 'extractive' states. They argue that this relationship creates a source of exogenous variation which allows them to show that the different colonization strategies were the cause of different levels of development in the 1990s. Going further, a follow-up paper (Acemoglu et al 2002) argued that this same mechanism explains a 'reversal of fortune' in which regions of the world which were wealthier in 1500 wound up being poorer by 1990.

In both these papers, the definition of 'extractive states' and their alternative remains broad. Other work in this area is more precise in the institutions it highlights as significant. La Porta et al (2008) make similar arguments about the legacies of colonial institutions, but look specifically at the legal systems exported to the colonies through colonial rule. They find that common-law countries, which were primarily colonized by Britain, performed better on a variety of economic metrics than those with systems of Roman law, owing to stronger protections for corporate shareholders and creditors. In distinguishing between, primarily, British and French colonies, this paper joins a longer tradition arguing that there was something distinctive about the rule of different colonizers which shaped the experience and legacies of colonialism in their particular colonies (Feyrer and Sacerdote 2009; Bertocchi and Canova 2002).

Through their use of settler mortality as an instrument for the type of colonial institutions, Acemoglu, Johnson and Robinson (2001) place great emphasis on the role of European settlers in shaping colonial policies. However, beyond broad claims about institutions, they are not explicit about what Europeans actually did in the colonies. Easterly and Levine (2016) link the share of the European population during the colonial period to recent development outcomes, arguing that even small communities of settlers improved development outcomes through the transmission of human capital and technological knowledge.

Emphasis on European initiative as a key foundation for economic divergence between colonies is not restricted to states or settlers. Missionaries are also credited with important influences in the economic legacies of colonialism through their role in the provision of education. As Chapter 6 discusses in greater detail, colonial government investments in education were minimal until the very end of the colonial period. Thus only a relatively small share of colonized people was able to access education. However, those who did so generally did it through mission schools (sometimes subsidized), in which the vast majority of students were enrolled (Frankema 2012). There was an uneven distribution of mission schools both between and within colonies, which has been used to explain later gaps in levels of human capital (Nunn 2014) and the structure of political institutions (Woodberry 2012).

Such broad narratives are always vulnerable to critiques about how these stories fit with the particularities of specific times and places. One source of criticism of much of this work is the data used in the quantitative analysis. Construction of such global datasets inevitably requires reliance on assumptions and proxies to fill gaps in the historical record. Albouy (2012), for example, challenges the settler mortality data used by Acemoglu, Johnson and Robinson (2001). In the legal origins literature, addressed in more detail in Chapter 5, several papers have argued that the division between common law and Roman law colonies made by La Porta et al (2008) is too neat, and does not take into account the importance of hybrid legal systems in places colonized by more than one European power, or the continued role of indigenous institutions (Klerman et al 2011). Historians have also criticized the empirical structure of this work, which links historical events or data to current levels of income or other measures without much consideration of what comes in between. Historians have tagged this with various labels, from 'leapfrogging legacies' (Cooper 2005) to 'compression of history' (Austin 2008).

In none of this work are indigenous institutions or responses to colonial rule considered in much detail. Rather, it treats precolonial regions largely as clean slates on which to project the 'modernizing' potential of colonial rule. This runs counter to the overall tendency in the writing of imperial history in recent decades to de-emphasize the role of European states and instead portray colonial rule as a series of interactions between colonial states, indigenous actors and various other stakeholders, including settlers, merchants and missionaries.

Indigenous origins of comparative development

The validity of claims about the legacies of European rule depends at least partly on assumptions about the capacity of the colonial state and related European actors to implement policies of their choosing. However, such assumptions can be challenged on two fronts. The first is the documented history of indigenous responses to the economic change. Elites in what became European colonies were not oblivious to the opportunities offered by global economic trends. Their responses to these opportunities were independent of the demands of the colonial state but often provided the trade on which the finances of colonial states depended. One example is the introduction of cocoa in West Africa, which would become the leading export for the British Gold Coast, French Cote d'Ivoire and to a lesser extent British Nigeria. Cacao trees are indigenous to the Americas, not Africa, and it was Nigerian merchants who first brought it to the mainland (Hopkins 1978). The importance of indigenous elites and producers in shaping colonial economies was such that Bayly (2008: 8) asks 'how far were there any truly "colonial" origins of Indian development?'

A second objection to Eurocentric approaches to empire is that empirical research on the history of colonial governance has consistently shown that in many parts of the world, the comparative advantage that colonial states had in military capability did not necessarily translate into the capacity to get things done once the process of conquest was complete. Perkins (1981: xi) writes that the 'imbalance of military and economic power may be offset by differing intensities of motivation'. There is considerable evidence, both anecdotal and quantitative, that the limited enthusiasm for colonial expansion in metropolitan states limited both the motivation and capacity of colonial governments. Former colonial officer turned historian Anthony Kirk Greene (1980) published some basic statistics on the number of European colonial officials in the British Empire. While he documented various periods of expansion and contraction in the size of the colonial service, the overall impression from the numbers is of a skeletal administration for governing impossibly large territories and population – to the point that it might appear to be 'a huge game of white man's bluff', which was able to survive through a combination of military power and, crucially, cooperation with indigenous institutions and elites. Peter Richens (2009) extended and elaborated this analysis for Africa, applying it to the literature on colonial legacies, which, he argues, 'overestimates the capacity of the colonial state', and the extent to which it relied on strategies of indirect rule and the integration of indigenous institutions and hierarchies for its survival.

These two arguments are both linked to the question of colonial legacies, and in particular the extent to which colonial institutions and economies were really shaped by the relatively skeletal European presence. Bayly (2008) stresses the importance of an indigenous commercial class in explaining comparative economic development, whether in Japan or in India. At the same time, comparatively weak colonial states relied on these same elites to maintain their rule. John Iliffe (2007: 193) describes colonial states before 1914 in Africa as 'mere skeletons fleshed out and vitalized by African political forces'. Historian David Killingray jokes that the ideal exam question for a course on African colonialism might be: 'During colonial rule, Africa was mainly governed by Africans. Discuss' (Institute of Commonwealth Studies 2013).

Building on these arguments, a parallel literature has argued that it was not the comparatively weak European institutions that shaped development outcomes, but rather the indigenous institutions to which people turned to resolve disputes and enforce their rights in the absence of a strong central authority. For India, Iyer (2010) compares areas in India which were under direct British rule with those under indirect rule, and finds that provision of roads, schools and health centres was more generous in the latter.

From a quantitative perspective, the role of indigenous institutions is often more difficult to investigate than national institutions owing to limits in the documentary record of indigenous states and businesses in many colonies. However, proxies can be found in anthropological research. A key measure of indigenous institutional capacity is an index of what is referred to as 'jurisdictional hierarchy', or the number of political units above the village level, compiled by George Murdock (1967). This is interpreted as a measure of state centralization in indigenous communities, which can then be associated with more recent development outcomes. In general, more 'centralized' indigenous states are associated with higher levels of contemporary income (Michalopoulos and Papaioannou 2013; Bandyopadhyay and Green 2016).

The anthropological data used as a measure of 'precolonial' centralization is potentially questionable. For Africa in particular, the period of observation of the societies included in the Murdock Atlas starts in 1830 at the earliest, with the 1920s as the most common decade of observation (Henderson and Whatley 2014). By the earliest point of observation, therefore, African states had undergone numerous upheavals linked to globalization and the slow end of the slave trade. The 19th century saw migrations, conflicts and political instability in various forms through much of the sub-Saharan region (Iliffe 2007: 164–92).

All of these papers explain their findings with reference to systems of indirect rule. However, 'indirect rule' is a phrase with many meanings. The ways in which indigenous institutions were incorporated into the colonial state ranged from the Indian princely states or the Kabaka of Buganda, who governed with little intervention from colonial officials, to indigenous appointees with little power outside their association with the colonial government. One example of the latter was the 'warrant chiefs' of colonial Nigeria, who were so called because the only authority they had came from a colonial 'warrant'. In this case there were also differences between colonial powers in the extent to which they prized the apparent legitimacy of indigenous rulers. Britain, in general, paid more attention to establishing this than the French, though this varied and they did not always get it right.

These debates aside, what this literature establishes is that the European presence in most colonies was minimal and, despite advantages in terms of technology and coercive capacity, often under-resourced. This leaves little room for the kinds of top-down explanations for divergences in economic development presented in the previous section. As Bayly

(2008: 405) puts it, 'historians and development specialists need to understand the actual mechanisms by which apparently benign European institutions were transformed and appropriated – or, for that matter, rejected – by people of non-European societies in the light of their own persisting social organization and aspirations'.

Local conditions and decisions

A third category of explanations for differences in colonial administration, and thus differences in economic paths after independence combines the first two approaches, in which local circumstances – particularly but not exclusively geographical and environmental – influenced the decisions that both colonial administrators and indigenous actors made. The emphasis in this area of work is often on the varying geographic resources or endowments of what were a far-flung and diverse set of colonies, and the argument is that different types of colonial institutions emerged in response to the incentives created by these resources. This was not necessarily the result of deliberate decision-making by European governments, but rather the outcome (sometimes unintended) of a series of decisions made by a range of actors, both European and indigenous.

Perhaps the best example of this work are the theories of Stanley Engerman and Kenneth Sokoloff (2013), who use this approach to try to explain an apparent reversal of fortune in the Americas. In the early modern period, the colonies of South America and the Caribbean seemed to contemporary observers significantly better off than those of North America. However, in the long run, it was the latter that achieved sustained economic growth and ultimately acquired colonies of its own. They argue that the climate and soils of the southern colonies, along with the survival of larger indigenous populations, favoured the production of crops by large slave plantations. This economic structure led to high levels of inequality during the colonial period, which ultimately underpinned policies aimed at maintaining those levels of inequality, for example limited investment in public schooling. In much of North America, where the biogeography favoured relatively small mixed farms, levels of inequality were low, and governments adopted more growth-promoting policies later on.

Engerman and Sokoloff (2013: 66–7) give as one of their motivations for this study their doubts about what they call 'a traditional and popular explanation' for the divergence between North and South America which 'credits the success of the North American economies to the superiority of English institutional heritage, or to the better fit of Protestant beliefs with market institutions'. However, they argue that this explanation neglects 'the fact that various British colonies of the new world evolved quite distinct societies and sets of institutions, despite beginning with roughly the same legal and cultural background'.

Other contributions also challenge the idea that French or Belgian colonial rule differed, for example, from British or Spanish. Rather, all colonizers adapted their policies to the circumstances they faced in each place. Ewout Frankema and Marlous van Waijenburg (2014) use the structure of tax systems in British and French colonies in Africa to compare the two strategies of governance, and find more systematic differences between the coastal and inland colonies of both colonizers rather than a specifically French or British 'blueprint', with coastal colonies relying more heavily on the taxation of imports while inland colonies developed systems of direct taxation. Chapter 4 returns to the use of tax systems as a way of understanding colonial institutions.

The notion that economic resources, rather than some ex-ante policy decisions, shaped colonial strategies is not new. Samir Amin (1973) proposed what remains a widely used classification of African colonies based largely on their economic resources and colonial strategies to develop them. 'Labour reserve' colonies were those in which foreign enterprises, from capital-intensive mines to plantations to settler farms, required large supplies of indigenous labour. A second category comprised those colonies without minerals or large settler populations, where colonial policies and economies were oriented towards the export trade. The third category, which Amin referred to as 'Africa of the concessionary companies', included colonies with limited export production and low population densities where the responsibilities of governance were effectively outsourced to private concession companies in exchange for various monopoly rights. Each of these styles of colonial rule, he argued, had different legacies for post-independence states.

This approach, which considers the dynamic relationship between local conditions and colonial policies, can also offer a different perspective on some of the issues raised in the previous two sections. For example, the presence of settlers was not necessarily the result of a one-off decision at the beginning of colonial rule. Rather, it was shaped by an ongoing negotiation between potential settlers, indigenous people and the colonial state (Frankema et al 2016). Similarly, mission locations shifted over the course of the colonial period based on both economic conditions on the ground and African demand for their services (Jedwab et al 2019). Systems of indirect rule and parallel legal systems did not preserve indigenous institutions in whatever form they were first observed by colonial authorities. Rather, they also changed over time, as indigenous elites reacted to the incentives offered through cooperation, or not, with colonial governments. Bolt and Gardner (2020) use new data on the capacity of 'Native Authorities' in British Africa to show that their capacities were not merely the result of early levels of centralization as observed in anthropological records, but rather could emerge during the course of the colonial period.

Finally, and perhaps more importantly, is the link between these interactions and the kinds of geographic conditions central to Engerman and Sokoloff. John Tosh (1980) argues that the extent to which West African producers could respond to new demand for agricultural and forest products depended to a significant degree on geography, particularly proximity to export hubs and the length of the growing season which influenced opportunities to produce for export without reducing food supplies. Geographic endowments were also influential in structuring the indigenous institutions and capacities (Fenske 2014). Roy (2014) finds that variation in geographic resources accounts for much of the variation in economic performance which Iyer (2010) attributes to institutions in her comparison of direct and indirect rule.

According to work in this area, economic divergences between colonies and former colonies are difficult to attribute to the actions of one set of actors alone. Rather, colonial institutions across the colonial period represented the outcome of a dynamic process by which both indigenous actors and Europeans responded to the constraints and opportunities of local environments. Most colonial economies depended heavily on the export of a few commodities in which that particular location specialized. Thus the methods of production of those commodities, whether small farms or plantations or large capital-intensive mines, had important implications for who held power and which institutions mattered.

Conclusion

The study of colonialism and its links with the emergence of large gaps between countries has experienced a revival after several decades of relative neglect. The overall aim of this chapter is to demonstrate the complexity of the question. New data on the economic performance of countries in a variety of regions over time suggests there is no neat linear narrative connecting colonial rule and economic change. Differences in European policies, indigenous institutions, or geography and climate do not fully explain why the experience and legacies of colonial rule differed so dramatically between countries. The aim of the book is to integrate quantitative and qualitative research to provide a broader foundation for understanding the economic impact of colonial rule, and generate a dialogue between scholars working in these two fields.

Subsequent chapters address themes and questions raised here in greater detail. What explains the rise of 'modern' European empires and how does this link to the broader economic changes of the period related to industrialization, globalization, and changing business structures (Chapters 2, 3 and 9)? How did European governments motivate and justify their decisions during the colonial period and who gained and lost from their policies (Chapters 4 and 5)? What determined the structure of colonial states and the ways they reacted to a rapidly changing world (Chapters 6 and 7)? How and why did empires end (Chapter 10)?

Note

[1] 'Responsibilities of empire', *The Economist*, 16 June 1900, p. 843.

2

Origins of Colonialism:
Is There One Story?

Most general accounts of the origin of colonialism since the 18th century consider the motives that drove the Europeans to seek opportunities abroad and the means with which they served these motives. Written from the perspective of European societies, and with an eye to the actions of people who seemed to gain money and power from having foreign territories, these accounts do suggest definite patterns of origin.

And yet, when we look towards Asia or Africa, it is hard to see any pattern at all. Some colonies started from trading enterprises, while others were a result of conquest. Some started as occupation of territories by settlers and groups and the state became involved later. Writing in 1883, the British writer John Seely remarked, 'we seem, as it were, to have conquered half the world in a fit of absence of mind' (1914: 10). But the 'scramble for Africa' was anything but an absent-minded act. Instead, it was the endpoint of a long process of negotiation over borders and territorial control.

Can there be a general theory of the origin of colonialism at all? This chapter argues that there can be a general story, but it needs to integrate Europe's expansion with conditions in those regions that were later colonized. These varied so much that not only the process of colonization but also the states that emerged from the process could differ a great deal. The combination of global or expansionist forces and local political and economic conditions gave rise to four distinct pathways of origin: the mainly political or militaristic pathway (for example Algeria in the early 19th century); the mainly commercial one (in India from the late 18th century, and Indonesia and the West African seaboard in the 19th); the inland-settler pattern (southern Africa from the 17th century, East Africa in the 19th); and the island-settler pattern (plantation societies of the Atlantic and the Pacific Oceans). The next section extends the discussion on patterns of origin, and the rest of the chapter follows that with a review of the major regional experiences.

Patterns of origin

Until about 30 years ago, standard works in 'imperial history' explained the origin of colonial empires by focusing on British or French society in the 18th and 19th centuries. The phrase 'European expansion', first used by Seely, or 'European world economy' popularized by the World Systems school, implied that for a sufficient explanation for the origin of empires we only need to study Europe's social and political history.[1]

This approach has the advantage that it makes a universal theory of the origin of imperialism possible. All we need to do for that purpose is to study the European empire-builders, their motivations and their means. If we follow this line, the origin of empires becomes a mainly political and cultural story. This story is not entirely wrong. The earliest and some of the latest colonial acquisitions in Africa were politically engineered. France invaded Algeria in the 1830s and the 1840s to restore its reputation lost in the Napoleonic wars. Forty years later, the carving up of Africa by British, French, German and Italian powers was driven by mutual distrust and fear. Culturally speaking, 19th century liberalism in Britain assumed that the western civilization had a mission to improve the lives of the backward Africans and moribund Indians, a view that made denial of liberty a good deed.

The stylized origin story that starts from Europe fails to persuade, for three reasons. First, notwithstanding these two episodes that bookend the colonization of Africa, there was enormous diversity in the time and the way empires emerged. The Europeans who went to the tropical world as merchants or missionaries in the 18th century did not carry a vision of an empire nor, as far as we can know, the desire for one. Those who did plan to acquire and govern lands appeared much later and were a minority among those who went abroad. The expansionist European came in many forms, from concession-hunting companies to adventurers, missionaries, settlers, explorers, scientists and politicians in London, Paris or Berlin. Their actions do not add up to one story. The companies, politicians, missionaries, settlers and traders rarely acted together or shared the same stake in the empire. Further, the very process of state-making created new conflicts among these groups.

Second, whereas politics explains the possibility of an empire, it does not explain the motive. The emergence of empires roughly coincided with the enormous growth of trade, investment and migration, the like of which the world had not seen before. Surely, profits from trade related to political expansion. This is the central message of Marxist theories of imperialism, though they do not explain the chain of causality – whether capitalism made colonialism or colonialism made capitalism very well. Still, the economic motivations must be acknowledged. By the end of the 19th century, colonization was firmly driven by the desire to keep commerce going, settle European farmers in the African highlands, and extract resources like rubber. In the pursuit of the two latter aims, violence and coercion were routinely used. But often these attractions of colonies revealed themselves after the colonization process had begun.

Third, neither the political account of the European expansion nor the Marxist economic account of European expansion says anything about the conditions in the regions that were colonized. In fact, the actions of the expansionist European were contingent on conditions in Asia and Africa in the 19th century, which made these fertile grounds for new political formations to emerge. The great empires of Asia – the Ottoman, the Persian, the Mughal and the Chinese – were going through a bad time in the 18th century. The abolition of slavery and the decline of the Atlantic slave trade had weakened several inland states in West Africa that had built a stake in the trade (see Box 2.1). As their decline progressed, the British and the French built power bases in mutual rivalry along the West African seaboard, making opportunistic use of that internal disarray. In North and East Africa, in Sudan, Egypt and Zanzibar, the slave trade continued well into the end of the 19th century. The level of brutality and violence, if not the scale, in the Arab-Islamic slave trade was as bad as the Atlantic counterpart. So many states and powerful actors had a stake in the slave trade that British efforts to suppress it created new conflicts and interstate rivalry. In turn, these very conflicts allowed for colonial states to emerge in parts of the East African coast and in Sudan. British motivations were as much commercial and political as humanitarian, for by then the Suez Canal (1869) had emerged as the lifeline of British trade. In Tunisia and Egypt, bankrupt governments threatened European investments, creating a justification for occupation.

Collaboration and alliances were again vital to the emergence of colonial states. Africa and Asia were neither peaceful nor egalitarian societies before the European rules began. Brutal oppression, slavery and notions of racial superiority and inferiority were ingrained in

Box 2.1: Slavery and colonialism

The Atlantic slave trade reached its peak in terms of numbers of slaves taken from Africa during the late 18th century, before declining slowly over the next century. Abolition by Britain and a number of European countries in the early 19th century checked, but did not stop, the trade, and exports continued to parts of the Americas until around 1880. Other African slave trades, including the trans-Saharan and Indian Ocean trades, also continued through the 19th century.

The relationship between the slave trades and the beginning of European colonialism in Africa is complex. In popular writing, the two are often conflated. However, the lines connecting the two are both indirect and frequently debated by historians.

The slave trades themselves did not in most cases require territorial conquest by Europeans. Rather, European merchants and companies remained on ships and in coastal forts. For the supply of slaves from the interior, they depended on African rulers, merchants and other intermediaries. By the time Europeans began to draw the colonial boundaries of Africa in the 1880s and 1890s, the trade in slaves had been displaced by the so-called 'legitimate' trade in agricultural products like palm oil and groundnuts.

This chronological separation does not mean the two were not related. Slavery and other forms of forced labour continued to be used in the production of export crops, and, while European rhetoric justifying colonial conquest often referred to abolition, colonial governments did little to enforce such rules and often depended on forced labour themselves in public works projects and staffing colonial administrations.

In his 1973 classic *Economic History of West Africa*, A.G. Hopkins proposed that the end of the slave trade resulted in a 'crisis of adaptation' among African states dependent on revenue from slave exports, while at the same time cash crop exports provided a new source of social mobility for those looking to challenge traditional elite structures. According to this argument, these two trends led to political instability in the region. Europeans were drawn into intra-African conflicts as useful allies and ultimately faced limited opposition in the process of colonial conquest.

This interpretation, particularly the extent to which African states really faced a crisis due to the end of the slave trade and the rise of cash crop exports, has been disputed. However, it is clear that the 19th century was a century of considerable political upheaval in West Africa, which, along with the development of malaria prophylaxis and a growing advantage in military technology, facilitated the rapid expansion of European territorial claims.

Further reading

A.G. Hopkins (1973) *Economic History of West Africa*, London: Longman.

Robin Law (2009) 'Introduction', *From Slave Trade to "Legitimate" Commerce: The Commercial Transition in Nineteenth-Century West Africa*, Cambridge: Cambridge University Press, pp 1–34.

these societies. Fierce contests for fiscal resources generated local warfare. The Europeans found no shortage of allies in this divided landscape. Further, nomadic and small polities in the arid tropics had limited financial resources with which to fight wars or build armies and were often happy to befriend Europeans or retreat before their advances. Much of the Sahara fell into European hands in this way without serious contests. When these political actors faced each other, it was usually in the interest of the weaker party to offer concessions and treaties. That was as common a pathway to colonization as was warfare and violence.[2]

The prehistory of maritime trade also shaped local conditions. The world's oceans saw a trade boom in the 18th century. While Europeans dominated sea trade, their business could not exist without the collaboration of the indigenous merchants who dominated overland and coastal trades. From the indigenous merchants' point of view, their dominance in the seas made the Europeans attractive partners.

A growing imbalance between land-based polities and sea-based ones explains to some extent the emergence of empires in India, Indonesia and West Africa. While the sea was of marginal interest to the states and empires of Asia and Africa, Europeans controlled seaborne trade, which was a cheaper mode of trade and therefore grew faster. 'Hee that commaunds the sea,' said Walter Raleigh, 'commaunds the trade.' Andre Gunder Frank and others claimed that presence in several continents gave the Europeans access to a universal means of exchange: silver. Even without the silver factor, maritime power could make a difference. Following a well-known economic principle, if maritime trade could grow faster because it was cheaper to conduct, it could potentially draw resources away from other activities, and undermine the political and economic capacities of inland states.[3] In this way, European commercial expansion might organically lead to sovereignty over the worlds that they traded with.

Why were the Europeans successful in this game? Many formidable land-based powers resisted colonization, from the Maratha in the 18th century to the Zulu in the 19th. Why did they fail? From the 18th century, imbalances emerged between the colonizing and the colonized regions on several points. One of these was access to cheap finance. State building and trading in a hostile world were expensive enterprises, and Europeans could invest more money into them. As Immanuel Wallerstein (1979) observed, the emergence of East India companies with global ambitions from London and Amsterdam in the 17th century was not an accident. These cities had deeper financial markets than most cities of the time and could sustain the heavy investment in defence and shipping that dominance in international trade entailed. Any state (or even a firm) that had even an indirect link with the money markets of London or Amsterdam was more capable of sustaining military campaigns than its potential rivals.

A second and related source of imbalance was the capacities of European and indigenous actors to create viable states. Owing to their situation in the semi-arid tropics or equatorial lands, states in Asia and Africa were generally poor. They earned little money by taxing resource-poor agriculture. Conflicts made them even poorer. The British state could find financial backers both to advance imperial expansion and to run states. Europeans, and later their colonial territories that received direct or indirect help from the parent states, were better off in this respect.

While the profit motive or resettlement motive might explain the drive to expand, and politics explain the prospect of acquiring territories with little bloodshed – the ideal model – the means to acquire colonies could still be variable. Economists, especially institutional economic historians, tend to believe that the Europeans commanded some superior means to establish rules, like secure property rights or the joint-stock company. Trade historians similarly point at useful knowledge like maps of oceans and technology like gunboats. The truth is, none of these advantages were advantages in all battlefields, nor were they used all the time. Asian and African societies had some form of property rights, and had well-functioning commercial institutions. Even if behind on military technology, they tried to catch up, and did so quite quickly. In 18th-century India, the Marathas employed French advisers to build armies that posed a formidable challenge to the expansion of British power. All tropical regions imported European guns (and mercenaries) from the 18th century to fight internal battles, sometimes weakening indigenous states even further (Hoffman and Roy 2021).

So, in terms of the means and the mechanisms at their disposal, the Europeans were not necessarily at an advantage everywhere. Instead a variety of means were employed. In some places, the European states and occupiers found themselves able to bully the local elite, if they wanted something from the latter. Mercenary armies formed easily and conducted raids. The state had limited means to punish them. Concessionary companies sometimes took the lead in imperial expansion. Communication channels like the telegraph and, in the 20th century, demonstrations of the machine gun subdued potential troublemakers. Equally, allies could be found everywhere. Diplomacy, protectorates and indirect rule were as common strategies as coercion to bring a region into the folds of the empire.

This may all sound chaotic, but these initial remarks do permit us to identify four broad patterns of origin. The rest of the chapter will explore these paths more fully with regional data. First, there were acquisitions like Algeria or Sudan, engineered by states and military actors, and with no visible economic motivation to drive the process. Many smaller and Saharan lands divided up during the scramble for Africa would fit a similar model of acquisition. Second, in India, Indonesia and West Africa, European power and interest originated in trade rather than politics. Here, local commerce and commercial actors both gained from colonization, and influenced the process, be they the Chinese in Indonesia or the Parsis in India. Third, in East and Southern Africa, colonialization followed settlers, farmers and economic fortune-hunters, or promoted their interest. And fourth, in the island economies, colonization again followed settler interest, but the relationship was often at arm's length, and complicated by slavery, abolition and migration. These four paths show that expansion began long before states became involved in a serious way. Who took the lead? And what difference did they make?

The facilitators: missionaries and explorers

Before the late 19th century, empires existed as a possibility in the actions of three sets of actors: missionaries, merchants and settlers. With few exceptions, that possibility crystallized on the seaboard. Here, traders and missionaries were already working, sometimes for generations, before the settlers and the administrators arrived. Missionaries wrote systematic descriptions of the regions because unlike the merchants, they lived away from home for longer years. The writings of Father Alexandre de Rhodes (b. 1591), for example, were the authoritative source on Annam until the 19th century, well into the consolidation of French power in Vietnam.

Missionaries were followed by an undefinable set of people often called 'explorers'. Coming from a variety of livelihoods, their only distinction was to write detailed accounts, sometimes knowledgeable and sometimes fantastic, of lands far away from the seaboard. This knowledge was a vital resource in the colonization project. Like the missionaries, these people were not usually driven by a profit opportunity.

Knowledge was key to European success in state-making. In however unsystematic a fashion, explorers and writers in the Sahara, in Congo, in the central African Lakes, and the great river basins, such as Niger, Gabon and Senegal, documented trade routes, located the position of oases, collected data on navigability of the water bodies, and described local culture, custom, language and states. They created a body of knowledge that the French imperialist expeditions used successfully. Their travels continued in the Sahara until the end of the 19th century. These travels, in turn, created a unified map of the immense region, which made any force possessing that knowledge a formidable contender for power. Most indigenous states lacked such a comprehensive view.

In the scramble for Africa, medical knowledge was added to this set. A book review published in the centenary of Cecil Rhodes (1953) in the *British Medical Journal* wrote that Rhodes' Pioneer Column, though 'deficient [in] their knowledge and equipment by modern standards, ... carried quinine and anaesthetics and applied the principles of asepsis. It was a relentless struggle against savagery, disease, and climate' (Anon 1953).

In popular perception, explorers are sometimes clubbed with the imperialists; their significance is seen in being a wilful facilitator in the colonization process. Such an interpretation would be overdrawn. A character from the 17th century, Claude de Rochefort in Senegal, was unlikely to have carried an imperialist vision in the modern sense. Even the late 19th century figures like Savorgnan de Brazza (1852–1905), Henri Duveyrier (1840–1892), David Livingstone (1813–1873), H.M. Stanley (1841–1904), and the painter Thomas Baines (1820–1875), who lived through and often took part in imperialist warfare and expansion, were not exactly partners in the project. Stanley came close to that status, having been inducted into King Leopold II's commercial enterprise in Congo. The king later sidelined him suspecting that he was too soft in dealing with the local elite. The popular interest in and sponsorship of these travels was only partly political in origin. No matter, the knowledge they produced shaped the pattern of imperial expansion, especially in the case of French intrusion into tropical and equatorial Africa.

The political route

The 'political' route involved conquest, invasion or the imposition of a protectorate status, without a definite economic gain in sight. Once, however, a territory was possessed, settlers would move in, and economic interests would feed the desire to hold on and shape economic policy. Indeed, the prospect of emigration and resettlement was a powerful motive driving some of these conquests.

The colonization of Algeria was one of these acts, which opened a northern route into the Sahara. Tunisia had a stronger government, but a bankrupt one. In 1881, it became a French protectorate with little resistance. In Morocco and Spanish Sahara, France and Spain muscled their way into creating protectorates out of states weakened by conflict and warfare. In Morocco, this development encouraged migration of French settlers in the early 20th century.

A spate of colonization occurred between 1884 and 1914. The Berlin Conference had effectively delivered all of the Sahara to the French, a region they knew better than the other Europeans, and the French and local forces now advanced to take possession of these territories. Chad came under French control in the early 1900s, and Mali around 1892. When Mauritania was occupied in 1904, there was little resistance to the French from the nomadic polities. Niger was occupied in the early 1900s, against nomad resistance. In the spirit of Berlin, Italy and Germany made moves into Africa in the early 20th century, Italy taking Libya from vassals of the Ottomans, and Germany taking over territories in Southwest Africa, East Africa and West Africa. German colonization was strongly influenced by the desire to export people to the colonies, and will be discussed later in this chapter in the section on the settler route.

These occupations greatly weakened the Islamic polities and states in North Africa. The process reached a peak with the fall of the two great provinces of the Ottoman Empire, Egypt and Sudan. Egypt became a British protectorate in 1882 following a war. Britain's interest in the war was to retain control over the Suez Canal, and generally over eastern Africa. The last great frontier of expansion was Sudan, part of which had been under Ottoman rule since the early 19th century. The rule was not backed up with either a strong military or a strong government and ended with uprisings. The conflicts left much of Sudan exposed to European merchants, colonizers and missionaries coming to it from the north (Egypt), west (Congo) or east (Kenya). By 1898, Sudan was in British hands and, in the spirit of the scramble, the French and the Belgians relinquished their claims to the southern border zones.

The scramble for Africa

The scramble for Africa, if we mean by that term bilateral agreements on internal borders, started in the 1860s and became a somewhat urgent matter in the 1880s. The secret Belgian plan to colonize the Congo alarmed the British, French, Germans and the Italians already based in Africa, and led to the Berlin Conference of 1884–85 where these powers sought a negotiated settlement of international borders. Whether the conference was of mainly symbolic value, or it decided anything of long-term significance, remains an open question. The hype over the Berlin Conference where the Europeans agreed to live peacefully with each other provided each knew who owned what may lead us to think that this was a momentous event in the history of colonization. Contemporary cartoons showing kings carving up Africa like a stuffed turkey suggest so. The truth is, it was a post-facto step taken to avoid a disastrous military contest when so many borders had appeared from scratch.

Berlin, however, did change the rules of the game. In Europe, it made it easier to draw up bilateral treaties, except where the Portuguese were entrenched. Once the division was done, the new landlords had to take the possession of territories. Some of the most damaging wars and oppressive modes of transfer now followed. Local commanders sometimes led military campaigns with a capacity for brutality and violence that surprised their masters.

In the long run, the project to create countries according to the control exercised by the armies of Europe was a disaster at many levels. Countries emerged in odd shapes, with volatile ethnic mixes, and often too small for the development of infrastructure or substantial domestic markets. This was not a universal outcome of colonialism, for in British India, there was territorial consolidation rather than fragmentation. In Africa, in the process of carving up territories, the participants also redefined lands that they did not know much about. Where the lands were located far away from the seaboard, the partitioning was based on a remote understanding of what these lands might contain or who ruled them. With knowledge of the economic value of the possessions being so limited, we may think that the immediate impetus behind the scramble was not economics but security. However, more detailed investigations of trade between Europe and Africa suggest that the scramble occurred at a time of commercial transition, with relative prices (and supplies) of West African commodity exports on the rise (Frankema et al 2018). There was always the expectation that colonization would force open markets for manufactures and food and material.

The maritime route: Asia and West Africa

The maritime route to colonization was one in which merchants had considerable agency. It was a qualitatively different process from outright conquest, because trading involved partnerships with local merchants and producers. Therefore, the emergence of European states depended on collaborations on the ground.

In coastal Africa, India and Indonesia, the Portuguese explorers and traders first established settlements in the 16th century. From the 17th century, the Dutch and the British East India Companies expanded their business enterprise in India and Indonesia. In both India and Indonesia, empires emerged from states that the Companies had taken over. The Companies generally governed these territories with a light touch, and a commercial outlook. The states took over governance much later (in 1858 in India, and 1816 in Indonesia).

British rule in India began from territories over which the British East India Company acquired control around 1770. Behind the first step, a tacit agreement between the businesses then prominent in Bengal and a coterie of Company officers was instrumental. It is difficult to generalize this story into one of across-the-board collaboration, for in the regular dealings between European and Indian merchants, contractual failure and feelings of mutual distrust were common. Nevertheless, merchants remained silent partners and beneficiaries of the Company state, freely migrated to the cities that the Company had established, and supported the regime with money and material during its worst crisis, the Indian rebellion of 1857 (Roy 2016).

The rule expanded from Bengal in eastern India towards north, west and south India via strategic alliances formed with friendly powers against hostile ones, and a series of battles to subdue the hostile powers. While fighting these battles, the British needed to raise more money and a reliable standing army. Most Indian states relied on military-cum-feudal lords for both taxation and the supply of soldiers, but their loyalty often failed. The British took a different road and raised an army of paid soldiers. This was done by reforms of the land tax system that turned the village landlords from military agents into landowners. In the process of this gradual transfer of power from the landlords to the state, the Company created a state that could collect more tax per head and operated a more powerful military machine (Roy 2013).

Towards the end of the 1600s, the Company's local officers had set up three bases on the coast – Madras, Bombay and Calcutta. Until 1740, these were small settlements of merchants and soldiers. Their role changed thereafter. In the 18th century, many Indian merchants and bankers fled the embattled princely states and moved into the safety of these three cities. The richest people in these towns around 1820 were Indians, with interests in shipbuilding, Indochina trade, coastal trade, Arabian Sea trade and overland trade.

In 1858, the Crown took over control of the Company's territory in India. At that moment, British India had three strengths with no parallel in South Asia. First, the centrally controlled army had created a degree of political unification that South Asia had not seen before. Thanks to its military might, the British could bully the independent princes into keeping their own forces small and their markets and trade routes open. Second, because of this arrangement, the region was emerging as one huge integrated market. Third, the seaboard, which earlier traded a lot with Asia and Africa, now also traded with Europe, thanks to the three port cities. Indeed, these three cities were among the world's biggest hubs of maritime trade at their peak (around 1920).

The start of Crown rule coincided with Britain's Industrial Revolution, and big changes in transport and communication. The Industrial Revolution created a huge demand for food and industrial material – a lot of which came from tropical regions. The expansion of British hegemony over almost a third of the globe allowed for trade, migration and investment to increase manifold. The British Indian state at no point announced an economic policy statement. From 1858 until 1920, it functioned as if its main aim was to keep this exchange going, an exchange dominated by Britain and of which India was a crucial part. From the mid-19th century, the importance of the Indian territories to sustain growth in foreign trade and investment flowing from Britain started to increase, leading to deeper forms of state intervention. The state invested in irrigation, guaranteed profits of railway companies, made numerous laws dealing with contract, companies and commercial instruments, and raised debt in London to fund capital expenditure.

Like India, Dutch colonization of Indonesia began with the trading enterprise of the Dutch East India Company (Vereenigde Oostindische Compagnie, VOC). The VOC started in 1602 and throughout the

17th century, it was embroiled in sometimes violent rivalries with the Catholic Portuguese agents in Asia. Its colonizing ambitions were limited. Between 1677 and 1755, the VOC took sides in the war of succession of the Mataram Sultanate. By the conclusion of the third of these wars, much of Java had been reduced to a protectorate of the VOC. By then the VOC had a sound governance system in Batavia, the main trading city. This was expanded to create a governmental system for Java.

A state needs an efficient fiscal machine. It is a survival issue for states caught up in warfare or conflict. Both the British in India and the Dutch in Indonesia hoped to expand the revenue base from agriculture to plantations, mining and commerce to raise more money. The Dutch feared the Javanese population of the island as potential rebels, but valued Chinese presence. At least commercially, 'little would have been accomplished in Java by the East Indian Company without the aid of the Chinese' (Vandenbosch 1930). Via such connections, the colonial world of Asia became magnets for migrants from Asia at large.

During the Napoleonic wars, the VOC lost control and then was disbanded (see also Box 2.2). After the end of the war, the Dutch government took over the administration of these territories. As in India, rapid economic change encouraged the government to take a direct interest in the economy in the 19th century, beginning with the culture or cultivation system when the state tried to increase and regulate production for export. Dutch rule over the islands and distant territories relied on indirect rule, that is, a notional rule that used the services of local chiefs and notables. Dutch power was no more than symbolic in many of these islands.

Like Indonesia, Dutch colonization of Suriname in the 18th century was similarly a product of the West India Company that passed on to government rule in the early 19th century. However, Suriname was not an established maritime trade zone like Asia. Suriname developed as a settler plantation society. Here, the plantation workforce was drawn from India from the 1860s.

The island colony of Ceylon (Sri Lanka) had a maritime trade origin rather than a settler origin like many other islands (to be discussed later). Portuguese attempts to establish secure power bases succeeded more in the western seaboard of Ceylon than it did in India. By the second quarter of the 17th century, the Portuguese had established territorial control over a large area, which induced the Kandyan kingdom that ruled over much of the island to form an alliance with the Dutch. The conflicts that followed saw a Dutch takeover of the colony, and a retreat of the Kandyan kingdom as well. During the Napoleonic

Box 2.2: The Napoleonic Wars

Napoleon's successful campaign in the Mediterranean in 1795–97 allowed him to capture Egypt and plan to either invade or extend French influence over India, and thus break Britain's commercial empire in the east. One root of that policy was the notion that England's wealth was spread throughout the world wherever its naval commerce had a presence. Another root was the 18th century tendency to take Europe's wars overseas and into Asia, Africa and the Americas. And a third one yet was the realization that the Ottoman Empire was too weak to hold Egypt, technically one of its provinces, alone. All three elements indirectly played a role in the expansion of European rule in Asia, though few people engaged in these conflicts would have foreseen that.

Napoleon's plans or suspected plans had significant repercussions on the immediate course of world politics. The French hold over Egypt that lasted until 1801 had apparently made Wellesley, the Governor General in India, anxious to assert British supremacy in India, campaign harder among potential allies, and fight wars when necessary. These moves were not all pre-planned and made Wellesley's bosses nervous that he would complicate the British campaign in West Asia. The Dutch East India Company's territory in Indonesia had been nationalized, on the bankruptcy of the Company. Between 1806 and 1811, this territory was ruled in effect by France. In 1811, it fell to the British East India Company's forces. In 1810, battles broke out in Mauritius, where French rule had become shaky. French privateers raided British merchant ships and invited the attacks that saw the end of the rule. In the Americas, the French, who had briefly regained control over the Louisiana territory from Spain, delivered the territory to the United States in 1803. The Spanish American wars of independence followed the battle for control over the Iberian Peninsula (1807–14).

The wars changed the governance of empires in Asia. Christopher Bayly called the rule between 1780 and 1830 the British imperial meridian, when an opportunistic form of power transformed into a directly governing one, in turn engaging the home government in foreign rule more deeply than before. The end of conflicts and military threats was necessary to make that transition possible. French imperial ambitions and policy too underwent significant, and somewhat similar, changes after 1814.

Further reading

Christopher Bayly (1989) *Imperial Meridian: The British Empire and the World 1780–1830*, London: Routledge.

David Todd (2011) 'A French Imperial Meridian, 1814–1870,' *Past and Present*, 210: 155–86.

wars, the British took over the Dutch colony. Within a few years the much-weakened Kandyan kingdom fell. Having so far been a trading station (cinnamon was the reason the Portuguese came to Ceylon in the first place), from the mid 19th century, plantations emerged as a major livelihood, employer of wage labour, destination for British capital, and the principal exporter of Ceylon.

In Vietnam, the French East India Company was drawn into taking part in local conflicts, much as the British and the French did in India, in the late 18th century. A deal to obtain the port of Tourane in the last days of the Tay Son rule, in exchange for French mercenary support, did not materialize as expected. However, British successes during the opium war turned the attention of the French towards East Asia. After a joint Franco-Spanish expedition ostensibly in defence of the missionaries (1859–1862), the inland empire was forced to hand over large territories in the Mekong Delta (Cochin China) to the French. Almost at the same time, Cambodia accepted French protection. The conquest of Northern Vietnam (Tonkin and Annam) was the result of a series of military expeditions, much like the scramble for Africa. A drive for military security led the French to make these moves, though the actual colonization process was not a quick affair.

In the seaboard of French West Africa, the various strands – explorers, merchants and military campaigners – came together in the 19th century. Sporadic French expeditions to the Senegal coast and river in the 17th century did not lead to either substantial trade or settlement due to the hostility of the Dutch traders in West Africa. By the end of the century, however, the French navy had taken over several trading sites. In the 18th century, the French influence extended from Senegal to the Guinea coast to Dahomey. Individual explorers travelling to the trading cities of the Sahara supplied useful information about indigenous and European trade. Although European warfare saw the sites under French control pass on to British hands and back again, after the Napoleonic wars, they were firmly in French hands.

Where the lands contained a seaboard, the missionaries and traders were already stationed there, usually with a force to protect them. With the growth of legitimate commerce in West Africa, British influence was growing along the seaboard, and the French responded to that threat by building forts and securing the support of the navy to protect French trade. Where the lands were in the arid interior, the navigability and commercial use of the two main rivers – Niger and Senegal – defined a zone of European influence.

In Senegal, French power was entrenched in the seaboard in the 1810s. The expansion into the interior through a series of conflicts and negotiations started in the 1850s. By the 1870s, when Pierre Savorgnan de Brazza's famous explorations had made many geographical and political features of equatorial Africa familiar to the colonizers, the French could think of its territories from the Mediterranean to Senegal to the Congo as one unified colonial empire.

In the 1880s and the 1890s, a series of military expeditions tried to secure that aim. On the West African seaboard, and the river floodplains, the French military had to deal with British forces guarding trade and colonies. Border disputes between the French and the British were already quite frequent. There were other territorial conflicts too, as a result of which Savorgnan de Brazza's journeys were cut short by the rival explorer H.M. Stanley and the Congo Free State. The Anglo-French rivalry in West Africa was eventually settled, but not before 1897.

Between 1895 and 1904, a unified government for French West Africa, an area of 2.3 million square miles and a population of 9 million, came into existence. A governor general ruled over the territory, answerable to Paris, with Lieutenant-Governors and commissioners appointed to rule individual countries or regions. The most successful innovation of the government was not fiscal, but military. A military force made up of African soldiers and camel brigades that was available for deployment in any part of this immense empire proved effective in containing local conflicts. The force did not affect inter-imperial conflict, which was largely contained through negotiations, except in the eastern Sahara.

Coastal French West Africa was a quite different world from other French territories in the region. The French ended up with a lot of interior, desert territory which needed to be subsidized by Senegal and other coastal territories. The economic divergence between the commercialized port cities and the dry, semi-nomadic, agrarian interior persisted throughout. The states were too poor to bridge the gap. Conditions for rapid economic change to happen existed in the seaboard cities alone. In these port cities, with private investment coming into roads, railways and internal navigation, business grew rapidly. The cities emerged as the main hubs of trade, manufacturing and education.

The settler route

Under the settler route, it was settlers who led colonization or governments whose intentions for resettlement were the objective behind colonization. Portuguese traders and missionaries were the first European settlers in Africa. In Mozambique and Angola, European entry began with Portuguese traders in the 15th century. Both remained under Lisbon's control until the mid-20th century. In Mozambique, the transformation from trade to colony happened in the 17th century when Lisbon began to give out land grants to Portuguese settlers, though immigration of settler-farmers took on a significant scale only in the early 20th century. The main commercial activity, besides trade, was the export of labour. Mozambique was a large source for slaves and a conduit for the slave trade. After the abolition of slavery, labour coercion and forced migrations continued, with tacit or covert government help. In a region with relatively low population density, the demographic effects of forced labour were damaging (Isaacman and Isaacman 1983). Angola's colonial history followed a similar trajectory, from slave trade to colonization to forced labour employed in settler agriculture (Clarence-Smith 1976). In the 20th century, diamond mining became the focus of commercial activity and labour deployment policy, with many of the details left to the company that owned the mines and enjoyed concessions from the Portuguese government, making it a state within a state (Cleveland 2018).

In the Arabian Sea, port cities like Mombasa and maritime states like Oman and Zanzibar were relatively independent until the turn of the 19th century. Europeans operated in East Africa, but it was not the main axis of trade for them. During the Napoleonic wars, with the rumour that Napoleon, having secured Egypt, would cut a channel through the Isthmus of Suez to control the Red Sea and eventually capture India, the control of East Africa and the Asia–Europe overland trade route became a vital concern for the British. 'Thereafter, the British did all that was in their power to forestall any local, regional or western power from challenging either their political or commercial hegemony in the area' (Bhacker 1992). With the end of the Anglo–Mysore wars in 1799, the British were a substantial state in India. Using that power, they could turn Mombasa, Zanzibar and Aden into effectively British protectorates.

In South Africa, Dutch settlement started in the 17th century was a consequence of maritime trade. The centre of Dutch settlement was in the pastures and farmlands in the interior, where the Boer Republic came into being in the 19th century. The British colonized much of the seaboard during the Napoleonic wars. Both these colonies had to contend with the rise of black African states in the river valleys, and in adapting to this potential threat, exploited divisions and conflicts within these states.

The discovery of diamonds intensified the three-way contention for power. The British eventually won the battle but not without heavy human and material losses. An offshoot of the Boer threat to British power was the bloodless acquisition of a vast tract of the Kalahari later called Bechuanaland. The British feared that with its control over that region, the Boers could disrupt trade between central and southern Africa. With the end of these wars, another contest became intense, that between the settlers who wanted independent policymaking powers and the British state. The Cape Colony had a measure of self-government and was treated differently from other British colonies in that respect. With the grant of independence to the Union of South Africa in 1910, the British Parliament conceded the contest, though full formal independence took 20 more years to come.

Until the 1870s, serious efforts at colonization of the East African highlands, accessible with difficulty from Mombasa, did not seem either feasible or profitable, though trading and missionary activity existed in the mountains. Once settlement was identified as a strategy for colonial development from 1903, some very active encouragement by the colonial state, and the construction of the Uganda Railways connecting the coast with the Great Lakes between 1896 and 1901, drew European settlers into the highlands (Mosley 1983). These areas were still thinly populated, but had abundant grazing land, fertile soil, timber and water. Thereafter, settlers engaged in plantations formed the backbone of a new political economy in colonial East Africa.

In popular history of the expansion of British power in southern Africa, the business interests of Cecil Rhodes and the British South Africa Company that he led receive a great deal of attention. Rhodes was only the last and most successful figure in a long line of people who tried to do what he did. One of the more consequential of these attempts had been made in 1847–52 by the soldier and governor of the Cape Colony Harry Smith. Rhodes succeeded where Smith and others had failed because of a combination of business acumen, diplomacy, a credible military force, and the power to persuade British politicians that he should be left alone. Despite being an imperialist in instinct, Rhodes' business interests had made him many allies among African states and settlers, and that factor limited London's interference in what came to be known as Rhodesia (from 1895). Although occasionally dependent on British military assistance and command, in the long run, Rhodesia was effectively an independent settler-ruled state. 'Having control of its own military forces placed Rhodesia in a quite different position from the settler systems in Kenya and Algeria' (Good 1974). This specific legacy of Rhodes, a settlers-only army ruling over a much larger and disaffected African population, however, proved unsustainable in the long run.

German colonial expansion started in the late 19th century largely in reaction to British and French expansion in Africa. From the time of German unification, public and academic discourse advocated emigration to relieve population pressure upon domestic resources. By mid-century, industrialization added another dimension to the discourse, the need to have control over a resource-generating hinterland (Smith 1974). The Great Depression of the 1870s raised the fear that the more successful colonial powers might try to push German business out of Africa. With so many motives for empire-building already in place, Chancellor Otto von Bismarck gave shape to his intention to create an overseas empire, declaring protectorates in New Guinea, Southwest Africa, Togo, and the Cameroons (1883–85). In these areas, German missionary and trading activity were present on a substantial scale. By contrast, British or French territorial claims were as yet undefined. The Berlin Conference in 1884–85 legitimized German claims over some of these areas, and in turn, opened up scope for disputes over drawing borders that would continue for years.

German colonialism thereafter followed two very different trajectories. Togo saw the establishment of direct administration, and its economy was based on trade. In other areas, concession-hunting companies and private armies carried on the business, and settlers engaged in agriculture and mining were powerful in running the state. Settler power in south-west Africa was strong enough to convert this territory into a colony or province of South Africa in the interwar period.

The most famous acquisition by the second route happened in East Africa. In 1885, a German teacher and Anglophile Carl Peters formed the German East Africa Company. His programme started with leasing in land in the interior from the coastal rulers of Zanzibar who had neither the means nor the interest to govern these lands. Peters' project received Bismarck's assent. His ambitions to move into Uganda and Congo were held in check by Frederick Lugard, the representative of the Imperial British East Africa Company, and Leopold II. Uganda, in the course of this conflict, ended up as a British protectorate.

In the islands of the Atlantic, Pacific and the Indian Oceans, settlers-cum-planters established spheres of European occupation.

They were useful to the parent states, but saw little direct governance. Still, slavery and abolition did draw the states into the governance of these territories.

The islands

In most parts of the Atlantic, early European settlements appeared chaotically, and not as part of a grand plan. Settlers in this world were the direct or indirect creations of the Iberian empire of the Americas, and became British or French citizens only in the 19th century.

In the Caribbean, colonization was preceded in the 17th century by settlements that followed the movements of British and French explorers and privateers. Barbados was a kind of penal settlement. Oliver Cromwell's Western Design plans (1655) to attack Spain in the Caribbean saw several thousand soldiers end up in Jamaica without a war to fight. In Barbados, rivalries between a small set of 17th-century English and Dutch merchants laid the foundation for a colony, as they campaigned in England on the economic value of the island and on the legitimacy of their status as landlords. Danish colonization in the region started in a more benign way, via occupation of uninhabited islands and purchase of territory from the French.

These settlements found a solid economic basis only in the 1730s, with their transformation into slave-owning plantations. Many of the planters faced limited opportunities at home. Economic desperation and the absence of legal restraints made for savagely brutal forms of labour discipline in the plantations. In the 18th century, the British and the French states at home took a direct interest in governing the territories to protect the interest of planters, sustain the slave trade that supplied labourers to the plantations, civilize the planters, and increasingly, reduce slavery.

In the end, they proved so useful to the societies seeking sugar or tobacco, that the planters got away with their semi-independent status. Cane sugar was the most successful export from the region, followed by rum and cocoa (in Grenada). As Burnard (1996: 792) argues, 'The West Indian colonies were more important economically to metropolitan interests than were the North American colonies.' The relationship between the two partly explains the absence of a strong repercussion of American independence in the West Indies.

The French Revolution, however, did not spare the island colonies. In Saint-Domingue (Haiti), a French plantation island where the vast majority of the population were slaves brought from Africa and their descendants, the French Revolution encouraged a slave rebellion.

The French revolutionaries did not seem to know how to react to this event, but Napoleon attempted to regain control of the island, unsuccessfully. 'This protracted and bloody struggle set off a wave of alarm in all those parts of the Americas where slavery was to be found, prompting slaveholders and public authorities to look to extra guarantees and new political alignment' (Blackburn 2006). Haiti, however, did not set off a serious chain reaction among other slave populations in the Atlantic. Because it did not, Haiti's export economy was left devastated by international isolation and the collapse of the plantation system. A military elite governed a countryside getting steadily poorer. Elsewhere in the Atlantic, slavery and the plantations continued to flourish together.

The Napoleonic wars led to the transfer of power from French to British hands in both the Indian Ocean and the Atlantic. Trinidad was a Spanish possession settled with French planters, before its takeover by the British in 1797. Tobago later joined Trinidad. Tobago was a French colony. With the abolition of slavery, colonial rulers had to work harder to save the plantations. The British knew where the solution to the labour shortage was: British India. Import of workers from India was seen as an option in Trinidad, Tobago and Dutch Suriname. From the 19th century, the presence of Creoles of French or British ancestry, Spanish, black, Indian and white people in the islands gave European colonialism in this field a local character, shaped more by relationships between migrant groups than by top-down imperialist designs. This feature carried over into the historiography of colonialism after independence, with the emergence of a range of contesting narratives about what colonialism really meant, especially in Trinidad (Brereton 2007).

The Trinidad and Tobago experience suggests two general points about the plantation complexes in the island colonies: they had their own pressing problems to handle that the British or the French politicians neither understood nor deeply cared about, and they were a very different lot one island from the other. Numerous pamphlets in English in the 19th century written by settlers in St Lucia, Jamaica, Guyana and elsewhere complained about disaffection among the slaves, threats to livelihood, economic pressures and natural disasters. Dependence on sugar and rum hurt these economies in the long run. These pamphlets were meant for London but did not produce results. These once 'gems of the British Empire ... were reduced to the "slums of the empire" in the late nineteenth and early twentieth centuries' (Keagy 1972: 9).

A large scholarship on Indian indentured workers in the island economies has underscored how very diverse the colonial economic experience was in this world. The scholarship developed partly in response to interpretations of indenture that saw it as slavery in another name. The indentured workers never saw themselves that way. They struggled hard to acquire assets and carefully preserved an Indian identity to distance themselves from the indigenous and Creole populations. The diversity emerged not only from identity politics and demand for rights, but also from the varying degree in which workers became farmers or merchants, and contests for economic resources that took on communal colours.

The second cluster of island colonies in Melanesia started as unplanned European settlements until their potential to become plantation economies was used more fully. Fiji, with its larger land area, emerged as a sugar and cotton cultivation zone, powered by indentured Indian immigrants. Its colonial history started in 1874, in the wake of disputes within the weak kingdom, and a series of brutal conflicts between the indigenous islanders and settlers.

All of these examples suggest that occupation and the start of a new kind of rule were two very different things. If colonialism means a distinct state with its own laws and policy and rule by a professional ruling class, when did colonialism begin? The answer to this question varies, and depends on which of the four routes – politics, commerce, inland-settler or island-settler – mattered to the emergence of a formal colony.

Conclusion

Can there be a general theory of the origin of colonialism? Despite the diversity of it, the raw material discussed in this chapter does suggest a general theory. It has two ingredients, only one of which is European expansion. The phrase means different things at different times. In the 18th century, overpopulation in Europe pushed a huge number of people to seek opportunities abroad. In the late 19th century, expansion involved the agency of the states and military power, and commercial interests motivated such action. No matter when we look, the expansionists were so diverse in interests and capacities and timing that they do not explain colonization in an easy or direct way.

To explain the origin of colonialism we need to look outside Europe. In the tropical regions, states were fiscally weak and had diverse institutional structures. When trying to grow they often ran into internal and external conflicts. The rise of sea trade made the maritime traders, both European and indigenous, politically ambitious.

This rise also took resources away from state building to warfare. For example, the most successful export from Europe in the 18th century, guns, hastened the downfall of some of the tropical polities where Europeans moved in.

The motives and capacities of indigenous actors mattered to the origin of colonialism and shaped the pathways towards the formal rule. With the merchant hoping to make profits through associations with European merchants, there was a hint of a strategic alliance behind the emergence of colonialism. In India, Indonesia and parts of West Africa that element was present. Where there was a failed state like Sudan under Ottoman rule, the indigenous actor was the local political elite willing to help the colonizer take over power. Where the actor was a weak nomadic polity of the Sahara, neither was resistance likely nor a complicated negotiation necessary. A protectorate emerged quickly.

The settler colonies in South and East Africa, and the islands, appeared in regions where settlers made the first viable state-like structure. Because they did, they also wanted independence from the colonist nation. When European planters and miners claimed privileged access to land and minerals, a tension emerged. Allocation of land rights to these people would sometimes entail taking away customary rights from the indigenous farmers. Not only the indigenous farmers but also the missions opposed the idea of privileged rights for the settlers. In all colonies where the settlers operated, administrative officers struggled with this conflict. In some colonies the policy tilted heavily in favour of the settlers. Thus, there emerged a difference between the mainly trading colonies – French and British West Africa, India, French Indochina and Indonesia – and the mainly settler colonies like those in East and South Africa and the island economies.

In trading colonies, by contrast, there was more collaboration than conflict between indigenous merchant groups and the European ones. In Indochina, Malaya and Indonesia, local and migrant Chinese took part in new forms of commercial enterprise. In India, business communities that had established a hold in the port cities during the 18th century gained significantly from commercialization. These processes will be discussed more fully in Chapter 9.

Notes

[1] European expansion means 'the processes by which the nation-states of the West attained domination over all other civilizations and culture areas'; see Adas (1999: x) or Wesseling (1997). Published works with the phrase 'European expansion' or

variations of it in their titles are too many to cite. See, however, Bentley (1997), which offers a more diverse view of what the phrase might mean.

[2]   Several essays in Belmessous (2015) consider whether treaties were a serious alternative to wars in the emergence of colonialism, and claim that they were.

[3]   Some scholars of 19th-century East Africa suggest that the growth of a world economy based on oceanic trade undermined the power of the inland states; see Alpers (1975) and Sheriff (1987).

3

Colonialism as an Agent of Globalization

A period of intense inter-European rivalry and military contest had come to an end in the mid-19th century, leaving Britain and France to pursue empire-building with relative ease. Economic globalization gave them a strong reason for doing so. A definition of globalization is helpful to understand why imperialists were keen to extend their influence overseas.[1] A basic definition – unprecedented growth in the scale of trade between 1820 and 1920 – is useful but insufficient. No doubt British export of manufactures formed a significant part of the growth of world trade and British industrialists had some influence on colonial policy. Still, making a direct connection between the direction of trade and the geography of colonialism is difficult. The emerging economic relations in the world contained other ingredients besides trade. These included the integration of commodity, capital and labour markets across continents and the increasing geographical mobility of firms. State support mattered in all cases because the states were multipurpose instruments that could play a variety of roles. They could, as the need arose, make laws, protect trade routes, negotiate openness, subsidize investment and validate indentures.

By playing these roles, colonial states not only acted as an agent in globalization but also as a conduit for the transmission of technologies and institutions. Trade was largely tariff-free at least within the British Empire. Barriers to the movement of labour, capital and technology were also generally low, especially so between countries within an empire. The gold standard and international banking contributed to broad stability in exchange rates and balance of payments. In effect, there was increasing institutional and policy convergence in the laws on contracts and companies. This allowed firms to hire trusted partners from home to run operations thousands of miles away. Europeans made use of this freedom to import skills. So did the Asians who migrated to Britain's tropical colonies to conduct trade there.

Was ownership of territories necessary to achieve globalization in this varied sense? Not necessarily. Agents of the states put pressure on weak states, as between Britain and the Ottoman Empire or Britain in Latin America, or with Commodore Perry in Japan. Negotiations occurred under threat (see, for example, Pamuk 1987). Still, the outright takeover of states through warfare and diplomacy, though a costlier option, was sometimes useful and increasingly necessary to deter rival powers from doing the same thing. Some large colonies, like India or Indonesia, were simply a handy inheritance from an earlier time.

This chapter explores the many-sided connection between globalization and colonialism. Although descriptive, it builds around a theme. Globalization of economic activity created uncertainty, and colonization reduced that uncertainty. The source of the risk and the instruments available to the states to mitigate these were neither predictable nor very well-defined. Therefore, it is not easy to turn this interdependence into a causal model of colonialism. Still, an interdependence did exist, and the chapter builds on that idea.

Globalization and colonialism: is there a causal chain?

In the 1970s, the World Systems School and neo-Marxist accounts of world economic history called the joint process of globalization and colonialism the 'incorporation' of the third world in a Europe-dominated economic system. In this view, the prospect of economic gains to be made from market integration motivated the use of political and military power the Europeans exercised over the rest of the world. Karl Marx's labour theory of value indirectly supported this idea, by suggesting that trade under colonial conditions entailed a transfer of economic surplus from the colonies towards Europe. Colonialism not only sponsored globalization but generated world inequality.

If, in this story, power is the cause and capitalism the effect, business history suggests that power sometimes followed the capitalists. Financial capital was mobile before states were. Mobile firms like the East India Companies created the foundation for globalization. Colonialism was at least in part an adaptation to that process. Studies on 19th century communication and transportation development, initially led by private investment, suggested again that empires followed tracks first opened by firms (Winseck and Pike 2007).

Still, businesses needed friendly states. In the Marxist account, business relied on power in order to force open markets, protect trade routes, divert trade from local to international markets, and repress wages. Again, these mechanisms overstate the political dimension of doing business. More recent accounts of the relationship also stress the role of institutional innovations and reduction in transaction costs. Becoming global via trade, investment or migration carried risks for everyone. Governments helped mitigate risks, but they were one of several agents working for that purpose. Business firms also relied on their own resources like networks, connections, access to capital markets and collaborations with local magnates.

Colonial territories were subjected to a deeper form of institutional intervention than the poor independent economies in the 19th century. Intra-empire market integration gained from 'the use of a common language, the establishment of currency unions, the monetisation of recently acquired colonies, and the establishment of preferential trade agreements and customs unions' (Mitchener and Weidenmier 2008). Two common strategies adopted to develop and sustain trading arrangements between the colonist and the colonized countries were currency unions and preferential trade. Colonialism sustained the relatively peaceful trading conditions of the 19th century and institutional convergence.

Trade

Trade, of course, was a key element and a reason for the expansion of territorial rule, though colonialism was not required for trade to grow. One of the first estimates of the share of imperial trade in international trade of the British Empire placed the share at 41 per cent, and observed that 'the Imperial share in supplying the Empire's needs has [in the immediate pre-war years] grown somewhat faster than the foreign share' (Rosenbaum 1913: 743). Later, cross-country statistical work offered a strong confirmation of the interdependence between the growth of colonial power and commercialization, finding that 'belonging to an empire roughly doubled trade relative to those countries that were not part of an empire' between 1860 and 1913 (Mitchener and Weidenmier 2008). In recent literature, the correlation between colonialism and globalization has been called the empire effect (see also Table 3.1).[2]

The 19th century did not just bring about a huge rise in the scale of trade, but also a change in the composition of trade. The tropical colonies supplied food, raw materials produced on land, animal products and some minerals to Europe, whereas manufactured goods dominated intra-European trade and European exports. India

Table 3.1: Colonial and metropolitan shares (%) in trade

	India		Indonesia	Indochina		
	1900–1910	1938–1940	1929–1933	1929–1933		
Metropolitan share in export	29	35				
Metropolitan share in import	62	23	17	55		
	Britain		France		The Netherlands	
	1900	1938	1900	1938	1900	1938
Colonial share in export	8	8	4	9	1	5
	1900	1938				
Share of Britain, France and the Netherlands in world exports	39	31				

Sources: Booth (2007b, Chapter 5); Roy (2011); United Nations, 'International Trade Statistics', https://unstats.un.org/unsd/trade/imts/Historical%20data%201900–1960.pdf (accessed 15 December 2019).

exported cotton, wheat, rice and tea in the late 19th century. West Africa exported groundnuts, cocoa, coffee, bananas, timber and gum arabic. East Africa exported tea. Malaya exported tin and rubber. The Irrawaddy delta in Burma exported rice. But trade did not mean the same thing for all supply regions. The export trade of the larger-sized countries in this system, like India, rose but did not exceed 10–12 per cent of national income around 1900. The proportion was almost certainly much higher for most other colonies and smaller countries in the system, and the export basket was less diversified too. In the mid-20th century, groundnuts and related products formed 90 per cent of the exports of Senegal, Sudan and Niger; whereas in French Guinea and Dahomey, bananas and oil palms formed 80–90 per cent of exports. All territories imported cotton piece-goods from Europe, capital and intermediate goods such as machinery, metals and chemicals. Africa also imported manufactured foodstuffs, hollowware, rice and sugar.

It would be a mistake to see the commercialization mainly through the lens of a core–periphery model, where Europe was the independent core region calling the shots and the colonies the dependent periphery following Europe's lead passively. A core–periphery model suggests a relationship of one-sided dependence, and in this case overstates the colonist-and-colony trade. Commercialization instead created numerous previously unexplored communication channels between regions in Asia and Africa.

Trade patterns reflected regional specializations which meant that Europe sold one thing and the colonies sold another. This might suggest that older patterns of exchange among neighbours in the tropical regions came to an end. For example, Indian textiles or Arabian horses or Chinese silk had once exchanged among segments of the Indian Ocean. European textiles and guns put an end to some of these local exchanges in cloths or warhorses. This is true, up to a point. Colonialism enabled new intra-regional networks of market exchange as well. It drew the territories within the tropics into a closer relationship with each other by political means, leading to easier migration of capital and labour between these territories. Indian workers went to British colonies in the Pacific, the Caribbean, in Africa and Malaya, to work for wages or do business there. Bankers and traders from China and India resettled readily in East Africa or Southeast Asia. Colonial power effectively imposed an integrated marketplace on the semi-independent states next door. This was the case with the Indian princely states and in coastal Africa. 'Singapore and Peninsular Malaysia, together with Sabah and Sarawak, ... evolved under British rule into a single economic system' (Ken 1979). Conflicts did exist because the coastal world and the 'hinterland' were very different worlds, but colonial power contained these conflicts.

Shipping history suggests again that dividing the world into a core and a periphery would be a mistake. Much of the growth in international trade was carried by ships. The seas in the tropics had long seen networks of local and short-haul shipping transporting goods among segments of the ocean. The Arabian Sea, for example, contained a network of transport routes connecting western India, East Africa and the Arabian Peninsula, before the 19th century, conducted by merchants based in the coastal towns. Transoceanic steam shipping, by contrast, was European and North American in ownership. It modified the local networks, broke up some of them, and redirected a part of the trade towards Europe. The new shipping hubs were cosmopolitan port cities like Bombay, Muscat, Mombasa, Karachi and Aden, instead of Surat, Zanzibar or Hormuz in an earlier era.

But did steamships cause a decline in coastal, short-haul and sail ships that were once the dominant mode of cargo carriage locally? Did steam take away trade from sail, or did the overall growth of commercial activity thanks to steam stimulate local networks? Satisfactory evidence to test these hypotheses does not exist. However, descriptions of the business of coastal merchants, or the trade carried by the 'dhows' of the

Arabian Sea (locally manufactured lateen-rigged boats) do not suggest a decline and fall story, rather the opposite. The expansion of steam and colonialism in the Indian Ocean region forged stronger local links, between India and China or India and Africa, for example. In turn, these links attracted new groups like the Parsis of Bombay and Surat into short-haul maritime trade.

These arguments hint that colonial links cannot be modelled completely into a dominance-dependence trading relationship. The so-called dependencies charted their own course and found business opportunities created by colonial power but not used by European capitalists. Therefore, the specialization was not a fixed thing either.

Indian merchants, for example, set up cotton textile factories in the manner of Manchester. Merchants who made profits in food and raw material trade built factories in the port cities of the colonial regions. Some British merchant houses raised capital in the London money market and invested it in manufacturing in the colonies. In this way, the coastal cities of the colonies shaped a development trajectory that resembled the western European model more than any indigenous model of economic change or entrepreneurship. Capitalists invested in industry in regions that had specialized in the export of commodities, and where the cost of capital was often quite high. Economic historians of world trade have overlooked this apparent anomaly; business historians are more aware of it.

The colonial trading arrangement was beginning to retreat after the First World War, leading to deliberate attempts to revive it. The share of regions outside the empires in the exports and imports of colonies rose rapidly, especially in Asia, where the government of Japan, and merchants, shippers and bankers from China and Japan, increased their economic influence in South and Southeast Asia. The history of pan-Asian links tends to be studied as an effect of independence after the Second World War, and the deliberate attempt to forge friendship among developing countries and develop ties between countries 'non-aligned' in the Cold War. As one historian usefully reminds us, this is a limited reading of pan-Asian links. In fact, 'the dynamics [of colonialism] set into motion a new set of inter-colonial Asian connections' (Goscha 2009). In the interwar years, Singapore emerged as 'a large provider of internationally-traded services, and as a regional service centre had a fundamental role in promoting Southeast Asian economic growth' (Huff 1993: 24). The redirection of trade and trade-related services induced the French, Dutch and British rulers in the region to strengthen customs unions with the territories they ruled, with modest success at best.

To sum up, a study of colonialism-induced trade cannot simply be a study of the dependence of Asia and Africa on Europe, for two reasons. First, a huge field of local and overland trade made this overseas trade possible. Whereas the Europeans dominated the latter, indigenous capitalists dominated the former. In this sense, Europe was the dependent partner. Chapter 9, on business, considers this interdependence more fully. These local networks of exchange consolidated, especially in interwar Asia. Second, while colonial trade did often cause rivalries between foreigners and locals to break out, trade also empowered indigenous merchants in unpredictable ways. A case study of British India helps us illustrate these propositions.

India: a study

During the 90 years of Crown rule (1858–1947), commerce and manufacturing within India changed in fundamental ways. The volume of foreign trade to and from India more than doubled in 1865–1914. The volume of trade through the British Indian ports increased from 1.6 million tons in 1863 to 8.6 million tons in 1913. The figure dropped after that to recover to 10 million in 1937. These numbers included short-haul and coast-to-coast trade as well as international trade. The ratio of foreign trade in national income increased from 8–10 to 20 per cent in 1865–1914.

The Empire was the main destination of Indian export in the pre-war years. There was some diversion of trade from China to Britain and parts of the world where British merchants had easy access. Likewise, Britain was the only major source of India's imports until the First World War. While Indian exports in the 18th century consisted of artisanal manufactures, its 19th century exports were dominated by primary products such as grains, seeds, raw cotton, hides and skins, oilseeds, tea, jute textiles and raw jute; imports consisted of manufactures, mainly cotton textiles and metals.

Whereas European capitalists dominated the port-based export trade, jute textiles and tea grown in the plantation estates, Indians dominated the railway-borne trade in commodities coming from the interior. There was a similar division in banking and finance. Export finance came from corporate banks in which the Europeans had a substantial presence; finance for agricultural production and commodity trade came from Indian bankers and moneylenders. The Indians, in other words, had a significant stake in the globalization process. Commercial law and policy reduced their business risk just as much as that of the Europeans. Therefore, some of them could consider investing trade profits into the manufacturing industry, like cotton textiles. At independence in 1947, India possessed the world's fourth-largest cotton textile mill industries.

Indian industrialization was a paradox because the region was always short of capital. Agricultural trade made a big draft on available capital, and long-term investors had to pay a large premium to draw money away from it. The Empire provided a limited means to overcome the obstacle. Indian capitalists, for example, had easy access to British technology and British, European and American engineers. Hiring abroad posed no difficulty except the requirement to pay a higher wage. British shareholders invested in India. And profits earned in commodity trade were reinvested in manufacturing. From the interwar years, manufactured goods dominated Indian exports.

Industrialization in turn changed the dynamics of globalization. In the interwar period, the share of Britain in Indian trade fell. India was trading more with Japan, the USA, Germany and Italy. Infant industries in metallurgy and chemicals needed the USA and Germany as partners, more than Britain. Asian trade was stimulated by the emergence of a modern cotton textile industry in Japan from the 1890s.

The Asian surge worried the colonial administrators and was the impetus to the Imperial Preference treaty of 1932. Britain now tried to create a customs union among the British colonies. Paradoxically, Britain was no longer a useful trading partner, and nationalist platforms underscored that point. Commodity trade and industrialization had made the indigenous bourgeoisie stronger economically and more ambitious politically. In India and Southeast Asia after the First World War, this was an unmistakable trend. For the British in India or the French in Vietnam, the choice was to concede modest self-representation and more state support to indigenous business lobbies, through tariffs for example, and thus turn these lobbies away from a more extreme form of nationalism.

Finance

The empire effect was not confined to trading but extended to capital and labour mobility. Consider capital first. British colonies could borrow in London more cheaply than independent territories. There remain debates about why. Ferguson and Schularick (2006) argue that it was because their currency and fiscal systems were deemed more stable and trustworthy. In contrast, Accominotti et al (2011) claim that lower costs of borrowing in the colonies were not linked to colonial institutions per se, but rather to the fact that colonies were subsidiaries

Figure 3.1: British capital exports (£), 1865–1913

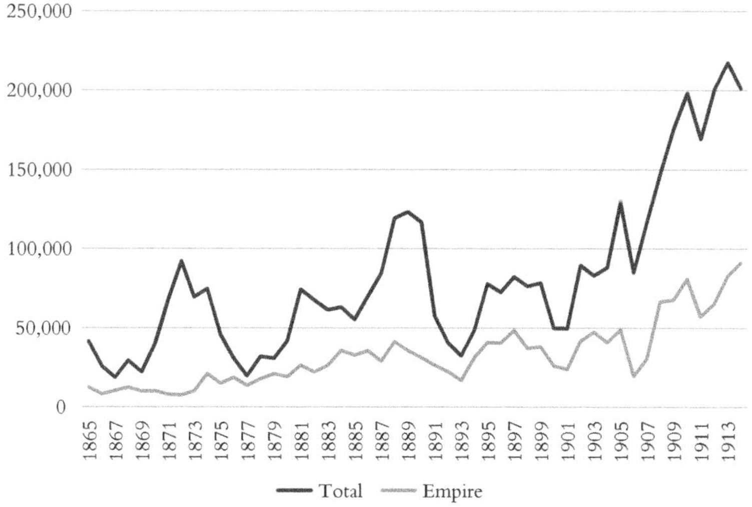

Source: Stone (1999)

of the British government. Their credit was therefore, essentially, the credit of the British government.

The joining of global finance with colonialism is a very British story and a story that unfolds in the 1880s. Between 1875 and 1913, the stock of British overseas investments rose from £1 billion to £4 billion (see also Figure 3.1). The empire's share was 43 per cent in 1913. Overseas holdings accounted for about a third of British capital stock in the mid-20th century (Pollard 1985). Peter Cain and Anthony Hopkins (1993) have shown that finance, more than trade, sustained Britain's interest in overseas territories where it exercised some form of political influence, though the cost of fighting the world wars put an end to this influence.

The British radical writer J.A. Hobson called finance 'the motor-power of imperialism' (cited in Chapman 1985). The phrase implies that surplus capital held by the banks drove imperialist expansion. Hobson's own experience in South Africa informed his theory. He overstated the drive somewhat. Contrary to this implication, banks cautiously followed imperialist expansion, and only when it seemed safe to do so, staked any money. Most banks in London were conservative in their choice of clients and investments, and enterprises in the colonies almost always entailed uncertainty and incomplete information. Financial firms of the City were occasionally able to advise and prevail on politicians with a say in colonial affairs, but only occasionally.

Hobson was still right to observe that the relationship between the City of London and the colonies was rapidly getting closer in the late 19th century. The banking system had two features that made it willing to stake venture capital in the colonies. First, it was diversified enough to contain a segment that was willing to speculate, in railroads, mining and bonds. Second, the core set of financial houses systematically collected information and prepared reports on foreign governments, new enterprises, funded individuals on fact-finding missions, and hired a diversified set of 'information intermediaries', whose role in the bond market was crucial.[3]

A well-studied example of the dependence between finance and colonialism is investments in gold and diamond mining in southern Africa (see Box 3.1). It is worth noting that South Africa received the vast majority of British capital flows to Africa as a whole (Frankel 1938). Gold was discovered in the Witwatersrand in 1884. By 1900, Transvaal produced a quarter of the world's gold output, and shipped nearly all of it to London, the financial centre of the world and the centre of the international gold standard. The early interest shown by German and British banks in southern African mining often resulted in losses. While European banks thus hesitantly drew closer to African mining, the colonial enterprises needed the banks the more. In the 1880s, before the consolidation of the business of diamond mining in Kimberley, the enterprise was perpetually short of working capital and labour and exposed to excessive competition. The stock markets did not help. In this backdrop, a partnership emerged between Cecil Rhodes and the Rothschilds that was crucial to the success of the consolidation under De Beers. The partnership was not an easy one, for the London end was wary of Rhodes' imperialist ambitions, but it survived.

Between 1886, when gold was found in Transvaal, and 1914, the beginning of the end of the international gold standard, the association between Wernher, Beit in gold, the London merchant banker N.M. Rothschild and Rhodes in diamond was a driver behind the expansion of European power in the region. The success of the collaboration had owed to an intimate knowledge of conditions of the mines and the capacity to manipulate the share market.

The success of these associations made Rothschild the world's manager of gold and induced them to invest in copper and oil (Ferguson 1999). Mining business still carried high risks and high returns, but with the knowledge that the risks could be managed by better production practices and saving in marketing gold, much of which was sold in the

Box 3.1: Gold and diamonds in South Africa

While there were many links between the growing European demand for raw materials and the expansion of empires, minerals perhaps deserve particular emphasis in the story of African colonization. It was demand for minerals – diamonds and gold – which set the territories which became South Africa apart from the rest of the continent in terms of the volume of both European capital and migration.

The first diamond was discovered in the Eastern Cape in 1867. Within only a few years, thousands were trying their luck in the open quarrying of small plots. However, it was soon discovered that the richest deposits were too deep for individual prospectors to reach and required more capital-intensive techniques. This resulted in the swift and complete consolidation of the diamond mines under Cecil Rhodes' De Beers Consolidated Mines.

This trend towards capital-intensive production of minerals and the domination of large firms was continued with the discovery of gold in the Transvaal in 1884. Gold production expanded rapidly, and investors across Europe scrambled to purchase land in the region around the goldfields and the new town of Johannesburg, founded in 1886. Growth in financial and other services as well as chemicals industries linked to mining helped make Johannesburg the leading commercial centre in South Africa. The investment boom prompted by the mineral discoveries also extended to infrastructure. Owing to the needs of the mining industry, the Cape Colony soon had the densest railway network in sub-Saharan Africa.

South Africa's experience generated anticipation among European investors that other mineral deposits of similar scale were yet to be discovered in other parts of the continent. The desire to secure such deposits, both real and imagined, lay behind the conquest of other territories, such as much of what was then the Congo Free State and the Rhodesias. It also generated mini investment bubbles related to other mining centres which turned out to be much less valuable, including gold mines in the Gold Coast and Southern Rhodesia. Even where other mineral deposits turned out to be substantial, such as in the case of copper in the Belgian Congo and Northern Rhodesia, those other minerals often lacked the unique price stability of both gold and diamonds, and thus the mining of these deposits often did not have the same impact on investment and development.

Further reading

Charles Feinstein (2005) *An economic history of South Africa: conquest, discrimination and development*, Cambridge: Cambridge University Press.

Alfonso Herranz-Loncan and Johan Fourie (2017) '"For the public benefit"? Railways in the British Cape Colony', *European Review of Economic History*, 22: 73–100.

bullion market of London, it attracted capital from the stock markets all over Europe.

Financing the railways in India again involved N.M. Rothschild as a lead underwriter. This was a different type of enterprise from mining. With the British Indian government standing as guarantor of the profits of the railway companies, the investment carried little risk. In turn, the merchant bankers' role reveals growing 'mutual dependence between the City and Whitehall in the financing of the British Empire's largest investment programme' (Sweeney 2009). Again, the success of these investments did not just depend on cooperation with the government, but also crucially on information collected (especially after the great Indian famine of 1876) on the earnings expected from new railway projects.

The third field of City investment was commodity trade. 'City firms were at the center of colonial trade, linked by personal networks as much as the supply chains of international commodity trading' (Mollan and Michie 2012). Commodity trading involved trading in financial products like futures and derivatives, especially in the 20th century. Some traders (like miners, Wernher, Beit) became financiers. The cluster of banks called British India exchange banks was global in operation and financed Asian trade.

By contrast with commodity trade, commodity production received little foreign investment. Plantation complexes in India, Ceylon and Malaya represented a mild exception to the bias displayed by foreign investment to avoid agriculture. Even here, the tea and rubber companies that received the investment tended to be in the cities whereas only their production sites were in the interior of the country.

Sovereign bond markets were a more complex field. Governments are reliable borrowers because they have access to taxes. If they do default, they cannot be disciplined and punished, certainly not by a bank. The sovereign bond market in autocratic states, therefore, is attractive as well as risky. Colonial governments offered an offbeat field in this set. They were usually poor governments in terms of their direct fiscal resources, and yet their finances were seen as having an implicit guarantee from the colonist country. In the case of a large colony like British India, the gold exchange standard practically eliminated exchange rate risks and signalled safe housekeeping practices. Eliminating exchange risk was a universal goal. To take another example, in Vietnam, the Mexican silver piastre was probably the most widely circulating currency before the French takeover. Silver speculation at the end of the 19th century led to a gold exchange standard in 1903 and tied the piastre to the French franc.

British India used its links with the City to raise a complex basket of loans. The complexity came from the many deals the India Office struck with firms in the City. Transactions and instruments proliferated because the India Office was a part of the City's 'ecosystem' (Sunderland 2013). Debts, for example, came in a variety of forms, each serving a specific need, including government stock, sterling bills, war loans and loans of railway companies. These diverse operations became possible because knowledge of markets combined with reputations of the intermediaries mattered more to their success than political power. The system was not without friction. The terms of transactions were often fiercely disputed. Still, occasional crises aside, until the First World War these deals were profitable for the City, and helped to raise money for India, facilitate its trade and meet its balance of payments.

In French Africa, British India and Indonesia, nationalist and other critics of colonialism accused the rulers of draining the resources of the colonies in the guise of governmental transfers. These net payments from the budget occurred because the colony had to pay for the European officers, their pensions and debt raised in Europe. Private profits and salaries paid to managers and engineers in private firms were other net outflows. Maintaining a trade surplus was a vital means to pay for these net payments.

The nationalists criticized the outflow, calling it a 'drain' of national savings. Drain it was, if we can be sure that these payments were a kind of forced tribute and a payment by one country to another. The defenders of the imperial form of government argued that the payments were made for a service the colonies would not be able to do without (see, for example, Treub 1930). Besides, these payments were not exactly payments made by one country to another. Rather, they were transfers between departments of the same government. In current economic history scholarship, new measures of the scale of the transfer have been made. The interpretive issue – whether an

Table 3.2: Emigration and empires in the 19th century (millions)

Types of migration flow	
1	Indians going to the British, French and Dutch Empire countries, 1840–1920[a]	2.1
2	Indian emigration, 1840–1920[a]	2–3
3	Persons of Indian descent in major destinations in the formerly British, French and Dutch empires (1981)[b]	4.3
4	Persons of Indian descent outside India (1981)[c]	7–8
5	Chinese going to the British, French and Dutch Empire countries, 1840–1940[d]	12–16
6	Chinese emigration, 1840–1940[d]	19–23
7	Persons of Chinese descent in major destinations in the formerly British, French and Dutch empires (1963)	16
9	European emigration to the New World, 1846–1924[d]	45–50

Notes: The figures are estimates, and vary from one research work to another. Return migration flows are hard to measure. Some early works on world migration (for example, by the International Labour Office) gave up measuring Chinese emigration because the data was incomplete. African migration that dominated the previous centuries fell significantly in the 19th century, but firm estimates are rare.

[a] Net flows. [b] Excludes Burma and Sri Lanka where the British Empire was not the main factor influencing Indian emigration. The main regions of immigration were the Caribbean, Fiji, Mauritius, South Africa, Kenya, Malaya, Singapore, Hong Kong and Guiana. [c] Includes large post-1965 flows such as the one towards the Persian Gulf. If this is excluded, the figure should be 5–6 million. [d] Gross flows. [e] The main regions were Hong Kong (3.2 million), Indonesia (2.5), Malaya (2.5), Singapore (1.3), Vietnam (1.0), Burma (0.4) and Cambodia (0.3).

Sources: Madhavan (1985); McKeown (2010); Chang (1968); Hatton and Williamson (1994).

adequate value matched these payments or not – remains open, and impossible to resolve.

Migration

Between 1840 and 1930, possibly 3 million Indian workers were recruited to work in the coffee and tea estates of Sri Lanka, the rubber plantations in Malaya, and sugar cane plantations in Malaya, Fiji, Mauritius, Reunion, Natal, Guyana, Suriname, Trinidad and Jamaica. Like Chinese migration to the Americas in the 19th century, numbering near a million, Indian migration did not just mean transportation of workers but also entailed the migration of business firms selling goods and a variety of services used by the migrants. This second process was more visible in the 20th century and in areas closer to India, such as East and South Africa and Malaya. In the 1930s, around 4 million Chinese settlers were present in colonial Southeast Asia (see Table 3.2).

Organized overseas emigration from India began in the 1830s. The destinations were the British colonies in Southeast Asia, Mauritius, Burma, the Pacific and the West Indies. Calcutta was the main port of embarkation. Also, the Madras (later renamed Chennai) port sent several hundred thousand Tamils to Ceylon, Burma, Mauritius, South Africa and the West Indies. The French ports in South India were also active in the business. Overseas migrants, like migrants to the Assam plantations, came from certain regions; perhaps the most important was Chota Nagpur. 'Hill coolies', a phrase used in early 19th-century official documents, referred to a group of people who lived on the margins of the forests and were already familiar to the indigo planters of Bihar as reliable wage-workers. At a time when wage-workers were not easy to find, their reputation travelled to the European shippers of indentured labour in Calcutta and onward to the sugar cane planters in Mauritius and the Caribbean.

Colonialism was a direct partner in this enterprise. The imperial states took a special interest in the status of the workers. Migrants were imperial citizens like any other.

> The rights and interests of these settlers were protected in legislation, at least on paper. First, the government of India insisted that its indentured subjects be allowed to enjoy the same rights and privileges as other subjects resident in the colonies. It was a requirement repeated over time. ... When exceptional abuses came to light, India intervened with the threat of cancelling emigration. The threat was effective. (Lal 2012: 142–3)

Merchant migration was a different matter. Here, the agency of the imperial state was felt differently. Possibly 2 million more Indians went to Asia and Africa intending to work as merchants and bankers. They did not all circulate in imperial spheres, some went to Japan and Central Asia, for example, but being British Indian subjects mattered to their identity and security (Markovits 2003). In Southeast Asia, the colonial state was again involved differently. As British power extended into the interior in Malaya between 1874 and 1888, Chinese miners and farmers were invited to settle there. In Java and French Indochina, most of the Chinese settlers were engaged in commerce and transport. They were permitted to settle, but under no special state privileges, and relied mainly on their networks.[4]

Conclusion

Too often the history of international economic relations has been read as a bilateral relationship between the colonized and the colonizer. Seeing the role of colonial power in sustaining it, it seems easy to conclude that the globalization was a one-sided exchange that reinforced dependency of Asia and Africa upon Europe. The colonies' specialization in agriculture and mining and their dependence on the import of hi-tech textiles, metals and machines suggests that colonialism enforced a malign trade regime.

The chapter suggests that this is not a good characterization of the world economy. It is wrong for three reasons. First, globalization was built not on power alone, but also on technological and institutional convergence. Colonialism was not just about forcing open trade, but also making laws to enable trade, migration and investment. It was a channel for the formal legal emergence of institutions that capitalism would need. Because of this effect, exchange among the colonies, and within Asia and Africa, went ahead. Second, while the institutional development no doubt helped foreigners, it also helped many local entrepreneurs. European enterprise often depended on local capital and information, so that globalization also empowered these local agents. These indigenous actors moved in various fields, sometimes in rivalry with Europeans. When nationalist movements gained speed, their loyalty to the cause was crucial to the movement's success. Third, colonies selling primary products to industrialized countries that ruled them – a pattern that an older scholarship would call 'typically colonial' trade – was unstable and not all that typical of colonialism.

Notes

[1]   There is a debate in economic history on when globalization really began (see discussion in De Zwart and Van Zanden 2018). The debate turns on how globalization is defined, and whether it is defined as a process with certain potentialities, or as a set of effects that followed from trade, migration or investment. One contributor to this discussion calls the early-modern (17th and 18th century) globalization polycentric and one limited by transaction costs, but one that nevertheless 'altered the course of development in polities throughout Eurasia' (De Vries 2010). The chapter includes the early-modern because political development is the subject of the book.

[2]   Originally proposed to explain the cost of borrowing, empire effect is generalized to include effects of the empire on trade flows, see Mitchener and Weidenmier (2008).

[3]   On information intermediaries, see Flandreau and Flores (2009).

[4]   On these networks, see Pepinsky (2016).

4

Growth and Development in the Colonies

The previous chapter showed that the links between colonialism and globalization were complex and nonlinear. Further, the experience of colonialism was dynamic, and its impact varied over time and across space. Unfortunately, understanding how colonialism affected individuals and communities is difficult given the surviving data in many colonies. Most colonial governments collected data consistently on only a few economic phenomena, mainly related to public finance and trade. Recent work in quantitative economic history has, however, made innovative use of surviving sources to document how colonial economic change affected groups within colonies over time. This chapter reviews this evidence, emphasizing the diversity of colonial experiences as well as identifying some common patterns across regions.

Efforts to examine living standards in the colonies have addressed the paucity of data by combining a variety of measures (see for example Booth 2012; Bowden et al 2008). Inspired by wider debates about comparative living standards, researchers have used wages and prices as one way to test hypotheses about the ways in which colonialism affected living standards (Broadberry and Gupta 2015; Frankema and van Waijenburg 2012; de Zwart and van Zanden 2015). Another approach is to use data on average heights, which are influenced by disease environments and food availability in childhood (Bassino and Coclanis 2008; Földvári et al 2013; Baten et al 2013; Moradi 2009; Austin et al 2012). Literacy rates or other educational outcomes provide yet another measure of how colonialism affected the lives of the colonized (Chaudhary and Garg 2015; Wantchekon et al 2015).

By triangulating different indicators, research in this area has examined in a more nuanced way how colonial policies affected people living under colonial rule over time. Overall, the findings have emphasized diversity both between and within colonies, but a few generalizations can be made. The first is that people in areas which produced exports, or had access to export markets, fared better during the colonial period than those without such access, confounding narratives about 'extraction' to some extent. The second is that the colonial period saw rising inequality between individuals and groups based on proximity to markets and education. The third is that there was considerable change over time, with outcomes across a number of measures improving after the Second World War. However, the degree to which regions which lagged behind were able to catch up during the final stage of colonial rule varied.

Measuring colonial economic performance

Chapter 1 presented some basic statistics on levels of income and the patterns of growth and development in a select set of colonies. They showed that both colonies and independent countries experienced periods of economic growth and contraction during the period of colonial rule. There is thus no straightforward relationship between colonialism and growth – colonialism did not universally undermine growth in the colonies. Rather, efforts made by both colonial governments and indigenous actors to deepen integration with global markets can be linked to growth during good times as well as reversals when global economic winds shifted. This section considers the data on which these calculations are based in more detail, and dissects what they do and do not reveal.

The calculation of aggregate measures of economic performance for colonies, dominated by GDP, remains a relatively undeveloped field. For many colonies, particularly in sub-Saharan Africa, no such estimates exist until the period immediately preceding independence; most studies of African growth begin in 1950 or 1960 with the first systematic databases of national accounts. Subsequent research has pushed this back further for a select set of countries. Broadberry and Gardner (2018) provide estimates of GDP per capita for eight countries in Anglophone Africa dating back to the late 19th century. South Africa is better represented, with estimates for the Cape Colony in the 18th century (Fourie and van Zanden 2013) and for the Natal and the Cape Colony in the 19th century (Magee, Greyling and Verhoef 2016). Most African economies grew comparatively rapidly during the decades preceding the First World War, as the production of export crops expanded and transport costs fell. This was checked, to a greater or lesser degree, by sharp periods of negative growth during the two world wars and the Great Depression. Most then enjoyed a period of growth during the immediate post-war decades before suffering a further period of shrinking during the 'lost decades' from the mid-1970s.

For India, national income research is better developed. In addition to the series by Broadberry et al (2015) cited in Chapter 1, there are three other series available (Angus Maddison, Alan Heston, and the most detailed of the three by S. Sivasubramonian). The three series tell largely the same story: national income per head increased at an average rate of 1–2 per cent in the late 19th century, and at a rate near zero in the interwar period. The fall was partly a result of the decline of networks of market exchange centred in Britain of which India had been a part, and also partly India's population transition. Behind this bleak result lies a story of inequality. Business activities did well throughout, with trade, transport, large and small industry seeing not only overall growth but also significant productivity growth. The main site of the stagnation was agriculture, where a land-extensive process of growth came to an end as arable land ran out. As in Africa, average performance was often the cumulative result of periods of growth offset by periods of shrinking.

All of these series, for India as well as Africa, rely on highly indirect methods of measurement of income, particularly for less commercialized parts of the economy. Three sources of data are key to the measures discussed earlier: population, trade and government finance. Wages and prices are also central, but not always available at the right level of disaggregation. Combined, these data provide the foundations for understanding broad patterns of economic development which can be used to compare colonies over time, helping to understand how differences in the origins, structure and institutions of colonial rule shaped economic performance.

One challenge in assessing the economic impact of colonialism is finding the right starting point. For places which had sufficient administrative and political capacity before colonial rule, it is possible to measure economic growth before, during and after the colonial period. This is true for India, as an example (Broadberry et al 2015). For most, however, the data used to produce measurements like GDP originate only with the beginning of colonial rule. Historically, the lack of a documentary record has been interpreted to suggest that most colonies had subsistence economies prior to the establishment of colonial rule – an assumption used by, for example, McPhee to argue that colonialism had been an agent of economic growth. However, despite the lack of data, it is difficult to square this assumption with voluminous evidence – both quantitative and qualitative – for economic dynamism prior to the beginning of colonial rule. India, for example, was comparatively prosperous under the Mughal Empire in the 17th century, although incomes declined thereafter. For other places, where we are dependent on data collected by colonial governments, early figures hint at the precolonial growth we are unable to document for certain. Ewout Frankema and Marlous van Waijenburg (2012) calculate real wages for unskilled male workers in a selection of African countries from 1880 and find that in the late 19th century, these were higher in West African cities than in many Asian ones. Efforts by Manning (2004) and Szereszewski (1965) to calculate per capita incomes in precolonial and early colonial West Africa using trade data also support the idea that coastal West Africa was a comparatively affluent region prior to colonial rule.

During the colonial period, the collection of data by colonial governments makes it possible to reconstruct patterns of economic change over the decades preceding independence. Perhaps the most basic set of data used to understand economic change over time is population. In eras when more nuanced measures of income are unavailable, population density and urbanization are often used as a proxy, on the assumption that: 1) higher levels of population density suggest greater land productivity; and 2) urbanization requires a sufficient surplus in agricultural production for some share of the population to specialize in other trades. This is the measure, for example, used by Acemoglu et al (2002: 1232) to speculate about a 'reversal of fortune' between wealthier and poorer areas.[1] Understanding population dynamics is thus central to any broader study of economic performance. However, data are often speculative. Few colonies produced systematic population counts before the beginning of the colonial period, and estimates of population trends are often based either on proxy measures such as cultivated land area, or on backward projection from later censuses. Colonial census-taking was frequently indifferent and politically fraught. India is again an exception, and from 1881 onwards there exists substantial demographic information (Dyson 2018: 124). Elsewhere, the starting point for such backward projection is often the first systematic censuses of the middle of the 20th century (Frankema and Jerven 2014).

Despite these uncertainties, these data do support several stylized facts about the demographics of the colonial world. First is that population densities at the beginning of the colonial period varied enormously across and within different colonies. South Asian colonies had much higher population densities than Southeast Asian or African colonies, with significant implications for institutions of property rights and taxation (Frankema 2015). A second is that, on average, mortality rates fell and populations grew across the colonial period. There were notable exceptions to this, and the colonial period also included dramatic, and tragic, mortality shocks. Some of these, like the influenza pandemic of 1918–19 were global. Others were attributable to local factors, either specific environmental events like the rinderpest epidemic in East Africa in the late 19th century, or failures in local systems of food distribution, as in the case of the several famines in India in the 19th and 20th centuries. In both cases, underlying economic and health conditions contributed to the impact of the crisis. These shocks often slowed, but did not stop, the general trend towards population increase over the period, and the end of these shocks accelerated population growth. In India, for example, population growth during the interwar period was linked to a substantial fall in the infant mortality rate, and the disappearance of famines and famine-induced diseases in the region, testifying to the effectiveness of public health measures.

This rate of population growth figures centrally in estimates of economic output. In older estimates of colonial economic performance, agricultural production not intended for export – about which we have little or no data in most cases – was assumed to move in line with population. This reflected an assumption that outside the tradeable sector, most people produced only enough to feed themselves (Szereszewski 1965; Deane 1953). Data on international trade and government spending, which are much better documented, was then added to estimates of subsistence production based on population to produce an estimate of economic production. However, more recent work has questioned the assumption that food consumption would remain constant even as incomes from international trade rose. Smallholders also responded to opportunities offered by economic growth and, as Arne Bigsten (1986: 1151) writes, 'in recent years it has been practically impossible to find a smallholder who produces for subsistence only'. Instead, newer calculations of GDP per capita have used various methods to try to predict the relationship between the expansion of trade and the production of food – either by using historical data on wages and prices (Broadberry et al 2015; Broadberry and Gardner 2019) or by using data from later periods when information on both domestic production and trade are more readily available (Prados de la Escosura 2012).

These estimates are an improvement on earlier ones, but they do not capture everything. Trade data, for example, is based only on the goods which passed through colonial customs houses. Given the limited administrative capacity of the colonial state, it seems likely that at least some imports and exports escaped the attention of officials. Indeed, the reality of smuggling was widely known in some colonies. In the Gambia, a tiny British colony in West Africa separated from French

Senegal only by a long and unpoliced land border, estimates by colonial officials suggested that an average of a third of the groundnuts exported from what was then Bathurst (now Banjul) were actually produced in French territory. Senegalese farmers and merchants smuggled groundnuts across the border in order to take advantage of the lower tariffs on manufactured imports in the Gambia (Gardner 2015: 304–5). While the Gambia is an exceptional case, colonial governments often debated the costs and benefits of establishing customs stations at particular border crossings depending on the scale of the trade at that point, making it likely that some trading opportunities were missed (de Roo 2016). However, it is likely that these were relatively small in scale compared to what was measured.

A bigger potential shortcoming is that these data provide estimates of average per capita production across what could be large and diverse territories. How this was distributed, and how these changes influenced individuals, is more difficult to capture. Data on wages and prices can, at least to some extent, help fill this gap. In their study of African real wages – or nominal wages deflated by the prices of a basket of household goods – Frankema and van Waijenburg (2012: 896) argue that, when compared to GDP, they 'better reflect the living standards of *ordinary African workers*' (original emphasis). They find that real wages in West African cities were relatively high compared both to Asian cities as well as to East Africa. They attribute low real wages in the latter to colonial policies which aimed to keep the cost of African labour low to assist settler farms and plantations.

The overall picture painted by these measurements is one of growth through the late 19th and early 20th centuries, followed by setbacks of varying severity during the years of war and economic depression which followed 1914. While there may be uncertainties about some of the data used, this overall picture is consistent with patterns of growth in the developing world as a whole across this period, and suggests that the institutions of colonial rule were just one factor in shaping the economic performance of colonies. In both colonized and independent countries, growth was particularly tied to trade and the state of the global economy. The next section considers the specific sources of growth in colonial economies and the ways in which colonial policies played a role in shaping them.

Sources of economic growth

The brief review in the previous section on the methods used to construct measures of economic performance in colonial economies tells us much not just about those measures but also about colonial economies themselves. They show that expansions in trade explain much of the growth of the colonial period, which in turn had implications for the incomes of those who produced goods for domestic production. This section looks more closely at the sources of this growth, and how they influenced the structure of colonial economies.

The development strategies adopted by colonial governments focused on the rapid expansion of export production. At the same time, indigenous producers also looked for opportunities offered by connections to the global market. One question is therefore what explains the comparatively rapid growth of export production during the early colonial period, given that as previous chapters have suggested the initiative for building links to the global economy did not necessarily begin with colonial officials? Current research highlights two main sources: investments in transport and other technology, and the introduction of new export crops. These two factors helped facilitate the rapid expansion of colonial economies, but they depended on the actions of both colonial governments and indigenous producers.

Chapter 6 shows that, at least based on their budgets, investments in transport infrastructure were an important priority for colonial governments. This included a variety of investments, from roads to ports and harbour works. Arguably the most important such investment, at least based on their share of total spending before 1914, were railways. Colonial railways served both military and economic purposes, and their actual economic impact has long been debated. More recent quantitative studies of the economic history of Africa and Asia have made it possible to document their impact more systematically. These are motivated by the fact that infrastructure often represents a substantial share of contemporary aid programmes, but, as Dave Donaldson (2018: 899) puts it, 'we lack a rigorous empirical understanding of the extent to which transportation infrastructure projects actually reduce the costs of trading, and how the resulting trade cost reductions affect welfare'.

It is clear that the construction of railways represented a significant technological change in the transport systems of most colonies. Prior to their introduction, goods were generally transported by methods that were much slower, less reliable and more expensive. In much of Africa, the prevalence of tsetse flies limited the use of draft animals, meaning that most goods were transported using head porterage. This was costly in terms of both money and time. A 1931 report on Liberia, a West African country that retained its formal independence and did not construct its first railway until the 1950s, observed that the native products are brought down from the hinterland to the coast towns for barter or sale on the heads and backs of porters, one of the most expensive means of transport known, as these men are taken away from their homes and farms for periods as long as 30 days to make the trip to the coast and return.[2]

This same description could have been made of many of Africa's export trades in the 19th century, from East African ivory to West African palm oil. In the case of the former, export trades were restricted to high value-to-weight goods. In the latter, transport costs restricted production of export crops to a relatively narrow band of territory near the coast (Tosh 1980). Even where animals could be used, such as India's pack bullocks, transport was slow and restricted to inconsistently maintained roads (Donaldson 2018: 900; Hurd 1983: 738).

Research on the impact of historical railway construction often adopts what is known as the social savings approach, which measures 'how much extra society would have to pay to do what it did after an innovation, without it' (Leunig 2010: 776). Owing to the high cost of alternative methods of transport, colonial railways offered significant social savings. In West Africa, for example, Isaiah Chavez, Stanley Engerman and James Robinson (2014) find that the social savings for good traffic were positive and sometimes substantial, ranging from 0.8 to 6.1 per cent of GDP in different colonies at different times. In their study of the Cape Colony, Alfonso Herranz-Loncan and Johan Fourie (2017) also find positive social savings of 12 per cent of GDP.

This reduction in transport costs opened up many new possibilities for the production of exports in regions which had previously been too far from ports for such production to be economical. New centres of export production emerged even where this had not been the initial purpose for the construction of the railway. In northern Nigeria, for example, a railway constructed primarily for military purposes made it possible to export groundnuts profitably, establishing what became the region's most important export industry (Hogendorn 1978). Similarly, in the Gold Coast, the railway intended to connect the mining areas to the coast also opened up what became important cocoa-growing areas of the interior (Jedwab and Moradi 2015).

The impact of railways was not restricted to export production, however. In colonies that were large enough, they contributed to internal market integration. John Hurd (1983: 737) writes of India that 'from a country of many segmented markets, separated from each other by the high cost of transport, India became a nation with its local centres linked by rail to each other and to the world'. The increase in internal trade, which is documented systematically by Donaldson (2018), is an important indicator 'about the potential for gains from trade'. Centres of export production generated increased demand for other products, such as grain or other foodstuffs, which would also be shipped by rail. In a study of Kenya, Remi Jedwab, Edward Kerby and Alexander Moradi (2016) find that the construction of the railway across Kenya had a permanent and significant impact on the economic geography of the country, causing the emergence of urban centres in the interior (most notably Nairobi) which remained even after the railway itself had declined as a primary means of transporting goods.

As important as railways were, their impact was often linked to parallel developments in the economy. The comparatively high level of social savings contributed by the Cape Colony railway can be attributed at least partly to the mining boom which followed the discovery of diamonds in 1867. The railway 'eased the movement of labor, capital goods, foodstuffs and other necessities to the mining centers' (Herranz-Loncan and Fourie 2018: 74). In French Algeria, the railway had limited impact until cereal production became competitive 'thanks to new farming techniques and changes in trade policy' (Maravall Buckwalter 2019: 19). The intersection of railways with the introduction of new farming techniques – in this case, new crops – was particularly important in the Gold Coast, which became the world's largest cocoa exporter just decades after the crop was introduced to West Africa in part thanks to the link between the railways and the cocoa-growing areas in the middle of the country (Jedwab and Moradi 2016).

New technologies in both transport and farming thus offered opportunities for increased incomes, among both producers for export and others who supplied food and labour services to exporters. However, there were risks in a development strategy which encouraged specialization in a relatively small number of primary exports, and these are important to keep in mind along with the sources of growth. Rapid growth through trade is often associated with equally rapid reversals when global prices decline. There is evidence that limited appetites for risk among indigenous smallholders could at times restrict the production of exports. In Uganda, for example, smallholders generally adopted a model of partial commercialization, mixing food crops with cash crops in order to ensure sufficient subsistence (de Haas 2017). However, in other cases and depending on various local ecological factors, the production of cash crops required a reduction in food production or a shift to food crops which were easier to grow but less nutritious. Further, when prices for those exports did decline, there could be serious consequences for both producers and those who depended on them. This was perhaps most obvious in the mineral sector. When the price of copper declined in the 1930s, for example, thousands of African mineworkers on the Copperbelt in British Northern Rhodesia found themselves unemployed. The colonial state lacked the capacity to provide any substantial assistance to any but the relatively small number of European mineworkers, and expected – incorrectly – that the African workers would simply return to farming. However, there were also examples in agriculture. The slow decline of the Caribbean island colonies, from some of the most affluent parts of European empires to some of the poorest, began when sugar prices fell due to the production of European beet sugar. Even the success stories of the 20th century were not immune. When cocoa prices declined in the 1930s, there was considerable consolidation in cocoa farms as poorer farmers were forced to sell their trees – which take several years to mature – to those better able to ride out the downturn (Hopkins 1973: 258–9). This contributed to the increase in inequality discussed later in this chapter.

Even before colonial rule, indigenous producers and merchants were taking advantage of opportunities offered by the globalization of the 19th and early 20th centuries, as shown by comparatively high levels of income and wages in some colonies before or on the eve of colonization. However, new technologies, including colonial investments in transport technology along with improvements in agriculture introduced largely by indigenous entrepreneurs, provided further opportunities and opened up access to new markets. However, this growth also increased the vulnerability of colonial economies to global downturns. The next section examines the implications of growth and reversals for living standards and economic development more broadly defined.

Capabilities

The methods described in the previous section can highlight broad patterns, using averages and aggregates, but they say little about how individual people in the colonies experienced the economic and political changes of the period. For this, historians have long relied on qualitative accounts. However, to capture this experience in any systematic and comparative way has required innovations in the types of data used and the methods by which they are analysed. In recent decades, technological innovations have made such methodological innovations possible, allowing for the collection and analysis of data not possible using older methods. This section reviews some of these advances.

In modern definitions, there is more to development than just increasing incomes. In his *Development as Freedom*, Amartya Sen (2001: 1) defined development as 'a process of expanding the real freedoms that people enjoy'. This includes growth in income. However, the approach notes that

> growth of GDP or of individual incomes can, of course, be very important as a means to expanding the freedoms enjoyed by members of the society. But freedoms depend also on other determinants, such as social and economic arrangements (for example, facilities for education and health care) as well as political and civil rights.

Colonialism offered little in the way of political or civil rights to most indigenous inhabitants of the colonies, although there were opportunities for social mobility which may have given some individuals greater political voice than they had under precolonial political systems, which were in many cases neither democratic nor egalitarian. These were mostly a function of the limited 'facilities for education and health care' which emerged under colonial rule, which despite their limitations did help to reshape the social landscape of many colonies.

Perhaps the easiest of these to measure is education. Surviving data on government expenditures, the number of educational facilities, and enrolment levels make it possible to understand in some detail how the provision of western education, at least, changed over time. Data on government expenditures are discussed in more detail in Chapter 6. This section focuses more specifically on educational outcomes and their implications for economic development in the colonies. The two are, of course, linked – Latika Chaudhary and Manuj Garg (2015) find a strong link between government spending on primary education and rural literacy rates in India – but the question of interest here is less about government decisions on the allocation of resources and more on the impact of these on people living under colonial rule.

It should be admitted that the education system for which we have data represents only a part of what was available. Indigenous systems of education, along with those offered by non-Christian religious institutions, are much less well documented even though they probably represented the dominant system of education in some areas. Still, it was western education in particular which offered a path upwards in terms of education for those who could access it. Such access was not necessarily a function of colonial rule, and in some regions trade could also lead to improvements in education outcome. Gabriele Cappelli and Joerg Baten (2017) find higher levels of numeracy among coastal trading communities in West Africa as early as the 18th century, well before the beginning of colonial rule in the region. Leonard Wantchekon, Mark Klašnja and Natalija Novta (2015) find that in French colonial Benin, both the first cohort of students in mission schools as well as their descendants had higher living standards and were less likely to work in agriculture than their non-educated counterparts.

Data on literacy, such as that used by Chaudhary and Garg (2015), are not readily available for all parts of the empire. Whether someone can sign their name is often used as an approximate indicator of literacy. Marriage registers from Namirembe Cathedral in Kampala, Uganda, were used to measure literacy and occupations for the men and women marrying there from 1900 through the remainder of the colonial period. They find considerable social mobility among Protestant converts in Uganda across the colonial period. Both men and women showed rapid improvements in literacy, and traditional elites lost their relative position to educated Africans engaged in trade and other related activities (Meier zu Selhausen et al 2018). However, these conclusions have been challenged on the basis that those who married in Namirembe Cathedral represented an elite group rather than the population of Kampala as a whole, which lagged considerably behind the Namirembe group in terms of literacy (de Haas and Frankema 2018).

Where literacy rates are unavailable, measuring access to education (through proximity to schools and mission stations) provides a plausible proxy. Areas that were nearer to mission stations during the colonial period are often more affluent in subsequent decades, which some have explained as being the result of mission schooling and local investments in human capital (Nunn 2014). However, this raises the question of why mission stations located where they did. In a study of British Africa, Ewout Frankema (2012) argues that it was primarily African demand rather than European decisions that influenced where missions were located.

Access to healthcare is another aspect of Sen's 'economic freedom'. It also features in classical definitions of human capital. Workers suffering from ill health are less productive, and lower life expectancies reduce incentives for investment in other forms of human capital. There has been less work on the effectiveness of colonial healthcare than on education, but there are several indirect measures which can provide insights into the health of indigenous populations under colonial rule. The principal one used by economic historians is heights. Height data was often collected as part of military or police recruitment. Individual heights are determined by a combination of genetics and living conditions in childhood. Children who are frequently ill or short of food are likely to experience stunting, or growth below their potential. In consequence, barring any substantial change in the genetic composition of a population through, for example, migration, average heights across a population are a function of childhood living standards.

Height data shows the diverse effects of colonial economic development on living standards. Height data from before 1950 often comes from selective samples which, as in the case of military recruits, could involve a positive bias for tall people and which studies in this area have to adjust for. Subject to this qualification, height data shows that in most colonies, at least some groups and regions saw an increase in average heights, though not all the time. Other groups suffered declines in their average heights, and for all there were setbacks during periods of conflict or depression, whether local or global. Lance Brennan, John McDonald and Ralph Shlomowitz (1994) find that the heights of agricultural labourers in North India increased during an initial phase of commercialization linked to the expansion of transport networks during the middle of the 19th century, but then declined from the 1870s into the 20th century. Guntupalli and Baten (2006) find rising inequality in heights, particularly during the 1920s when caste was an important influence shaping individual heights. In Dutch Indonesia, average heights fell during the period of the 'cultivation system' in the middle of the 19th century (Baten et al 2013). Similarly, West African heights also declined during the early and mid-19th centuries (Austin et al 2012). In contrast, Moradi (2008, 2009) documents increases in heights in the Gold Coast and Kenya through the 20th century. However, these increases were unevenly distributed between regions and ethnic groups.

Colonial interventions in education and healthcare, however minimal, seem to have improved the standards of living of at least some living under colonial rule. For example, in 1951, the literacy rate in Sri Lanka (Ceylon) was 60 per cent, next to Japan in Asia, whereas that of India was 18 per cent. Both countries were colonies of Britain until recently. However, this is not to say that colonial interventions should be considered positive, and there is more work to be done linking colonial spending on, for example, healthcare and the outcomes of those programmes. Sara Lowes and Eduardo Montero (2018) study a series of French campaigns to eradicate tropical diseases in Central Africa from 1921–56. During the campaign, Africans were forcibly injected with ineffective medicines which had serious side effects. The legacy of the campaigns was not the eradication of disease but rather a persistent distrust in medical treatment which has influenced the effectiveness of future healthcare initiatives in the region. Further, other measures paint a less optimistic picture of the extent to which growth translated into better standards of living. Booth (2012) finds that in much of Southeast Asia, levels of food consumption were comparatively low and the share of their budgets that urban labourers had to spend on food was high, an indicator of poverty.

Inequality

Whether measured in terms of income or living standards, some people were able to gain from the interventions of colonial governments by taking advantage of opportunities for production, trade or education. But how widely were these benefits distributed?

The question of links between colonialism and inequality are linked to broader debates about the link between globalization and inequality, which have gained wider traction in the aftermath of the 2008 financial crisis. In studying the history of inequality, it is important to distinguish inequality between nations from inequality within nations. Since 1990, inequality between nations has fallen, driven largely by rapid growth in populous countries like India and China. At the same time, however, inequality within countries has risen. In contrast, from 1820 to 1990, both types of inequality increased, leading to a rise in global inequality, or the relative inequality of incomes among all people in the world regardless of where they live (Ravallion 2018: 621). The growth of many countries was not sufficient to catch up to the economic leaders of the world, and progress was often erased by reversals. At the same time, however, inequality within countries also increased.

There are various measures of inequality, but most involve relating an individual to the distribution of incomes in whatever the unit of analysis might be (a country, a region or even the world). The most common is probably the Gini coefficient, defined as the average gap between two individuals chosen at random from the particular unit of analysis (Bourguignon and Scott-Railton 2015: 18). Bigsten's (1986)

Gini coefficient calculations for Kenya show a steady increase in inequality from 1914 up to 1950, after which it declined slightly in the ten years before independence. The increase was particularly sharp in the aftermath of the two world wars. From 1914–21, per capita incomes on average decreased due to the trade disruptions of the war but there was differentiation within the 'modern' sector. From 1936 onwards, economic growth and rising inequality occurred side by side. The decline during the 1950s was due to growth in the agricultural sector and, after 1955, land redistribution programmes in the aftermath of Mau Mau. Dutch-ruled Indonesia saw inequality increases of a similar magnitude, although the peak was not as high as in Kenya, from the early 20th century up to 1942 (van Leeuwen and Földvári 2017). In Botswana – often hailed as an economic success story – inequality rose rapidly in the 1930s alongside the growth of cattle exports (Bolt and Hillbom 2016; see also Box 4.1).

Economic theories of inequality suggest that the economic expansion of the 19th and early 20th centuries could be expected to contribute to rising inequality irrespective of whether a country was colonized or not. However, it may be argued that the institutions of colonialism may have contributed to some types of inequality. In settler economies like Kenya, governments took steps to reduce the wages of the African majority and often adopted policies which favoured expatriate farms over indigenous smallholders. The limited reach of infrastructure investments benefitted some regions over others, as in the earlier example of heights in Ghana.

Another area in which colonial policies are thought to have contributed to growing gaps between groups within colonies is in terms of gender. Although gender gaps are not generally the subject of most work on inequality, they are another example of the uneven distribution of the benefits of colonial-era growth. Further, theories of development economics have emphasized that female empowerment, variously defined, contributes positively to living standards. In Africa, Emmanuel Akyeampong and Hippolyte Fofack (2014) have argued that colonial education systems undermined existing systems of relative gender equality by entrenching the patriarchal norms of western societies. While the extent to which precolonial African societies were really characterized by gender parity is debatable, other evidence also supports the notion that colonial education systems contributed to gender differentiation in education levels and occupations. The Ugandan marriage registers discussed in the previous section also show large gaps between men and women in terms of improvements in literacy across the colonial period.

Box 4.1: Inequality in Botswana

In many countries the colonial period included periods of economic growth as well as economic crisis. This raises the question of how the proceeds from that growth were distributed, particularly in the context of autocratic and fragmented political institutions. High levels of inequality are common in formerly colonized countries: does this inequality have its roots in colonial patterns of development?

The case of Botswana is instructive. Botswana has achieved consistently high levels of economic growth since achieving independence in 1966, even during the period from the mid-1970s to the 1990s described in most of Africa as the 'lost decades'. This growth, based primarily on the export of diamonds, has led numerous observers to label Botswana an African 'success story', an exception to an otherwise general pattern of persistent poverty. This success has been attributed to the inclusive nature of Botswana's precolonial institutions paired with minimal interventions by the British colonial state.

The distribution of these gains has been unequal, and Botswana also has one of the highest rates of inequality in sub-Saharan Africa. New quantitative research on Botswana's economic history suggests that the link between growth based on resource exports and inequality may also date back to the colonial period. Botswana had been a predominantly pastoral economy since before the beginning of the colonial period, and therefore had some degree of wealth inequality based on different herd sizes. This was compounded when the rapid expansion of cattle exports from the 1920s provided opportunities for those with large herds to increase their cash incomes. Those with smaller herds could not sell as many cattle without threatening the viability of their herds. Using social tables, Bolt and Hillbom (2016) document a rise in inequality in Botswana from 1921 and show a sharp rise coinciding with the increase in cattle exports. By the time diamonds replaced cattle as Botswana's most important export in the 1970s, inequality had already been rising for several decades.

As yet, measures of colonial inequality are restricted to a comparatively small number of countries for which the necessary data are available. However, the data that do exist suggest that colonial-era growth often benefitted some groups more than others.

Further reading

Daron Acemoglu, Simon Johnson and James A. Robinson (2012) 'An African success story: Botswana', in D. Rodrik (ed), *In Search of Prosperity: Analytic Narratives on Economic Growth*, Princeton: Princeton University Press, pp 80–122.

Jutta Bolt and Ellen Hillbom (2016) 'Long-term trends in economic inequality: lessons from colonial Botswana, 1921–74', *Economic History Review*, 69(4): 1255–84.

Conclusion

Economic growth was possible under colonialism, but its implications were not always wholly positive. There were winners and losers. The structure of the economies that emerged often left them vulnerable to global downturns, and many people who had gained from earlier phases of growth suffered sometimes severe setbacks during the Great Depression and the two world wars.

Attempts to link particular types of colonial rule and institutions to current development outcomes neglect the fact that the relationship between colonial rule and economic development in the colonies was complex, dynamic, and depended as much on global conditions and the initiative of indigenous people as it did on what colonial governments did. Nor were the interests of colonial governments necessarily antithetical to encouraging economic growth – if not broad-based development – in their colonies. Their ability to build a tax base and relieve metropolitan taxpayers of the burden of local administrative costs depended on it.

However, this did not mean that colonial governments aimed for the balanced development, in modern terms, of their colonies. It was not in their interests, for example, to encourage the development of manufacturing industries which have at least traditionally paved the way to sustained (rather than sporadic) economic growth. Despite this, there were some cases, like India or South Africa, where local interests achieved sufficient autonomy to adopt protectionist policies anyway. Similarly, many colonial officials saw little advantage in providing education opportunities to their subjects, beyond perhaps what was needed to staff government jobs. A few, like Lord Lugard, actually thought to do so was dangerous, and would lead to resistance against colonial rule (Lugard 1926). Despite these obstacles, some did manage to take advantage of the opportunities offered by export growth, urbanization and slowly expanding social services.

But not everyone, and the rising inequality between regions, individuals and to some degree ethnic groups often had significant political consequences both during the colonial period and after. Unequal access to land among the Kikuyu was one of the key drivers of the Mau Mau uprising in Kenya, for example (Anderson 2005: 10). Similarly, large gaps in the provision of education between southern and northern Nigeria prompted conflict after independence, when the new elected government sent southerners to administer the north (Osaghae 1998: 5). The high levels of inequality which emerged in some former colonies, such as Botswana, have persisted to the present.

Notes

1   See also Bairoch (1988).
2   Col. George Lewis, 'The Republic of Liberia', in US National Archives and Records Administration (NARA) RG 165 NM84 Box 2393, Declassification NND745020.

5

Debates about Costs and Benefits

Previous chapters showed that no single explanation can account for the timing, scale or scope of modern imperial expansion in the 19th and 20th centuries. Rather, it reflected wider changes in the global economy, including the spread of industrialization in Europe and North America, and the rapid expansion of trade as transport costs fell. Both indigenous and European actors responded to these changes in a variety of ways, and these shifts underpinned the accumulation of territory by a growing number of colonial powers through the 19th and early 20th centuries.

This process was costly in both human and monetary terms, and prompted fierce debates within colonizing states about whose interests were served by this process and whether the expense would be at all repaid for the economies financing colonial conquest. Historians have subsequently taken up these debates, using an approach Avner Offer (1993: 215) refers to as 'imperial accountancy'. Neither contemporaries nor historians have come to any solid consensus about the question of net cost or benefit to the colonizer or the colonized. One reason is the complexity and variation in colonial connections which emerged from the process outlined in the previous chapter. John Darwin (2009: 1) describes the British Empire as consisting of 'an extraordinary range of constitutional, diplomatic, political, commercial and cultural relationships'. While the British Empire was the largest of the European empires, the others were no less complex. Another reason is that the 'accounting' approach relies on surviving and accessible data, which necessarily restricts the range of questions that might be asked, and interests that might be considered. More qualitative questions on power and influence or the value of self-determination cannot be addressed in this way, and when applied retrospectively it is difficult for this approach to account for the range of possibilities imagined by contemporaries who often rationalized current costs with the potential for future benefits.

This chapter reviews these debates, but not with the intention of coming to any firm conclusion on the net balance by the end of the colonial period. Rather, its aim is to use these debates as a framework to investigate the relationship between metropolitan and colonial governments. While they are often discussed as one unit, debates about costs and benefits show that their interests were not often unified, and that much of imperial policy was the result of negotiations between metropole and colony on this very question. The chapter also aims to balance a generally heavy focus on the British Empire in this literature with discussions of other colonies, to highlight both similarities and differences between them.

'Imperial accountancy', then and now

The end of mercantilism and the corresponding move towards free trade in the 19th century brought a new perspective to the question of whether the possession of colonies could possibly repay the costs of maintaining them. Under mercantilist policies of the previous era, international trade represented a zero-sum game; markets captured by one country were lost to others. In this system colonies were captive markets for the exports of their colonizers, as well as suppliers of bullion and other valuable commodities. With the rise of a more open global economy, however, colonial markets were no longer closed and both opponents and proponents of empire had to grapple with the question of what value the possession of colonies held for countries which ruled them, in a context of the rising fiscal costs of maintaining those colonies. The question has remained a hardy perennial in the decades since the end of empires: as Offer (1993: 215) writes, 'every generation has had a shot' at answering it.

There are two sides of the 'balance sheet' conceptualized by these debates. On the 'credit' side, for the metropole, were whatever economic gains came from the possession of colonies. Proponents of imperial expansion often made the argument that, while the trade with particular territories might be small at that moment, colonial rule – with its import of capital, expertise and good government – would give rise to rapid economic expansion linked to the export of previously neglected natural resources. However, such anticipation sometimes did not pay off. According to O'Brien (1988: 180), 'historians have recorded many examples where British investors were "gulled" into anticipating supranormal profits'. To give just one example, Michael

Havinden and David Meredith (1993: 77) describe a 'mini gold rush' in the Gold Coast between 1880 and 1904, when 476 companies with a nominal capital of almost £43 million were registered for mining and exploration in West Africa. By the end of the period, however, only four of those companies had achieved an annual gold output of more than £10,000. Colonial reports often fed such miscalculations, with wildly optimistic predictions about the future developments of particular colonies. One such report, authored by a government committee in Kenya, argued in 1919 that Kenya only needed sufficient investment in transport 'to swell within one decade into a World-Mart comparable with the century-old growths of the Dominions' (quoted in Gardner 2012: 35).

With the benefit of hindsight, the outcome of these decisions can at least to some extent be measured. According to Patrick O'Brien and Leandro Prados de la Escosura (1999: 32),

> in every European case, for which data is available, interconnections through (i) the export and import of goods and services, (ii) migration, (iii) net flows of returns on investment overseas (interest, profits and dividends) and other economic connections with the rest of the world economy look immeasurably more important than links with empires.

During the 1880s, for example, when the scramble for Africa was ramping up, Portugal's African colonies only had a tiny share of Portugal's overseas trade – only about 3 per cent of exports and imports were traded with the African colonies (Lains 1998: 238–40). Dutch trade with Indonesia actually declined as a share of overall Dutch foreign trade across the decades preceding the First World War. Over that same period, an increasing share of Indonesian commodity exports went to destinations outside the Netherlands (van der Eng 1998).

Calculating the potential gain or loss from the absence of empires with any certainty, however, depends on what assumptions are made about the counterfactual world that might exist without empires. Michael Edelstein (1982) tries to do just this for the British Empire, assuming that if the trade conducted with the empire were to vanish, it would result in a decrease of 1 to 3 per cent in British GDP in 1870 and 1913, respectively. However, O'Brien (1988: 169) challenges the assumptions made, asking: 'why should an independent India have withdrawn from trade with the United Kingdom?' He also points out that more complex modelling would be necessary to understand how economies might have developed differently in a world without empires. If independent countries became more protectionist, for example, would that have led to a broader decline in international trade and specialization? Or would infant industries protected by these tariff walls have generated increased demand for capital goods from Europe and North America?

The same complications arise in considering the export of capital and returns on imperial investments. Measurements of these returns often rely on the limited sample of capital flows and companies for which data can be reconstructed from surviving sources. Lance Davis and Michael Huttenback (1986) use the finances of a large, if selective, sample of companies doing business in the empire, to argue that the British economy received little in exchange for the costs of running its large empire. Further, wider investigations of foreign investments in the era of 'financial globalization' from 1880 to 1914 show that, despite the apparent protections of empire, investors on average preferred to send their money to countries outside it.

For metropolitan countries, balanced against the potential benefits of trade and investment were the costs of acquiring and maintaining far-flung territories. Such costs were Adam Smith's primary complaint about the possession of empires. They could be substantial, particularly during the years of colonial conquest or conflict. Italy's conquest of Ethiopia in the late 1930s caused colonial expenditures to jump to over 10 per cent of GDP, from less than 1 per cent earlier in the decade (Federico 1998: 387). The heavy costs of the South African war for Britain were one inspiration for Hobson's critiques of empire (Krebs 1999: 22).

Even in peacetime, the cost of defending empires was a major fiscal concern, and a source of sometimes fierce political fighting within metropolitan legislatures. Adding to this were expenditures on the colonial civil establishment and development programmes. As O'Brien (1988: 194) put it with regard to the British Empire, while some individuals were able to profit from imperial expansion, 'the majority of English people cheerfully and even proudly shouldered a tax bill for an empire from which they derived very little in the form of tangible pecuniary gains'. However, there remain debates about the ways in which these expenditures were divided between metropolitan and colonial taxpayers, which are explored in more detail in the sections below.

Most of the 'imperial accountancy' work restricts its focus to the period before the First World War, the period from 1880 to 1913 often thought of as the high point of 19th-century globalization. Offer

(1993: 235) describes this end point as 'misleading' in that much earlier investment in the defence of colonies was repaid through colonial contributions to the war effort after the outbreak of hostilities in the First World War. During both world wars, metropolitan countries relied on their colonies for supplies of both manpower and commodities which, although quantitatively not always a large share of wartime mobilization, could be strategically important during periods when other supplies of commodities were restricted.

Relationships between colonies and their colonizers were to varying degrees redefined in the more protectionist world of the interwar period and beyond. Adam Smith, whose writings on empire were somewhat ambiguous, was also invoked by those arguing for imperial protectionism later on (Palen 2014). In some empires, policies of imperial preference had been introduced even in the pre-war period. An 1892 tariff had increased the share of Portuguese exports going to Africa from 3 per cent of the total to 15 per cent of the total (Lains 1998: 240). In particular, after the Second World War, colonial exports became important sources of foreign exchange for metropolitan governments (White 2011).

This changing picture emphasizes that the structure and purposes of imperialism were not static, as both economic theories of colonialism and the imperial accountancy literature tend to suggest. Rather, colonialism represented, as van der Eng (1998: 317) describes for the Netherlands and Indonesia, 'a dynamically changing bilateral relationship'. Conditions in both Europe and the colonies could and did shape this relationship in different ways over time. This gave rise to almost constant debates about the respective interests of metropole and colony, which played out in many of the arenas discussed in the accountancy literature. The next three sections explore these in greater depth in the areas of defence costs, development spending and trade policy.

Negotiating defence costs

The idea that colonies enjoyed access to an imperial defence establishment for which they paid little is an influential one in the imperial accountancy literature. 'Of all the subsidies enjoyed by the colonies, none was more lucrative than that for defense', write Davis and Huttenback (1986: 145). O'Brien and Prados de la Escosura (1999: 35) echo this point in their global survey of the literature: 'What seems clear (with the possible exceptions of India and Indonesia) is that the economies and populations of nearly all European colonies and dominions contributed very little towards the costs of their own defence from external aggression or from internal insurrection.' These claims have been challenged, on both conceptual and empirical levels. Can the cost of maintaining colonial rule be equated with the defence expenditures of an independent country? And is it possible to draw a firm line between metropolitan defence expenditures devoted to empire and those for generally metropolitan interests? This section examines these negotiations across the late 19th and 20th centuries.

One of the most prominent debates in this area is over the issue of British India. The scale of the Indian Army, which served both in India and in sometimes large numbers through the rest of the empire, was not matched by any other colonized region. To historians and contemporaries, this seemed to set India apart in terms of discussions about colonial contributions to defence. Others, however, challenge claims about India's contribution, pointing out that in terms of national income, India spent far less on defence than Britain did (O'Brien 1988). However, Offer (1993: 228) disputes the premise of the question, arguing that

> the so-called defence of India was really the cost of keeping India under British rule. The benefit of defence is the maintenance of liberty and sovereignty, the control over one's own affairs. An independent India might have spent the same or more, but it was not independent, and had no liberty to defend. It paid to support alien sovereignty.

This same argument could apply to most colonies, where the costs of imperial defence – whether funded by the colonies or by the metropolitan state – might arguably be said to serve imperial interests rather than the interests of taxpayers in the colonies. Colonial contributions to the war effort in both world wars could be described the same way, as people from the colonies were brought by virtue of colonial conquest into what was largely an intra-European war. Perhaps the most compelling example of this comes from French Africa. During the Second World War, French Equatorial Africa (AEF) remained under control of the Free French government-in-exile led by Charles de Gaulle after France fell to the Nazis in 1940. Soldiers conscripted in AEF colonies found themselves fighting against conscripts from French West Africa (AOF), which was under Vichy control (Jennings 2014).

Negotiations between imperial and colonial governments about the division of defence costs shifted in the final decades of the colonial period. Both financially and in terms of military capacity, imperial governments were weakened after the end of the Second World War. Rising political activism across the colonial world meant that the incidence of internal insurrections had increased. In these cases, imperial governments often did not step in until it was clear that colonial resources would not be sufficient. One example is the Mau Mau rebellion in Kenya, which upended the finances of the Kenyan colonial administration. For over a year after the uprising began in 1952, the Kenyan treasury used its reserves to cover both the cost of the counter-insurgency as well as decreases in tax revenue caused by the conflict. In 1953, Kenya's treasurer travelled to London to request financial support. However, the British government insisted that as Mau Mau was a local rebellion, the colonial administration 'would need to show immediate financial need before such aid could be granted' (Gardner 2010: 70). When the treasurer countered that the colonial government of Malaya had received aid in similar circumstances, the British Treasury responded that the conflict in Malaya was 'one facet of the world-wide anti-Communist struggle' rather than just a local affair.[1] It was not until early 1954 that the British government began to help with the costs of the emergency. Even then, however, costs were shared meticulously between the two governments.

As well as variation over time, there were also differences between imperial states in their ability to mobilize coercive resources in defence of their colonies. This, in turn, influenced the distribution of defence expenditures between colony and metropole. Alexopoulou (2018) compares spending on defence and policing by British and Portuguese colonial governments in Africa and finds that colonies of the weaker power, Portugal spent a much larger amount than their British counterparts. She argues that, as the larger empire, Britain enjoyed economies of scale in the deployment of military force. Portuguese colonies, on the other hand, had to a large extent to fend for themselves.

These examples suggest that arguments about a defence 'subsidy' from imperial governments to their colonies are too simple, even for the period before 1914. Rather than being a straightforward transfer from one to the other, access to imperial resources in response to either external threats or internal uprisings was contingent on negotiations between colonial and imperial governments. In turn, the outcome of these negotiations depended on the resources of both governments and the extent to which the conflict in question was seen to represent an existential threat to the empire.

Bargaining for capital

Access to capital for investment in infrastructure and other development schemes is another 'subsidy' discussed by the imperial accountancy literature. 'Guaranteed loans, grants-in-aid of official salaries, public works, and disaster relief all served to reduce the financial burden on the colonies', by taking those burdens onto metropolitan budgets (Davis and Huttenback 1986: 145). However, as in the case of defence, there remain debates both about the scale of these contributions and about whose interests they served. Subsequent studies of colonial public finance have often argued that metropolitan contributions to colonial budgets were limited through most of the colonial period, only increasing in its final decades. Further, can these contributions be seen as serving the interests of the colonies rather than metropolitan governments?

Metropolitan subsidies to colonial budgets varied, but were in general relatively small shares of overall colonial spending. An exception in some cases were the early years of the colonial period. Fairly quickly, however, colonial governments were expected to support most of their local expenses through their own revenues. How they did this, and the ways in which it influenced their relationships with indigenous populations expected to foot the bill, is the subject of the next chapter. For now, it is enough to note that for most of the colonial period, metropolitan subsidies to colonial governments represented only a very small share of total government spending. Huillery (2014) finds that on average between 1844 and 1957 the French government spent just 0.29 per cent of its total budget on its colonies in West Africa. The vast majority of this expenditure was devoted to the cost of 'conquest and pacification'. On the West African side, this accounted for an average of 2 per cent of the revenue collected in the colonies.

These broad averages mask sometimes significant change over time. In the final decades of colonial rule, colonial spending by metropolitan states often increased rather than decreased. As Cogneau et al (2018: 42) put it, 'after World War II, as their legitimacy was increasingly questioned, French colonial governments did not tax and spend less. They accelerated their modernization project and turned more developmental, in the hope of preserving their imperial dominance'. They were not alone; other colonial powers also increased their spending, in order to either quell rising opposition or to develop the production of specific commodities in demand in the metropole. Much of this spending was on development projects of various kinds, fitting with an overall post-war shift towards state-led development.

Beyond the preservation of colonial rule, many such projects were intended to meet specific commodity needs in the metropole. Many were also unsuccessful.

A good example is the Tanganyika Groundnut Scheme. Havinden and Meredith (1996: 276) describe it as 'a large-scale project which was intended to demonstrate what the state was capable of in tropical Africa when it harnessed modern Western technology and expertise' The scheme, which planned the large-scale production of groundnuts in East Africa through the use of heavy machinery, was intended to fill a gap in the supply of oils and fats in a Britain still under wartime rationing. Today, the scheme serves as a case study for many of the failures of large-scale state-led development in the late colonial period.

Metropolitan government grants were not the only source of capital for colonial governments. As the quote from Davis and Huttenback at the beginning of this section suggests, they could indeed borrow on better terms than independent states with comparable levels of income. In the 2000s, this was picked up again by financial historians investigating the reasons why investors seemed to see some borrowing countries as a better bet, part of the 'empire effect' discussed in Chapter 3. More recent takes have argued that it was specific features of colonial governance which reduced borrowing costs, including sound financial management or use of gold standard currency (Ferguson and Schularick 2006; Obstfeld and Taylor 2003). An alternative argument by Accominotti et al (2011) argues that colonies were able to borrow at cheaper rates because they were colonies, and therefore shared in some implicit way in the credit of the metropole.

However, as was the case with the costs of defence, access to such capital was not freely available to colonies but was rather the subject of sometimes protracted negotiations between colony and metropole. Low borrowing costs presented an implicit moral hazard, and metropolitan governments dealt more harshly with some colonial governments than others in preventing excessive borrowing. In the British Empire, those with large populations of European settlers were allowed to borrow heavily while borrowing was restricted for others (Accominotti et al 2009). Colonial governments wishing to borrow had to demonstrate to the satisfaction of metropolitan officials that they could afford to service any debts they incurred. The timing and amount of their debt issues were subject to approval by the metropolitan government, and some found their own requests reduced or delayed because of what were perceived to be the more pressing needs of a different colony.

Despite these constraints, it is likely that being part of an empire did help poorer colonies to borrow when they might not otherwise have been able to do so. While it is true that, on average, investors considered colonial governments to be safer borrowers than independent governments, they did not necessarily see them all as equal. Metropolitan interventions of various kinds were often required to make smaller, newer or poorer colonies attractive to investors. For example, three of Britain's West African colonies borrowed on the London market before 1914 to fund railway construction. Railways were a central pillar of colonial development policies in the 19th and early 20th centuries, helping expand export production through the reduction of transport costs. In all three of these cases, however, it required a variety of efforts by the British government to generate demand for their loans, including the advancing of money to fund the construction of railways before bonds to pay for them were issued – thus ensuring a quick revenue return – and 'market making' through the pre-arranged purchase of bonds by individuals and institutions with ties to the region (Gardner 2017).

Financial transfers from the metropolitan government to the colonies did at times ease some fiscal burdens for colonial governments, but the scale of such transfers was often small and they arguably served the interests of the metropole as much as they did the colonies. This is not to say that no local economic benefits accrued from colonial investments. However, such spending was not an exercise in philanthropy; rather, it was part of the dynamic relationship between colony and metropole which also shaped defence spending and, as discussed in the next section, trade policy.

Trade and protectionism

Another area of imperial policies which feature heavily in the imperial accountancy literature but which on closer inspection involved a set of bargains between colonial governments and metropolitan capitals was trade policy. The second section of this chapter showed that the share of trade between metropole and colony was one measure of the economic importance of the relationship to the metropole. This level of importance varied, but in general trade flows with countries outside the empire were more important. However, this did not mean that trade relations within empires were not at times politically fraught. The sort of open or preferential policies which benefitted the metropole were not always in the interests of economic elites in the colonies. These debates became increasingly contentious with the tightening of global trade more broadly during the interwar period. In his economic history of Africa, John Forbes Munro (1976: 157) describes these debates as a 'clash of interests on a grand scale – between different colonial and metropolitan governments, between the various producers of the same commodity or types of commodity, between producers and merchants – in which there were "losers" as well as "gainers"'.

Narratives about colonial extraction or the importance of colonial markets would suggest that trade between colony and metropole should be free of tariffs, or at least subject only to a revenue tariff. While this was true of many colonies, particularly during the second half of the 19th century, there was also considerable variation within and between empires in the trade policies adopted. A 1922 survey of colonial tariff policies by the United States Tariff Commission observed that one key difference between colonies was the 'location of tariff making authority', which could lie 'either with home government or with administration of colonies individually'. It was relatively unusual for colonial governments to have the sole power to set tariff rates – this privilege was accorded only to the British Dominions – but in others authority was often divided in various ways between the two governments. In some places – like in the American-ruled Philippines – rates could be determined locally but subject to a metropolitan veto. In others, the metropolitan government could set general restrictions on the level of tariff preferences granted to metropolitan products. This was the case, for example, in Portuguese colonies and in British Rhodesia. In Italian colonies and most British crown colonies (as distinct from dominions), tariffs were set by a governor on the orders of the metropolitan government.

This variety of arrangements, which also changed over time, meant that at least some colonies at some times had a degree of freedom in setting their trade policy. They often used this freedom to press for policies which served local, as opposed to imperial, economic interests. There were two key areas where interests often diverged. One was in the use of protectionist tariffs to help build local industries which might compete with metropolitan exports. The ability to use this strategy was particularly in demand after the economic upheavals of the First World War and the Great Depression illustrated to both colonial governments and to producers the dangers of specializing too heavily in the production of a small number of primary commodities. In India, a hard-won fight to introduce protective tariffs and encourage industrialization was finally won by the colonial government in the interwar period (Roy 2011: 253). Similarly, the 1923 tariff in Kenya was intended to facilitate the creation of local industries, particularly the light processing of agricultural products like wheat and tobacco (Gardner 2012).

The other area of dispute was over imperial preferences. Preferential tariffs like the one adopted by Portugal in 1892 could increase the share of trade with the colonies at the expense of other producers. One effect of such policies was to force colonial consumers to purchase what might be more expensive goods produced by the metropolitan countries. Where this affected the cost of living, imperial preferences could be the subject of either vocal complaint or, perhaps more often, evasion through smuggling or other similar mechanisms. In British West Africa, for example, the imposition of a preferential tariff favouring British textiles raised the cost of living for many consumers, for whom textiles were their main imported purchase and who preferred cheaper Japanese textiles which had recently come onto the market (Havinden and Meredith 1996: 188–9).

Empires of data

One consequence of the political salience of 'balance sheet' debates during the colonial period was a preoccupation with record keeping and data collection in the governance of empires. This was, in many ways, a unique characteristic of the 'modern' European empires, which Jasanoff (2012: 293) describes as 'obsessed with record keeping'. This is not to say that records were not kept by early modern empires. Certainly they were, and historians have used these to develop new pictures of how these empires operated (see, for example, Grafe and Irigoin 2012). However, the logistical challenges of communication over long distances before the age of steam and rail meant that the records of early modern empires were necessarily more decentralized. New transport and communications technologies, such as the steamship and the telegraph, developed as empires expanded. At the same time, European governments were undergoing a process of bureaucratization which aimed to eliminate the rent-seeking and nepotism of the past. It was during this period that, according to Adam Tooze (2008: 678), 'the production of economic data became quasi-industrial'.

Within the realm of imperial governance, one implication of efforts to stamp out the 'old corruption' of the early modern period was a shift away from reliance on personal networks to keep tabs on what was happening in the colonies and towards a more bureaucratic structure of information gathering. This created what Laidlaw's study of the British Empire describes as an 'information revolution'

(2005: 169) in colonial governance. Perhaps the quintessential example of such a change is the colonial 'Blue Books' of the British Empire, so called because of their blue cover. These annual reports of the statistics from the colonies, presented in standardized form each year, have become an invaluable source for the comparative study of British colonies over time. From 1822 onwards colonial governments were required to file annual reports on the trade and finances of their colonies, reports which were eventually expanded to provide data on the civil service and the operation of government departments (Laidlaw 2005: 170–1).

Historians, and particularly those doing quantitative history, have benefitted greatly from this obsession, which produced not only a wealth of quantitative data but also data that was at least intended to be standardized and comparable across different colonies. However, the tidy picture of standardization and comparability was often somewhat illusory, the creation of bureaucratic pressure rather than the centralization of colonial rule.

One example from tax collection in Kenya illustrates this tendency nicely.[2] Like many colonial governments, Kenya collected a flat-rate direct tax imposed on Africans from the first years of colonial rule. As will be discussed in more detail in Chapter 6, this was an important revenue source in colonies where the scale of foreign trade was limited. The tax was initially imposed on African dwellings (referred to at the time as 'hut tax') or on individual African men and sometimes women ('poll tax'). Collection of the tax was extended gradually through the whole of the colony in the first decade of the 20th century. However, some regions were less amenable to it than others. In northern Kenya, for example, the prevalence of nomadic pastoralism among the population made the collection of a hut tax impractical. Instead, local officials imposed a tax on cattle sales in particular population centres. This tax had no legal basis, but it was tolerated by the colonial government in Nairobi (and by extension the imperial government in London). After the first collection of this tax the Consul-General of the territory sent a letter to the Sub-Commissioner on the ground stating:

> I leave the details of tax-collecting to your discretion but you must remember that the revenue is subject to a strict audit and that the auditor will object not only to any defficiency [sic] out [sic] to any revenue collected irregularly. Therefore, though you may collect the Hut-Tax as you think best, you must be careful do describe it

as "Hut-Tax" or "commutation of the Hut-Tax" and not under any new name.

The tax on cattle sales was eventually abandoned after a legal challenge by a group of Somalis from the Northern Frontier Province, but only after it had been collected for a quarter of a century.

Further imperial records suggest that officials 'on the spot' were expected to resolve problems related to the inconsistency of local conditions to imperial policies themselves. One member of the British colonial accounting service, N.S. Carey-Jones (2017: 76), wrote later of his time in the colonial government of Belize.

> My only superior was the Director-General in London. In my early days I used to refer quite a lot of matters there, both for advice and support and to show how "on the ball" I was, until I received a demi-official letter from his deputy, saying that the D-G was worried about the stuff I was sending him as he had thought, when he appointed me, that I was competent to do the job. From then on, I never referred business "upstairs".

Not all imperial governments were happy to have their performance assessed and measured by outsiders, even in sanitized form. King Leopold II ordered the destruction of many of the financial records of the Congo Free State before the colonial administration was taken over by the Belgian government in 1908, and access to surviving records from the Free State period was restricted long after that (de Roo 2016: 19–24). In 2011, investigations into British policies during the Mau Mau uprising in Kenya in the 1950s revealed a set of records taken from 37 different colonies before independence and hidden in the Foreign Office for 50 years or more after independence (Anderson 2015).

While previous sections showed that debates about the 'cost and benefits' of empire were as much political as substantive in nature, this section has illustrated that the collection of the data informing these debates was equally political. Reports by the imperial government masked a dynamic and evolving tension between a desire for uniformity and the need to adapt to local conditions. This tension was a constant feature in the governance of the colonies. It also informed the areas featured in the costs and benefits literature, such as defence and foreign capital.

Conclusion

Few studies of the financial and economic 'balance sheet' of empire claim to have captured the whole of the experience of colonialism, for either people in the colonies or the metropole. Instead, most acknowledge that this approach to the study of imperialism has significant limitations. Hopkins (1988: 234) writes that 'the social and psychological effects of what some historians refer to as "the imperial experience" are excluded, and so too are moral judgments on empire-building'. Davis and Huttenback (1986) admit on the first page of their volume that they make no attempt 'to measure the social or psychic effects that the colonial experiment had on inhabitants of the imperial domain or, for that matter, on the British themselves'.

Such intangible factors may have been important for both sides of the equation. For its cheerleaders, empire was a source of what Offer (1993: 232) describes as 'psychic goods' of status or national pride. William Roger Louis (2006: 35) notes that 'the colours painted on maps over vast areas of Asia and Africa symbolized national power, prestige, and destiny' (Louis 2006: 35). In Italy, where the costs of colonial conquests were so high, it was reference to such prestige that convinced taxpayers to fund it. According to Federico (1998: 381), the use of imperial expansion as a political distraction by Italian leaders from Crispi in the 1890s to Mussolini in the 1930s 'would not have worked if the colonial issue had not struck chords with at least part of public opinion'. Advocates of colonial expansion had argued since soon after Italian unification that colonies were 'indispensable for any great power'. Belgian King Leopold II made the same argument in his search for a colony for his own relatively new state.

Despite these limitations, however, the 'imperial accountancy' approach does bring into sharp relief the fact that imperial and colonial interests could be – and often were – distinct. Decisions made by contemporaries and historians about what served the metropolitan versus colonial interests shape the calculations of net cost and benefit. They also provide a window into the extent to which imperial policies reflected the outcomes of negotiations between stakeholders on both sides of the political divide. In defence, investment and trade – three areas in which the accountancy literature has presented a somewhat static picture of imperial subsidies – the relationships between colonial and metropolitan governments varied over time. Efforts to balance these two sets of interests also generated an imperial interest in data collection which, though limited and specific, has made possible much of the research featured in this volume.

These negotiations also had important implications for institutions and governance in the colonies themselves. In particular, the need to account to parsimonious metropolitan treasuries shaped the policies that colonial governments adopted on the ground and the structure of their relationships with indigenous institutions and individuals.

Notes

[1] Memorandum on Kenya, 4 March 1953, in TNA T225/771.
[2] The following is drawn from Gardner (2012: 56–8).

6

How Colonial States Worked

The previous chapter showed that, whatever the varying motives for the acquisition of colonies, the minds of officials and politicians in colonizing countries were much preoccupied by the balance sheets of the empires they had built, and in particular of convincing sometimes reluctant voters that expenditures on imperial conquest and development would somehow pay off to their benefit. While, as Davis and Huttenback (1986: 1) put it, 'the last word may never be written' on whether those arguments were correct, making these arguments required at least a notional separation of the interests of the colonies from those of the metropole, and a consideration of how the costs and benefits of imperial rule were divided between them.

This chapter considers how this logic influenced the structure and operation of colonial governments in the colonies themselves, and thus their relationships to the indigenous people they claimed to govern. Building on the 'imperial accountancy' discussion, it focuses particularly on the finances of those governments, which in most modern empires were kept separate from those of the metropolitan state. The idea that colonies should be financially self-sufficient introduced specific political dynamics within individual colonies which did much to shape the experience and legacies of colonial rule (Gardner 2012).

Taxation and public spending by colonial governments are now the subjects of a literature which approaches public finances as a window into broader political and economic trends. This approach, often described as 'fiscal sociology', dates back at least to the early 20th century and the theories of Rudolph Goldschied and Joseph Schumpeter. The former wrote in 1917 that 'the budget is the skeleton of the state stripped of all misleading ideologies' (quoted in Schumpeter 1954: 6). Public finance, in other words, provides a language for understanding the intentions of the state and their relationships to taxpayers. Building further on this is a wider project in history and economics which uses taxation as an indicator of state capacity (Karaman and Pamuk 2013; Dincecco 2011). This approach to the study of colonial states provides an empirical handle on questions about the strength or weakness of the colonial state. In Africa, for example, Crawford Young (1994) characterizes the colonial state as *bula matari* or 'crusher of rocks', while Jeffery Herbst (2000) and Frederick Cooper (2002) stress the inability of the colonial state to broadcast its power much beyond colonial capital. How much revenue colonial states could raise, from whom, and how they spent it provide a more dynamic perspective on this question.

Several insights arise from this work. The first is that while the expectation of financial self-sufficiency affected almost all colonies, the methods used to achieve this (and indeed the extent to which it was ever achieved) depended heavily on local conditions in the colonies rather than only the intentions of the colonizers. That colonial governments could not always have it their own way is revealed by the extraordinarily diverse set of fiscal arrangements which could exist within the same region and the same empire. The second is that neither colonizer nor colonized represented unified groups. Operating in distant colonial capitals, colonial officials often resisted, either passively or actively, orders from Europe. Other European actors – settlers, traders, businessmen or missionaries – also had their own voices which could be more influential locally than in metropolitan policy. At the same time, indigenous elites often differed in their approach to colonial invaders. The interactions of these multiple political layers and interests were important in the operations of colonial states.

Collecting taxes

The principle of financial self-sufficiency implied that one of the first tasks of colonial governments, once the process of conquest was completed and order restored, was the collection of taxes. In building a tax base, colonial governments everywhere had to face a number of common challenges, ranging from limited knowledge of the people and economies they were intending to tax to resistance from the taxpayers themselves. Recall from Chapter 1 that even at the high point of modern colonial rule in the interwar period, the number of European administrators actually present in most colonies was extremely limited. The collection of tax thus had to be restricted to a limited number of places or to be delegated to indigenous intermediaries of various kinds, who had to be recruited and incentivized to work for the colonial government. What strategies colonial governments chose to cope with these challenges differed across space and time.

The first question to be asked might reasonably be about the effectiveness of colonial tax regimes. Were colonial states able to extract large revenues from their subjects? Such a claim is implicit if not explicit in Acemoglu et al's (2001) conception of 'extractive' states. Empirical evidence on tax revenues across a range of colonies suggests otherwise, though uncertainties in the data mean that the debate is far from settled. Frankema (2011) compares tax revenues across the British Empire, expressed in terms of unskilled daily wages – measuring, in other words, how many days' labour it would take to raise the amount of per capita revenue taken in by the state. He finds that colonies in Asia and Africa, which might be expected to be more 'extractive' actually raised much less revenue when compared to settler colonies. Measured as a share of local GDP, however, Cogneau et al (2018) find that levels of fiscal extraction in the French Empire (which includes colonies in North Africa, sub-Saharan Africa and French Indochina) were not particularly low – in fact, they were comparable or higher to those of other developing countries in Asia and Latin America, although still lower than metropolitan France.

That tax revenue in poorer colonies should be less than in wealthier colonies and, to an even greater degree, less than the metropolitan state should not be surprising. Taxation is linked to both the ability and willingness of taxpayers to pay. The first is determined by income, and historical studies of taxation show a strong relationship between levels of per capita income, economic structure, and tax revenue (Dincecco 2011; Chelliah 1971; Musgrave 1969). Even today, farmers producing for their own subsistence are extremely difficult to tax in part because they have little surplus with which to pay (Teera and Hudson 2004: 789). In most new colonies, subsistence farmers would have constituted the majority of the population. Where people do have surplus income, it is difficult to make them pay through coercion alone – as the previous chapter discussed, the use of force is costly, and without some degree of cooperation on the part of taxpayers, the costs of collection tend to outstrip the revenues collected.

The overall scope for tax collection in many colonies was thus limited, and there were many colonies which were not self-sufficient right away. Most received some form of transfer or subsidy from imperial governments in the first years.

It also meant that colonial governments needed to be selective about who they could tax. In virtually all colonies in the first years of the colonial period, the preferred method of taxation was through the taxation of international trade, either imports or, less commonly, exports. In many cases this was done through a low 'revenue' tariff of 10 per cent of the value of all imports, but in other cases taxes were focused on a particular commodity. Probably the best example of the latter was the tax on opium which represented a major, if not the major, revenue source for a number of colonies in Southeast Asia (Trocki 1999). Regardless of their precise form, trade taxes suited the constraints of colonial governments in that they could focus their attention on a relatively small number of trading centres, and on transactions which they monitored anyway. Taxes could also be collected from a relatively small number of people, who often depended in some way on infrastructure provided by the colonial government.

This worked in places where the value of overseas trade was already fairly high. However, there were a number of colonies where this was not the case, and the taxation of trade could only cover a small share of the local expenditures of the government. In these places, colonial governments had to turn to other methods, principally the imposition of some kind of direct tax. Both logistically and politically, this was a more difficult proposition. In some places, existing systems of taxation were simply adopted by the colonial state, adapted gradually from indigenous structures. Such was the case with the Mughal land tax in India, or a range of direct taxes already collected by the emirs of Northern Nigeria. Where there was no existing system to incorporate, colonial officials faced a bigger set of hurdles. They had little of the information required for establishing an effective system of direct taxation. How much could people afford to pay? When during the year would agricultural producers with seasonal incomes be able to pay? How should taxes be collected – by whom, and in what medium of exchange? All of these questions and more had to be worked out through a process of learning and negotiation, and direct tax revenues increased slowly and fitfully. Among colonial officials, there were heated debates between those who believed the payment of tax would provide a valuable lesson in citizenship for colonial subjects, and those more focused on the risks of organized tax revolts. Incidents like the Sierra Leone Hut Tax War of 1898 did little to reassure the latter group (Hargreaves 1956).

For taxpayers, objections were often less to the principle of taxation per se than to the little benefit they saw in return. In 1935, for example, the Kavirondo Taxpayers Welfare Association in Kenya – one of a number of such organizations emerging throughout sub-Saharan Africa during the interwar period – submitted a memorandum to Sir Alan Pim, a former Indian civil servant undertaking an investigation into

Kenya's finances. In it, they wrote that 'about £250,000 is collected in this Province in the hut & poll tax every year. The Africans get this money by wages earning sale of produce. Every year this money goes out of the Reserve and [very] little comes back to Africans to be spent by Africans in the Reserves'. They argued in the memorandum for the rate of tax to be reduced and for more of the money to be budgeted by African local governments known in Kenya as Local Native Councils.[1]

Direct taxes, particularly in the first years of colonial rule, were frequently collected in something other than the currency of the colonial government, usage of which often spread slowly. These could be comprised of either labour services or agricultural produce. Both could represent substantial shares of total revenue. In his study of the colonial state in Africa, Crawford Young (1994: 173) describes forced labour as 'of enormous importance' to colonial budgets. Using a unique dataset for French Africa, van Waijenburg (2018) estimates the approximate cash value of forced labour requisitions by the colonial state and finds that in the first decades of the 20th century, it represented a substantial implied contribution to colonial budgets which fell from 70–100 per cent of cash revenue in the early 1900s to around 20 per cent in the interwar period. In both of these examples, labour taxes were collected in the form of labour services, primarily work on the construction of roads or railways. In other colonies, coerced labour was used to produce export commodities. The value of this labour to colonial budgets can thus be measured in terms of the revenue realized by the sale of those commodities. In Dutch Java, the 'cultivation system' of the mid-19th century, which forced villagers to produce sugar and coffee, generated around a third of Dutch (note not Javanese) government revenue (Dell and Olken 2020: 172). In the Congo Free State, the infamous 'red rubber' regime operated by King Leopold II generated more than half of the total revenue of the colonial government (de Roo 2017). Revelations about atrocities committed by Belgian officials forcing Africans to harvest quotas of wild rubber created an international scandal and ultimately led to the Belgian state taking over governance of the Congo.

Colonial governments faced with the challenge of building a tax base had to make a set of difficult and often uncertain decisions about whom to tax and how. These decisions were influenced arguably more by local conditions and societies than by decisions made in metropolitan capitals. From the perspective of the latter, the important question was whether the colonial government could fund itself without access to a regular metropolitan subsidy. As the next section shows, the extent to which they could do this shaped the types of expenditures colonial governments were empowered to make. This, in turn, influenced both the ability and willingness of taxpayers to pay the expanding array of taxes collected by colonial governments – a dynamic relationship which struggled to cope with the economic changes of the 20th century.

Budgets and the typologies of colonial states

In histories of taxation, there is a close correlation between tax compliance and the taxpayers' belief that they will benefit from public spending. While the majority of taxpayers in colonies had little political voice, they did find ways of expressing their discontent, from letters like the one from the Kavirondo Taxpayers Welfare Association to passive evasion and in some cases outright rebellion. For colonial governments, avoiding the latter was a key priority – defence was costly – but beyond that their expenditure priorities were shaped primarily by the need for revenue and the limited means at their disposal for long-term planning. They were also influenced, at least to some extent, by changing ideas across the 19th and 20th centuries about what governments were supposed to do. This combination of global, imperial and local influences shaped individual colonial budgets in unique ways.

Historians have tried to capture this variation in how colonial governments allocated their resources using a variety of definitions or classification of the colonial state. These efforts date back at least to the middle of the 20th century. Morris D. Morris (1963: 615) coined one such classification, arguing that 'the British raj saw itself in the passive role of night watchman, providing security, rational administration and a modicum of social overhead on the basis of which economic progress was expected to occur. The Indian government obviously had no self-conscious program of active economic development.' This description of a 'night watchman' or 'gatekeeper' state gained considerable traction in descriptions of colonial states outside India (Booth 2007a: 242; Cooper 2002). One reason is that colonial budgets – particularly those from the early decades of colonial rule – were dominated by expenditures serving what Adam Smith might have described as the core functions of government, namely administration and defence. Despite the fact that, as discussed in the previous chapter, colonies could benefit from metropolitan defence spending, they did pay considerable amounts for local policing, raised at least to some extent from people in the countries they were in the process of conquering. In the first decade of the 20th century, for example, the Congo Free State spent an average of 46 per cent of its annual spending on defence, while

British Uganda spent 35 per cent on the same purpose. By the 1920s, these shares had fallen to less than 20 per cent (Gardner 2019).

However, even after this period administration was also relatively costly. The salaries of European officials were generally set based on the standards of the metropolitan civil service, and thus even a small number of them tended to weigh heavily on colonial budgets. In their study of the French Empire, Cogneau et al (2018: 35) show that the average public sector wage in colonies was often not far below that of metropolitan France, despite the fact that GDP per capita in these territories was much lower. In Indochina, for example, the average public sector wage paid to European officials in 1925 was 15,858 francs, while in France the equivalent figure was 17,049 francs (1937 ppp-adjusted). Other parts of the empire were lower – in West and Central Africa, for example, the average public wage was 6,504 francs. Still, as a multiple of GDP per capita, this was much higher than in France. Frankema (2011: 143) notes that 'administrative expenditures absorbed more than one-fifth of the budget in British Africa. By contrast, New Zealand's administration appeared a mere bargain, consuming just 5% of the same budget.' Pensions and other allowances contributed to these costs.

The restriction of colonial government spending to these core activities was not necessarily a matter of political preference among local officials. It could also reflect efforts by imperial governments to exert control over colonial spending. In the British Empire, for example, colonies receiving regular budget support from the imperial treasury were subject to greater scrutiny over their spending, in the form of a line-item veto by officials in London. This power was often used to restrict the range of colonial government expenditures. When colonial Nyasaland, for example, wanted to use an increase in its revenue collections for investment in agricultural research and railway construction, the British Treasury disallowed this spending until the grant-in-aid was eliminated (Gardner 2012: 26; Kesner 1981: 17).

The large share of spending on administrators and other imperial priorities was often controversial. Indian nationalists claimed that India purchased too many services from Britain, the payment for which was a 'tribute' and a 'drain' of resources, implying that had this money stayed in India it would raise investment in economic growth. The focus of the nationalist critics fell on three items of payment specifically: expenses of the Indian army which came from the Indian budget, interest on public debt, and guaranteed profits of railway companies in India. As discussed in Chapter 5, the British Indian budget paid for the

Indian army, which fought wars beyond Indian borders. Defenders of the empire said that the army protected the empire, and the empire protected the interests of the enormous diaspora of Indian merchants and workers. Without the empire's military might, Indians would not be business in Hong Kong, Aden or Natal. The nationalists thought interest on the public debt was a waste of money. A critic would say that borrowing in the cheapest money market of the world made sense. Without the railway guarantees, the railways might not have been built in India. The fact remains that the top end of the colonial bureaucracy and military received salaries at British rather than Indian rates, and since Indians were excluded from these levels until late, there was an element of monopoly rent in these payments.

Over time, spending on administration and defence generally decreased as a share of total spending in favour of a broader range of government activities, often dominated initially by investments in infrastructure and government services intended to promote trade (Booth 2007a: 245–6; Frankema 2011; Cogneau et al 2018). In the 1920s, expenditures on public works could absorb as much as half of the budget in some colonies in Africa (Frankema 2011). These numbers were lower in Southeast Asia, but still came to 20 per cent of total spending in the Federated Malay States and 30 in French Indochina (Booth 2007a: 252).

These expenditures provide grounds for challenging the 'night watchman' view of colonial states, in that they represented sometimes transformative interventions in colonial economies through the reduction in transport costs which, in some cases, provided a foundation for export production by indigenous as well as expatriate producers. Different authors interpret these expenditures in different ways, and that interpretation is to some extent what informs the classification of the colonial state offered in place of the night watchman state. Critics of Morris's arguments about the British Raj, for example, argue that it was not neutral but rather constructed to protect British capital and interests, at the expense of those of the indigenous population of the colony in question (Booth 2007a: 242–3). On the other hand, colonial officials were aware that the only way to build a larger tax base was to increase the incomes of the majority of taxpayers, generally through the promotion of trade (Frankema 2011: 139). The extent to which colonial states did this effectively, and thus became 'agents of globalization', is the subject of Chapter 3. In some specific cases, investments by the colonial state are used to argue that it was, or at least could be, 'developmental' in the limited definition of that phrase at the time.

One way in which 'extractive' and 'developmental' colonial states can be distinguished is by their attention to wider development aims beyond export production. Groups like the Kavirondo Taxpayers Welfare Association often complained that this single-minded focus on infrastructure and the export of primary commodities came at a cost of other potential priorities, including spending on education and medical services for the indigenous population. Across the board, and particularly before the Second World War, the shares of colonial budgets spent on such services were very low. In the French Empire, education spending was, on average, just over 7 per cent of the budget in 1925, as compared with 20 per cent in metropolitan France (Cogneau et al 2018: 29). Moreover, at least some of the colonial spending in this area was on education services for French settlers – the shares were much higher in North Africa (9.1), for example, than in France's sub-Saharan colonies (3.6). There were some exceptions to this – in the Philippines under American rule, close to a third of total spending was on education in 1931 (Booth 2007a: 252).

Owing in part to agitation by indigenous political groups, the share of education and healthcare increased in the final decades of the colonial period. In much of Africa, for example, there was a late colonial 'surge' in government development programmes, sometimes referred to as the 'second colonial occupation' (Low and Lonsdale 1976: 12). The degree of expansion in the budgets of the late colonial period should not be exaggerated; there was growth, but from a comparatively low base, and even more ambitious development programmes were constrained by a lack of resources (Gardner 2012). In a 1955 speech, John Butter, a former Indian civil servant who had been transferred to the Kenya Treasury, articulated the role of government finance in colonies as a purely negative one. Unlike the governments of industrialized economies, colonial governments had few ways of positively intervening to influence patterns of economic development, either through long-term planning or manipulations of the banking system. 'My conclusion,' he said, 'is that the role of the Finance Minister in a poor country cannot be that of a fairy godmother with a box full of Keynesian chocolates, but must rather be that of an unkind aunt who always – or almost always – says: "jam tomorrow!"' (Butter 1955: 38).

There is thus not one rule or definition which can describe the ways in which colonial states spent the tax revenue they raised. In each case, budgets were shaped first and foremost by the amount of revenue which could be raised, and secondarily by changing global ideas and the ability of various stakeholders to influence the budgeting process.

A common thread which did run through these various experiences was the desire to maintain order, and to do so at the least possible cost. However, what achieving that goal required differed across space and time, and, in particular, increased over the course of the 20th century.

Whose colonial policy?

All of the classifications and discussions in the previous section on the nature of colonial policies are based on using budgets set in colonial capitals. They focus largely on relationships between those colonial officials and imperial administrations in Lisbon, Paris and London, and whether the expenditures of colonial governments favoured imperial relationships or reflected local conditions. However, there was another set of political relationships which was perhaps more important for the experience of colonialism by the majority of the population, namely between the administrations based in colonial capitals and the local institutions and interest groups through which much of the policy made there was implemented. This section considers the influence of two groups within the colony which could also shape fiscal policies: 1) local interest groups – both foreign and indigenous – which could constrain the actions of colonial states as much if not more than the imperial government; and 2) local governments tasked with collecting taxes and, increasingly, implementing development programmes.

Previous sections have already noted that, despite the lack of political voice for much of the population, the process of bargaining between taxpayer and government which plays a major role in histories of taxation was not absent. Taxpayers had other ways of finding their voice, and they used it not only in the broader sense discussed earlier of forcing increased investment in social services, but also to shape local policies in ways suited to their particular interests. To the extent that they succeeded, they introduced local variations into what might otherwise have been uniform or at least similar imperial policies.

One example is in the imposition of more 'modern' methods of taxation, such as taxes on individual incomes and corporate profits. Historically, these have been important in expanding the fiscal base of the state. However, their intended targets were often the best able to act collectively to avoid or reshape the tax. One example is in the introduction of income tax across parts of the British Empire. In 1922 the Colonial Office circulated a 'model' income tax ordinance to encourage colonial governments to adopt the tax. Not all introduced an income tax in response, but even among those that did, the type of tax imposed – starting from the same basic legislation – varied depending on the influence of local interests. In Northern Rhodesia, for example, the minimum income on which the tax would be levied was £500 per annum – significantly higher than in Kenya, where it was £150. In the former, the income tax (which also included a tax on corporate profits) was essentially tax on the two major mining companies. In Kenya, by contrast, the European settlers and Indian merchants who were the main targets of the tax successfully prevented the colonial government from levying an income tax, not once but twice, by simply refusing to pay. The income tax was not imposed there until 1937 (Gardner 2012: 98–102). The failure of the Kenya income tax points more broadly to questions of distribution, either between regions or between groups, which inflamed discussions of both taxation and public spending. Decisions about the structure of tax and the allocation of public resources were at least in part political questions about distribution and, despite limited political voice through representation, local actors attempted to influence these decisions.

Similar debates occurred at the local level as well, and the structure of local rule was an important (if often neglected) ingredient in the colonial fiscal system. Systems of 'indirect rule', as this is often referred to, varied enormously across and even within individual colonies, shaped both by the initial structure of indigenous institutions and their relationships with the colonial government (see Box 6.1). The 'Native Authorities' or local governments established through this method were crucial links in the fiscal infrastructure of the state. In many places, they were the primary collectors of direct taxation. This was sometimes, but not always, the result of the colonial state building directly on indigenous tax systems, as was the case in Northern Nigeria or with the Mughal land tax in India. Even in these cases, taxes were often reshaped or restructured in various ways to fit the different needs of the colonial government.

In other areas, where existing systems of taxation and tribute were not readily adoptable by the colonial state, new taxes were introduced but indigenous actors were tasked with working out how to collect them. One consequence of this was enormous local variation in the ways in which taxes were collected. Local officials had tremendous discretion in applying central government policy. Colonial governments often did not have reliable data on the number or incomes of taxpayers, and relied on local authorities to adjust rates and collection methods to local circumstances. This placed tremendous power and authority in the hands of indigenous delegates. In much of British Africa, for example, Native Authorities and other African delegates in charge of collecting taxes were allowed to exempt taxpayers they felt were too

Box 6.1: Indirect rule

Histories of the colonial state and the legacies of colonial institutions often make reference to 'indirect rule', as for example an explanation for the persistent influence of precolonial institutions on later economic outcomes in the former colonies. But what indirect rule was and how it was supposed to work were subjects on which even colonial administrators could not agree. Lord Hailey, in his study of 'native administration' in Africa, refused to use the phrase as he argued it had 'no claim to precision'.

At least in theory, indirect rule was the practice of governing through indigenous institutions. Indigenous rulers would accept the superiority of colonial governments and, in return, they would enjoy the support of the colonial government against rivals and be left to govern their own subjects largely on their own terms. Such a system is often contrasted with 'direct' rule, in which European officials were responsible for day to day governance, and indigenous people acted on their direction.

In practice, the interaction between indigenous and colonial institutions was considerably more complex. There were areas where the practice came close to the theory. Lord Lugard, one of the principal proponents of indirect rule in the British Empire, developed many of his ideas about it in the development of treaty relationships with the powerful emirs of Northern Nigeria. India's Princely States occupied a similar position. However, where indigenous rulers were unwilling to cooperate, or where less centralized institutions made it more difficult for colonial officials to identify a single ruler with whom to negotiate, relationships became much more fluid. Elites with little or no claim to local authority could be appointed to positions of political power within the colonial government, as in the case of Eastern Nigeria's 'warrant chiefs', so called because their only authority came from the warrant of the colonial government. Alliances with rival powers were often used to weaken centralized states which refused to cooperate, as initially used by the colonial government of the Gold Coast and the rivals of the Asante state.

There were differences between colonizers, though these were often overshadowed by the practical necessities faced in individual locations. In Africa, British 'indirect rule' is often contrasted with French 'direct rule', on the basis that French colonial officials were thought to care more about French language skills and connections than about indigenous legitimacy. However, such generalizations should be taken with caution: across all empires, it was as much the structure and policies of indigenous institutions which shaped the manner of their involvement in colonial rule. No European administration possessed the authority to govern absolutely.

Further reading

Lord Hailey (1942) *Native Administration in British Tropical Africa*, London: HMSO.

Lord Lugard (1922) *The Dual Mandate in British tropical Africa*, London: W. Blackwood and Sons.

Stelios Michalopoulos and Elias Papaioannou (2013) 'Pre-colonial ethnic institutions and contemporary African development', *Econometrica*, 81: 112–52.

Adnan Naseemullah and Paul Staniland (2016) 'Indirect rule and varieties of governance', *Governance*, 29: 13–30.

---

poor to pay the tax from all or part of the total tax payment. There were often no records kept of such exemptions, but they both limited the effectiveness of increases in the tax rates and often resulted in complaints of corruption by tax collectors (Gardner 2010).

But who Native Authorities were, and what scope they had to use (or abuse) their authority, varied tremendously between empires, and even between different colonies of the same empire. Adnan Naseemullah and Paul Staniland (2016: 16) describe indirect rule as

> a conceptual category that contains a bewildering diversity of members: great and petty princely states, areas of tribal or customary administration, political agencies, entrepots and supposedly administered regions in reality dominated by local strongmen. These instances of governance exist along a spectrum of state authority between full direct rule on one end and independence from state sovereignty on the other.

They divide these various cases into three categories: 1) suzerain governance in which indigenous governments maintained full jurisdiction over their citizens, while maintaining an allegiance to the colonial state; 2) hybrid governance, in which authority is shared between colonial and indigenous states; and 3) de jure governance, in which authority officially rests with the colonial state but is in reality exercised by intermediaries.

Which type of rule was chosen depended on the interaction of a variety of factors, from the policies and attitudes of the colonial government in question (and sometimes the personalities of individual governors) to the degree of perceived political authority possessed by indigenous elites (Gerring et al 2011). Crucially, different decisions about the precise form of indirect rule were frequently made within colonies as well as between them. From the perspective of the fiscal system, therefore, these various types of rule manifested themselves in a patchwork of different systems of tax collection and distribution of public revenue. In Nigeria, for example, tax revenue was shared between the colonial government and the local Native Authorities which collected it. These were classified as 'organized' and 'unorganized' by European officials. Those deemed to be 'organized' were allowed to retain a larger share of their revenue and had greater 'discretionary' powers over their budgets (Bolt and Gardner 2020).

Colonial fiscal systems were not, therefore, exclusively the creations of either imperial governments or the bureaucrats they sent to the colonies. Rather, the structure and implementation of taxes and spending measures were shaped by a range of other interest groups and intermediaries. The next section considers how this patchwork system coped with the economic changes which occurred during the colonial period.

Coping with the contradictions

During the first few decades of colonial rule, a diverse set of systems of governance and taxation were established which varied not only between but also within colonies, reflecting differences in local institutions and the influence of a range of different social and economic interests. Colonial administrations had the dual task of maintaining order and promoting the economic growth which would help to expand the tax base. As the colonial period progressed, these agendas often conflicted with one another, and many of the shifts in colonial policies in the years before decolonization intended to address the gap between them. This section looks in more detail at the strain placed on colonial fiscal systems by the economic changes the policies had, at least in part, aimed to encourage.

The section borrows its title from one of the earliest papers to address the contradictions in colonial governance, by John Lonsdale and Bruce Berman (1979). In it they use the case of colonial Kenya to argue that the colonial state had to both preserve indigenous systems of social control while at the same time encouraging economic change which undermined these same systems. Their argument, which they claim applies beyond Kenya to colonial states more broadly, is put in terms of the Marxist theory popular in research on Africa at the time. However, more recent studies of colonial institutions have also highlighted similar tensions between the hybrid institutions of governance, which, through systems of indirect rule, relied on the codification and solidification of indigenous systems of rule as Europeans perceived them in the initial decades of the colonial period.

As argued earlier, colonial states – despite their limited capacity and in contrast to the 'night watchman' label – intervened frequently in colonial economies and societies in ways that could introduce considerable change. Investments in infrastructure opened up new markets and opportunities, a process examined in more detail in Chapters 3 and 4. Indigenous producers responded to these opportunities, through migration and by adapting existing systems for the mobilization of labour and capital.

Further, a growing colonial state presented opportunities of its own for mobility – occupational, social and physical. Latika Chaudhary (2015: 163) notes that a rapid increase in the number of private secondary schools was driven by 'Indian elites hoping to secure lucrative government jobs after graduation'. Responses to these new impulses could be both voluntary and compelled by the state. One outcome of these changes was sometimes significant shifts in the economic and human geography of many colonized countries over the initial decades of colonial rule. Capital cities and other urban centres, often based around mines or plantations, grew rapidly. Those living there included not only people in the direct employ of the state or production centre, but also people who provided services and goods to those who were so employed. Some built on earlier urban foundations, while others were the creations of administrative fiat. Missionary education, urban labour and the production of exports provided avenues of social mobility for those who were not necessarily members of a pre-existing elite. This was also true, although via a more difficult path, of some of the forced requisitions of the colonial state. After the Second World War, for example, conscripts into imperial armed forces often returned home with cash incomes, skills and experiences which made them into a relatively privileged and often influential group.

From the beginning, the piecemeal structure of colonial governments made it difficult for them to respond to such changes, in either positive or negative terms. The systems of flat-rate hut and poll taxes created in colonial Africa, for example, were ill-equipped to take advantage of rising incomes among a sometimes large number of taxpayers. In Northern Rhodesia, the rapid growth of copper mining transformed the financial fortunes of both the colonial state as well as mineworkers and others who moved to the growing cities of the Copperbelt. However, the best the colonial government could do in terms of taxing these higher incomes was to set a higher rate of taxation for the Copperbelt districts as a whole. This was, they admitted, a fairly blunt instrument, but they had neither the administrative capacity nor the legitimacy to introduce income-based taxation on the indigenous population.

Instead, colonial governments often relied on the Native Authorities or other local institutions to adjust taxation to individual incomes. The system of exemptions discussed in the previous section was one example. However, during the final decades of the colonial period, policies of fiscal decentralization took this further. Native Authorities were granted greater powers of taxation and, at the same time, responsibilities for the provision of many of the expanded set of services offered by a more interventionist colonial state, including education and healthcare. The rationale for these policies has clear echoes in more recent decentralization policies encouraged by the World Bank and other international development organizations: local governments are likely to have a better knowledge of the demands of local taxpayers, and it may also be easier for those taxpayers to hold local governments to account.

However, local governments established on a basis of indigenous structures also struggled to cope with the impact of economic change. In his landmark *Economic History of West Africa*, Hopkins (1973) argued that the end of the slave trade and the shift towards 'legitimate' commerce in the 19th century, discussed in Chapter 2, resulted in a 'crisis of adaptation' in West African political institutions, in which existing elites whose incomes were linked to the slave trade were increasingly challenged by new elites empowered by the production of new export crops. This narrative has been the subject of significant critique for the 19th century (see, for example, Law 2009). However, it could equally apply to the colonial period, when those who were able to take advantage of new commercial opportunities increasingly came into conflict with an existing elite structure solidified through policies of indirect rule.

Reforms in the local government system over this period were often intended to address these conflicts. Across British Africa, advisory councils were introduced as a way of incorporating mission-educated Africans or those with commercial experience into structures previously dominated by a hereditary chiefly hierarchy. These were intended to serve two purposes: first, to be an alternative outlet for the energies of an increasingly vocal political class; and second, to bring the human capital of these 'new' elites into an increasingly bureaucratic system of local government for which 'traditional' elites were often ill-prepared.

Just as the power of the chiefs seemed to be being eroded, however, economic growth could also consolidate the power of traditional elites by increasing the salience of the powers they held over the allocation of land and other resources. Rathbone (1996) argues that competition over increasingly scarce cocoa lands in Akyem Abuakwa in the Gold Coast sharpened the distinction between Akyemfo and the large number of migrant producers living in the region. Whether someone claimed to be the subject of the Paramount of Akyem Abuakwa or to some other ruler in their home region could be strategic, depending on the levying of local taxes and the allocation of land rights. Such competition also provided chiefs with valuable sources of revenue. Internal migration and urbanization made such ethnic definitions of citizenship 'disconcertingly messy and unresolved' as the colonial period progressed (Rathbone 1996: 515).

Conclusion

This chapter uses systems of taxation and public spending to understand the changing capacities and constraints facing colonial states. Expectations that colonial governments would at least mostly be self-sufficient placed tremendous pressure on them from the beginning to collect sufficient tax revenue to cover the local expenses of conquest, administration and any programmes of economic development. It also restricted their administrative and coercive capacity, forcing them to rely to varying degrees on indigenous institutions and other intermediaries, creating a system of hybrid and de jure forms of governance characterized by considerable diversity both within and between different colonies.

Assessments of how successful colonial states were in raising taxes vary. However, it is universally true that local economic and political conditions dictated what could be taxed and when. Where possible, colonial governments tended to favour taxes that were easier – administratively and politically – to collect, particularly taxes on trade. Where these were sufficient to pay the local expenses of the government, they represented an often substantial share of total revenue. Where they were not, however, a variety of direct taxes on incomes, land and production were required to supplement the state's income. These were collected in ways that reflected both the limitations of the colonial state, as well as the resources of the colony in question, and their precise structure was often heavily influenced by local interests of various kinds. Lack of formal political voice did not always mean lack of influence.

Tax systems and the revenue they produced determined the possible range of expenditures. In most colonial states, budgets were characterized by high levels of spending on administration, dictated in large part by exorbitant (in local terms) salaries for European civil servants, and infrastructure. The latter constituted the primary means by which colonial governments sought to expand the tax base. Most spent little on developing the human capital of indigenous populations, though this varied to some extent across space and to a greater extent over time.

The development of colonial fiscal systems illustrates that colonial states were the product of a 'complex historical process', rather than being the sole creation of either imperial bureaucrats or economic interests (Lonsdale and Berman 1979: 487). Financial dependence on local taxpayers meant that colonial institutions had to be, at least to some degree, responsive to their demands in the implementation of colonial policies. For taxpayers, the experience of colonialism – extractive, developmental or minimalist – would have varied enormously even within individual colonies. Finally, financial constraints and considerations shaped the ways in which colonial states performed other institutional functions, which are the subject of the next chapter.

Note
[1] Quoted in Gardner (2012).

7

Did Institutions Matter?

European rule deeply influenced the institutions that mattered to business or agriculture in the colonized regions. This old idea received a new emphasis in the 2000s when economic historians inspired by NIE started to use it to explain the origins of world inequality since 1820 (see Chapter 1). They divided the world according to the institutional legacies of colonial rule and showed that these divisions were correlated with differences in long-term economic performance measured in per capita income growth. The literature laid stress on the laws of property and contract, making two propositions about their origin and effects. First, whereas in the normal course, laws evolved through changes in jurisprudence and the context of practice, in the colonial societies, laws came from the outside, they had western roots and were unilaterally imposed on the colonized peoples. And second, the quality of this inheritance shaped comparative economic growth in the modern world.

The attempt to draw a causal link between colonialism and comparative growth via institutional effects did not go unchallenged. Critics felt that the attempt overstated the value of institutions and the European lead in institutions, and underestimated the weight of indigenous traditions and the power of other drivers of comparative growth such as geography. Whoever wins this debate, we must explain the difference that institutions and colonial legacy made. Explaining comparative growth is not the only reason to be interested in that legacy. Besides economic growth, institutional change might have contributed to the capacity of societies to take part in globalization, or to inequality within the colonial societies. These are also good reasons to be interested in institutional change.

The chapter explores two questions. How did colonialism reshape institutions? And what was the effect of that process on the subject societies? The chapter begins with a fuller survey of the recent scholarship connecting comparative economic growth with institutional change induced by colonial rule.

Colonial institutions and comparative economics

Although institutional economics has an older antecedent, the subfield known as new institutional economic history took shape in the 1980s, mainly through the writings of the economist Douglass North and his co-authors (North 1981; North and Thomas 1973). The difference between the old and the new was that the new emerged from a criticism of neoclassical economics, specifically the assumption that market exchange was a frictionless process. If it is not, then the prospect of economic growth would depend on attempts to mitigate frictions and the transaction costs. North and his associates suggested that the economic emergence of the West since the 17th century stemmed from a process of institutional development that reduced transaction costs in market exchange, allowing fuller play of market-led economic growth.

An obvious problem with this narrative was that its evidence came from Europe during its transition to a modern society and economy. A fuller test of the model would require evidence from the non-European regions. In response to this need, a scholarship connecting colonialism with economic growth outcomes emerged in the 2000s. The most influential publications in this set appeared in economics journals. We can call this the comparative economics approach to the economic history of colonialism. The comparative economics approach makes use of three core ideas linking institutions and economic growth. These ideas emphasize security of property, inequality and incentives, and the quality of the legal system.

One of the core ideas on which the importance of institutions depends is the risk of expropriation from property. If private property rights are vaguely defined or protected by a system that entails high costs of enforcement, the expropriation risk is high. The high risk will discourage investment and economic growth. One set of writings in comparative economics suggests that colonial rule had a systematic impact on expropriation risk.

Dividing the colonial world into settler colonies (temperate zones) and non-settler ones (tropical and equatorial), these works contend that in the latter, the risk of catching tropical diseases and an uncongenial environment for settlement by Europeans made the colonial agents 'extractive' or exploitative, leading to expropriation of resources by the Europeans and impoverishment of the locals (Acemoglu et al 2001).[1] In a related paper, the writers in this set contend that 'European colonialism led to an institutional reversal' (Acemoglu et al 2002). Colonialism established or strengthened extractive institutions in the regions that were relatively rich 500 years before and strengthened property rights in the relatively poorer ones. In the scholarship on comparative development, this thesis is known as 'reversal of fortune', after the title of the paper that makes this claim (Acemoglu et al 2002).

A further contribution from the same set of writers considers contractual law, the contrast between property and contract, suggesting that property right was more important than contract law in explaining comparative growth because expropriation risk gave property users no escape route from uncertainty whereas a poorly defined contract law left contracts open to negotiation (Acemoglu and Johnson 2005).

Whereas these writers claim that natural endowments and disease environment influenced the governance strategies of colonial rulers, others dispute that claim suggesting that geographical features shaped development directly rather than indirectly via colonial strategy (Bloom and Sachs 1998; Gallup et al 1998). Since most colonized countries were tropical and in regions with more pathogens and harsher climates, the dispute is difficult to resolve. Tests tend to rely not on good narrative histories but on a choice of instrumental variables in the models.

Another attempt to link the institutional legacy of colonialism with economic growth emphasizes inequality in the distribution of property, and its consequences on incentives and public goods. The key example is the divergence between North and South America in economic growth outcomes. Spanish colonialism in Latin America enters the colonialism-development debate through an unusual set of stylized facts. Growth of trade, import of European technology and people, and demographic crises caused by epidemics and slave trades 'raised per capita GDP in the Americas well above the achievements of the most advanced pre-Columbian societies', if at a great human cost (Coatsworth 2008). And yet, once European rule took hold, productivity in Spanish America stagnated whereas productivity in the British colonies in North America started to rise.

Settlers were the main landholders in both areas. In British North America, institutions encouraged market exchange and economic growth. Regimes in the South, by contrast, limited the access of most of the population to land and public goods, and weakened market exchange. More generally, concentration in landholding, by slowing down human capital accumulation, made the transition from agrarian to industrial economy difficult (Galor et al 2009). The divergence is attributed to a relatively egalitarian property rights regime in North America and ethnicity-biased property rights in Spanish America, suggesting the formation of two very different models of settler colonialism. The open frontier of land in South America saw European settlers occupy land. Concentrated land ownership, in turn, helped the formation of a regime that perpetuated inequality via public goods and other strategies (Sokoloff and Engerman 2000).

That an institutional divergence of some sort did exist in the Americas is widely acknowledged, but its origins are explained in quite different ways. In one view, the difference was rooted in Iberian colonialism as opposed to the British one. In yet another interpretation, the divergence emerged after independence from Spain and was a sign that the settlers were powerful enough to limit metropolitan interference (Coatsworth 2008).

Europeans occupied land belonging to the indigenous people everywhere in the Americas. In Spanish America, the process led to extraordinary levels of inequality in landholding. A study of dispossession in British Columbia explains the process succinctly:

> the initial ability to dispossess rested primarily on physical power ...; the momentum ... derived from the interest of capital in profit and of settlers in forging new livelihoods; the legitimation ... lay in a cultural discourse that located civilization and savagery and identified the land uses associated with each; and the management of dispossession rested with a set of disciplinary technologies. (Harris 2004: 165)

How did dispossession on such a scale take place? What were the institutional or legal foundations of land grabs on such a large scale? The first European settlers seemed to follow the Roman *terra nullius* principle, which sanctioned occupation of land that did not seem to belong to any sovereign and its conversion into private property. Much of this land had been held under communal tenure by the indigenous population, while joint or communal holding of land was not common in Europe. Furthermore, the state exercised law-making powers in the way the contemporary European states had done, but such powers often denied the non-European population citizenship and equality of property rights. Reversals and adjustments were made on both these counts, but late and partially (Metzer and Engerman 2004).

This literature illustrates the preoccupation of scholarship on the New World with the possession of land frontier and the retreat or decimation of indigenous populations. A similar set of issues do not appear in any region of Asia or Africa. In this sense the New World was exceptional in the economic history of colonialism. Large-scale land grabs and labour servitude were used in some of the 19th-century colonial acquisitions in equatorial Africa. By then these familiar strategies of extraction were in retreat in the settler societies, but they remained available for use where the Europeans could use them. They did not, however, have the backing from jurisprudence in the way the New World land grabs did.

The third core idea within the scholarship claiming that colonialism influenced economic growth via institutional legacies emphasizes quality of law, especially the process of dispute settlement. Sometimes called the 'legal origins' literature, it stresses differences in legal traditions that first formed in Europe and were carried over via colonial rule to other regions. Countries that adopted or received via colonization the more investor-friendly English common law system performed better than the ones that received the less investor-friendly French or German civil law systems or the socialist systems (La Porta et al 1999).

The scholarship lays emphasis on the contrast between common law and civil code or statutory law. A civil code is based on concepts and principles rather than judicial opinion; common law traditions form from cases and judicial opinion. Common laws, therefore, consist of norms established by past judgments and also allow judges discretion to set new norms. The prospect that common law judges, when faced with alternatives, could employ the benchmark of economic efficiency in making a choice leads to an inference that common law is efficiency enhancing. It needs stressing that regard for procedures, or to use the more common English phrase, the 'due process of law,' is necessary for norms to be treated as law. So, codes matter in common law too. In the recent economic history usage of the distinction between common law and civil code, British India, which inherited a common law system, is deemed to be better off than, say, Francophone Africa.

These ideas make comparative economics easier but do not make it easy to read the history of colonial law in any region. In most regions, colonial law contained elements of both common law and code-based law. Coded law tried to incorporate local elements by codifying local customs and norms into law. Both British and French empires contained vast areas where neither imperial authority nor its law were effectively in full force. Although the French technically declared all subjects as equal in law, the claim was qualified by many exemptions and privileges (Mann 2009). A collection of writings on the history of colonial law suggests that what Europeans really took from Europe to Asia or Africa were not French or British legal systems, but an idea of jurisdictional fragmentation (Benton and Ross 2013). This means acceptance of diversity of norms corresponding to the diversity of the subject people, and a reluctance to impose one homogeneous legal order on all. In the process, jurists got busy framing and defining customary law, often based on little information on what either custom or law meant.

The comparative economics studies foreground institutions in economic history. They are the reason a chapter on institutions exists in this book. But the focus on economic growth limits the scope of debates on institutions. For example, it constrains us to see the world in binary terms – extractive (non-settler) and progressive (settler); or common law (British colony) and civil law (French colony) – one of these two boxes had a higher average income than the other. The binary division makes the experience of all colonies of one kind (non-settlers or British) alike, which is an unacceptable premise. Many factors went into making each box differentiated within. For example non-settler colonies differed by the availability of a legal precedent, whether the colony was trade-based or based on plantation-mining complexes or based on peasant exports, when it was acquired, which imperial complex it was a part of, and where it was located.

The comparative economics literature makes several presumptions that are at least doubtful, and probably wrong. One of these is that we know which regions were rich and which were poor 500 years ago.[2] The contributors to the debate have also used population density as their measure of 'wealth' in earlier periods, which is arguably even less reliable than incomes. The second questionable presumption is that property rights were poorly defended in most European-ruled regions that had relatively low average income in the 20th century. There is little evidence to support this claim. In the institutional scholarship, it enters not as a claim founded on evidence, but as a canon.

This chapter does not share the aim of the comparative economics scholarship. The wish to discover the origin of world inequality need not be the only reason to study institutions. Indeed, it is not in this book. Another very good reason to study institutions is to investigate how societies in Asia and Africa became more unequal within, because colonial law could potentially lead to a redistribution of the assets or because enforcement of law and dispute settlement were costly, making the rich better able to play the game. Land grabs in the settler societies of East and Southern Africa were obvious examples of the legal origins of inequality. For another example, in British India, colonial officers felt that contractual law had made the hands of rich creditors stronger than that of the poor debtors in the countryside.

Therefore, even when we leave the debate on comparative growth aside, a set of important questions about institutional change remains to be answered. How did colonialism shape institutional change? Why did it act to reshape institutions? Colonist aims, we show in the next section, were no doubt important, but they were tempered by local conditions. The overriding aim of colonial states in designing new laws was to be able to raise money by promoting private and potentially taxpaying enterprise, be they planters, miners, merchants or peasants. But their ability to do so differed from place to place.

Local conditions: factor endowments and smallholders

Historians of colonial law have long claimed that European rulers used legal reform as an instrument to strengthen their rules over alien societies. But colonial states were constrained to act in certain ways to achieve these aims. The constraint came from three sources: contradictory aims, factor endowments, and the power and persistence of indigenous institutions.

The aims of the state could be contradictory. Political stability and business growth were both paramount objectives, but balancing the two aims was not an easy matter, because taxing the most successful economic agent, be they merchants or landholders, could be politically unwise or impossible. For example, a private property right in land was good for exchange and investment, but potentially dangerous if farmers mortgaged their land too often and lost control over it. Colonies would try to achieve this balancing act in different ways. In the British Empire, there was great resistance to taxing trade. Tariffs were generally low, and used more for revenue generation than protection of domestic enterprise. Taxing land was not easy when the land tax came from poor peasants who had in the past rebelled against the state over such matters. Taxing plantations was logistically easier but could anger settler–planters who often had considerable political influence.

Factor endowments added another constraint. An argument that has become known as the land abundance view of precolonial Africa suggests that land abundance and labour scarcity induced the emergence of regimes of labour coercion in precolonial Africa (Austin 2008, 2009; Fenske 2013). The land abundance thesis connects three features of precolonial Africa: relatively low population density, the presence of slavery, and group rather than private rights over land. Land being abundant, private property in land was poorly defined. However, labour being scarce, private property over labour was well-defined and coercive.

Land abundance suggests ways in which colonial markets and institutional interventions worked to transform African societies in the

19th century. One of the questions asked is: did coercive institutions persist? Not only did they persist, they were even reinforced at times because new patterns of business needed to divert labour away from subsistence agriculture towards plantations or mining. In French colonial territories, unpaid and forced service (*corvée*) made a substantial contribution to government revenue (van Waijenburg 2018). At the same time, where peasants led cash crop exports, these regimes weakened and made way for freer labour markets. Population growth and rising land value created areas of land scarcity and stimulated land markets.

The factor endowments story suggests a divergence between peasant economies and plantation and mining economies. In the former, smallholders were engaged in subsistence agriculture or were the major suppliers of export goods; in the latter, European settlers controlled the most lucrative economic resource. Property right reform in the former case tended to preserve existing rights and indigenous precedence, founding these rights on new procedures, courts and written codes. The state batted for the settlers in the latter case.

Local conditions: plantation–mining complexes and settler power

In several plantation–mining complexes, especially in eastern and southern Africa, the colonial state promoted the formation of 'native reserves', forcing indigenous tribes to live in a designated area, with the explicit aim to convert these areas into supply sources for cheap labour. The reserve lands were generally, though not always, less productive than other areas. Their low fertility combined with population growth to induce a steady migration into mines and plantations (Frankema 2010).

In peasant production systems, the state could achieve this purpose via directives on labour or land use. Formally, colonial rule may be said to start when the state announces that it is the owner of all land in a territory that it already controls. This announcement came in at different times in the career of European rule. In India ruled by the East India Company, this right was framed around the last quarter of the 18th century in the course of land reform. Company rule began (around 1757–65) by occupation. The assertion of sovereign rights followed later (around 1793). In Indonesia, a sovereign right was established during the Napoleonic wars. In Africa, the signing of bilateral agreements following the Berlin Conference of 1884–85 represented the moment when claims to ownership of territories were announced and accepted by potential rivals. Here, colonialism began with exaggerated claims of ownership, measures to occupy and governance of the land followed later.

Does the formal announcement of sovereign rights to all land matter? It does in an indirect way because it usually signals the state's right to define and allocate property right over land and minerals. The assertion of individual land tenure overriding collective or shared rights was quite universal and would not be possible without the state first claiming ownership over all land. In India, West Africa and Southeast Asia, the assertion of ownership also entailed recognition of peasant rights over already cultivated land and customary rights over the commons.

Once the state became the owner of the land and the peasants the tenants of the state, legal expropriation became a possibility. The state, when it wished to drive labour towards preferred types of activity, could use threats of force. For example, in the Cultivation or Culture system in Indonesia under Dutch rule, peasants were forced to allocate a part of their labour to growing sugar. In Sudan under British rule, the Ghezira Land Ordinance of 1921 forced peasants, who were tenants of the state, to grow cotton over part of their land.

In the island economies after abolition, again, the state sought to ease labour shortages, now via the use of indenture contracts. The strategy was strikingly successful in the British tropical colonies in the Caribbean, Mauritius and Fiji, and in Dutch Suriname, where hundreds of thousands of Indians were imported to work as wage-labour. Sometimes merchants, bankers and service workers followed. The indenture contract was technically voluntary, but since most workers in the mid-19th century would not be able to read the contractual document, they often entered work with limited knowledge of what their rights were.

In the plantation and mining economies, property right reform was more disruptive and often biased towards settlers. These settlers, as we shall see, were not always Europeans. The reforms were destructive in their impact on indigenous institutions. For example, in the plantation-mining complexes of Africa, the colonization process occurred too quickly to be orderly. Where the mainstay of the economic system was plantations or mining, 'the exploitation of resources during the colonial era diminished the significance of mutual assistance relationships within the community' (Sahn and Sarris 1994: 283). Labour coercion (in Mozambique, Tanzania or Malawi, for example) damaged farming and indigenous land tenure systems, and communities and chiefs sometimes lost their authority to control and allocate property.[3]

The plantation and mining economies, thus, would seem to support the prediction that concentration of natural resources reinforced inequality of economic and political power, with some bad growth outcomes. This is the second of the three comparative economic arguments. The settlers gained from exploiting resources and exploiting slave labour, became rich, practised policies that in effect alienated land from the poor landholders, and denied the majority access to public goods.

But these generalizations are neither wholly realistic nor applicable to all plantation complexes. For one thing, the businesses that gained from plantation-mining complexes were not always European in origin. The Chinese were the leading settlers in Indonesia and Malaya. Australian capital gained from the sugar export complex in Fiji. For another, labour reserves were not a static thing, but constantly changing due to migration and, in the islands, conversion of indentured workers into farmers, shopkeepers and merchants. After all, 'indenture,' an account from Fiji declared, 'was a journey undertaken to find security in this life, an ingredient largely missing in village India' (Ahmed Ali, cited by Knapman 1985).

Plantations were located at a distance from the capital city so that production and labour conditions were often hidden from public view. These sites were sometimes criticized for exploitative practices such as coercion of workers or discriminations against smallholders. These practices were not illegal; in fact, labour contract legislation in India sanctioned harsh penalties for breach of contract on behalf of the worker. The model of such penal law came from early modern Britain, but it meant one thing in an English city and another in a remote tea estate in the highlands of a colony. In British Malaya, land policy and export quota systems favoured the estates over the smallholder.

Harsh measures and biased land policy, however, were not necessary conditions for plantations to grow, especially after 1900. Commercial and financial institutions, like auction houses in tea conveying information on quality and the stock market, were more important. The close collaboration that had developed between banks and mining firms in southern Africa (see the section on globalization) is another example of the point that innovations in finance and marketing rather than exploitative practices in production sustained the main forms of colonial business.

Local conditions: persistence of precolonial institutions

The persistence of coercive labour regimes inherited from the precolonial times represents one significant example of how indigenous institutions shaped colonial policies, when these systems served commerce or the government interests. Compromise with indigenous law acted as a further constraint on the state's capacity to act freely. One type of compromise followed from 'indirect rule'. Colonial states had limited administrative and military capacity and traded off direct governance for loyalty and open markets when they could. It is said with Africa that indirect rule systematically limited the power and will of the state to carry out institutional change.[4] Critics of this view consider it too one-sided and 'Eurocentric', among other reasons because it implies that in directly ruled regions, colonial regimes had unlimited power to make laws.

Where the indigenous state systems were large, complex and sufficiently bureaucratic before the colonial takeover, the colonial state was more likely to inherit laws rather than make them. In late 18th-century India, colonial property right reforms tried to achieve a modern aim by making a partial compromise with tradition. The modern aim was to expand the state and create a market for land so that the more efficient cultivator could bid for more land.

In meeting these aims, the British Indian state scored partial success. The land market remained less active than expected because people held on to land for lots of reasons. But the state succeeded in raising significantly larger amounts of money in taxes, mainly from land, between 1770 and 1840. This aim it could achieve by disallowing the right to collect taxes – formerly enjoyed by landlords – and redefining the right to own land as the only legal right on the land. The move led to the conversion of militaristic landlords and warlords into landholders and increased the state's share of tax collection.

The Indian case challenges several assumptions of comparative economics analysis of colonial law (see also Box 7.1). The literature overstates the case that laws were a purely western inheritance. British Indian law, in fact, had a mixed origin, indigenous in property and land law, and western in commercial law. Because it was a mixed product, it gave rise to theoretical debates as well as contestations in the courtroom. In matters of succession and inheritance of property, the new legal codes closely followed indigenous legal codes as these were written down in Sanskrit or Persian by jurists and experts serving the local states. The reference to tradition, it was expected, would give the colonial state a legitimacy in Indian eyes. In landed property, maintaining peace and stability was of paramount importance to the state, especially after the Indian Mutiny (1857–58), which nearly put an end to British rule in India (Roy and Swamy 2016).

In practice, the compromise with Indian tradition created new problems. In land law, it made the work of the courts and the judges

Box 7.1: Colonial law

Whereas economic historians take an interest in law for the consequences that it might generate, historians take an interest in law for what it tells us about systems of governance. These two scholarships often diverge in their accounts of the origin of colonial law. This box intends to capture some of the key points of the historical discourse.

Colonial states derived laws, especially those on property and inheritance, from a variety of sources, of which four were especially significant: Europe, which divided into common law, Germanic and Napoleonic codes as models; religious law such as the Sharia or Hindu codes; customs with legal implications or adat in the Islamic regions; and intercolonial transfers, more common in company, contract, procedures and other commercial law.

While this issue raises a complicated question of what was used where and why, it also raises a puzzle about governance. Surely a universal system of law would be the preferred model of any state to assert its power over subjects. And surely, by allowing custom and religion a say, the state would deliver some of its governance power to the communities. Why, then, a fragmentation that weakened the state? A simplistic answer to the question is indirect rule or rule by proxy, a precondition for which was sharing the power to make laws. This is an incomplete answer because the law that the partners of the colonial regimes preserved was usually a recreated system and not a system that they had traditionally followed. Another answer to the question is that the colonial regimes consolidated their power by exercising the authority to define and sanction laws deriving from custom and religion. In other words, the sanctioning of a heterogenous set of laws represented their power.

A second set of questions concerns the instability that was built into these hybrids. There were several roots of instability. One of these occurred when recreated custom sanctioned the property rights of clan or kin or the joint family over that of the individuals, following on the European preconception that oriental or African societies were ruled by clan, caste and kin. That principle conflicted not only with British law of inheritance but also the Sharia. Problems like these added an enormous burden to the courts system, underfunded in all empires, and led to departures from the original model. A third set of questions concerns the different mix between the four elements that emerged in the European-ruled regions. There is no one comparative history that explains why the Dutch strengthened custom relatively more, whereas the British and the French strengthened religious law.

In commerce, contract and company, the universal practice was to borrow from Europe, and for the later colonies to borrow from the earlier ones. Thus, British

East Africa borrowed English law on contracts and procedures via India, at the same time making Indian case law as admissible in the East African courtroom.

Further reading

William R. Roff (2010) 'Customary law, Islamic law, and colonial authority: three contrasting case studies and their aftermath,' *Islamic Studies*, 49(4): 455–62.

David Gilmartin (1988) 'Customary law and Shariat in British Punjab', in Katherine P. Ewing (ed), *Shariat and Ambiguity in South Asian Islam*, Berkeley CA: University of California Press, pp 33–62.

---

more complicated, because the disputants sometimes preferred British to Indian law in matters of succession and inheritance. For example, Indian law upheld the right of the 'family' over individuals in the inheritance of property. British law allowed for more explicit testamentary powers of the head of the family. The latter feature was attractive to some Indians, especially when the head of the family was a successful entrepreneur or landlord. In Punjab, where the local states and peasants did not join the Mutiny, the local administrators were aggressively pro-peasant and favoured the conversion of local norms into laws.

Reference to indigenous tradition also failed in commercial contracts. In precolonial India, commercial law was embedded in customary practices and norms of business communities. As the scale of market exchange increased, and especially with European presence in trade and finance, the absence of coded laws recognized in the courts caused problems, often resulting in violent trade disputes like the indigo mutiny of 1859–60. Indigenous contracts, framed by scribes and priests rather than merchants, were no good as guides. This vacuum led to a drive to legislate on commercial law as globalization took roots in South Asia. These laws built on British precedence almost entirely.

In British India, the average number of 'supreme government acts' passed every year was 0.6 in 1835–50, 1.8 in 1880–1900, and fell rapidly after that. The most frequently used among the new laws were those related to procedure in general, and business procedure specifically. For example, the Code of Civil Procedure 1908, the Indian Contract Act 1872, the Evidence Act 1872, Limitation Act 1908, Stamp Act 1899 and Registration Act 1877 accounted for 70 per cent of all High Court suits settled in 1900–10. The actual pattern of legal reference also suggests that the legislative process responded to problems of business transaction. By the same logic, legislative dynamism weakened later because international business was in retreat after the First World War.

Legislation was one thing and enforcement was another. Making laws is a comparatively low-cost activity, but enforcement requires a system of police and justice, which can be costly. In most colonies, the states were too poor to invest enough in this system. The business of the cities was less affected by the underinvestment, for they operated from areas where the legal infrastructure was dense enough. But away from the port city, the existence or roots of law became an academic question, as no law of any kind was backed up adequately. In British India again, cases piled up in the courts from the interwar years because the capacity of the system fell behind the demand placed on it.

Institutions and inequality

Because institutional reform was tempered by local conditions, the process had very different implications for inequality and globalization. One channel of impact of colonial rule was the difference between property regimes. A paper on Indian land law suggests that in those districts of British India where the colonial rulers had delivered property rights to non-cultivating landlords or zamindars (in 1793), rather than to the cultivating peasant, agricultural productivity was higher and investments lower in the post-independence period. The underlying argument is that in the landlord areas, conflicts and lack of cooperation between the elite and the peasants became more likely and made lobbying for resources in the post-independence period less successful (Banerjee and Iyer 2005).

In most large countries, the cities and the countryside usually differed substantially, especially in the operation of commercial law and ease of dispute settlement. Whether in India or Indonesia, the effects of globalization and state institutional support to that process did not have much transformative power over the interior. Much of the action was confined to the port cities and their satellites, and agriculturally well-endowed and vanguard regions. This inequality was large and systematic in India (Roy 2019). Governance and laws transformed Java, which contained 10 per cent of Indonesia's land area and over half of the population (in 1930), but distant islands were barely touched by colonial rule institutionally speaking.

Does the identity of the colonizer make a difference to the pattern of institutional change? There is a view that the British relied on indirect rule more than the French did. The difference between direct and indirect rule could also influence the pattern of political evolution in late colonial rule. An exploration into such legacy compares post-colonial Ghana with Ivory Coast to conclude:

> In Ivory Coast French colonial institutions fostered the emergence of a landed elite. That elite ardently supported ... promarket, proagrarian policies. In Ghana British institutions helped create a small peasantry. Unable to mobilize politically, this group did not effectively challenge Kwame Nkrumah's decision to adopt pro-state, pro-urban policies. (Firmin-Sellers 2000: 268)

Within cash crop producing economies ruled by the same colonial power, surprising divergences can be discovered. Comparing three cases, Malaya, Sierra Leone and Zambia (all British colonies), Frankema (2010b) offers two results. First, political imperatives and not only economic ones often led to policies of land alienation. Second, 'the nature of indigenous institutions played a decisive role in shaping the political, economic context in which such decisions by indigenous rulers were made' (446). In Malaysia and Sierra Leone, local institutions changed little because they did not need to change or were too costly to alter. In Zambia, tribes and chiefs 'traumatized by slave raids and endemic tribal warfare' (447) handed over control of land in exchange for military protection.

The comparative economics discourse on institutions places a heavy emphasis on property rights. That emphasis carried on into studies of colonialism and institutional change in Asia and Africa. Relative to land law, little research has gone into the evolution of commercial law in the non-European world where, presumably, European precepts and precedence were transplanted almost intact, as the Indian example would suggest.

There was almost perfect equivalence between colonized and colonist countries in the laws of contract and companies. How do we explain the equivalence when in property law there was so much divergence between regions? The reason may be threefold. Law relating to the joint-stock limited liability company would have come from Europe, because the concept was used more there if not invented there. Commercial law was earlier less coded and more intrinsic to the shared practices of business communities. There was little written tradition for the colonialists to draw on. As globalization progressed, both indigenous and foreign businesses would want convergence in law. The implicit demand for a global law in commerce, therefore, was shared between foreigners and locals, and between colonists and the colonized peoples.

No matter the root, compatible law encouraged trade, migration and capital export. Empires achieved that equivalence. But this was not an uncomplicated borrowing that always led to a good result for those engaged in these transactions. The use of the contract in employment and rural credit in India was deeply controversial among colonial administrators, many of whom thought that mortgage law or indenture law strengthened the hands of the rich, literate and powerful employers and creditors, and discriminated the poor and illiterate borrowers and workers (Chaudhary and Swamy 2017; Gupta and Swamy 2017; Swamy 2015). If there were any truth in this claim, then westernization of law would aid inequality while it also aided globalization. Further, in some cases, the colonial law of joint-stock corporation led to misreading and suppression of indigenous systems of pooling capital (Chung 2003).

Conclusion

How did colonialism reshape institutions? What difference did that process make? Recent interest in questions like these derive from an economic history discourse aiming to explain the origin of international economic inequality. It makes the following claim: whereas in the normal course a legal system evolves via an interactive change in theory and practice, in the colonial societies, key institutions like property and contract law were an imposition from the modern West; and the quality of that inheritance varied between settler and non-settler colonies or between French and British colonies.

The chapter concludes that in colonial societies, laws were not just imposed from the outside, but that they were shaped by settler power, factor endowments and precolonial laws. The quality of law depended on this mix, as well as on systems of justice or systems of enforcement.

There was no doubt a great deal of transplantation of European ideas and precepts. Still, local situations limited the capacity of the states to put these ideas into practice. States relied on indirect rule, recycled and reinvented precolonial institutions, deferred to 'tradition' to gain legitimacy in the eyes of subject peoples. In some places, colonial states helped the elite and settlers capture economic resources, thus empowering the settlers. Elsewhere colonial governments did not come to their aid. There is no one story about how these constraints worked.

One systematic pattern can still be recognized in the way institutions developed in the colonies: while landed property systems were extremely variable, and shaped by local conditions as well as imposed political trends, there was convergence in commercial law. In the definition of landed property rights, all these local constraints usually mattered a lot, and everywhere. In the commercial law of contract or corporations, local situations mattered less, and colonial states freely borrowed from European precedent. That freedom was crucial to the successful pursuit of projects that made 19th-century globalization – like indentured labour migration, free trade, capital flow and railway construction.

Enforcement is another area neglected by the literature. A well-functioning rule of law requires clearly defined laws as well as a system of courts, justice, procedures and police. Colonial states concentrated on making laws. They had neither the money nor an urgency about investments in the systems of justice. The legal infrastructure in most countries was seriously underfunded and had little presence or effect beyond the port city. If colonial law aided globalization, it made societies more unequal.

Notes

[1] When these works appeared, there was already an extensive literature arguing that African living standards had declined during European rule. The scholarship held institutional interventions in the settler colonies responsible for the decline. More recent research challenges that view. The debate is discussed in Fibaek and Green (2019), and covered more fully in Chapter 4.

[2] Such claims usually rely on Angus Maddison's dataset. Maddison delivered an enormous service to economic history by compiling a dataset on average income of countries over centuries. But Maddison often set a number for the average income (or population and urbanization) of a country for a time when neither data nor the country existed. The fact that the number exists creates the illusion of knowledge, but it is no more than an illusion. On Maddison's dataset and research to improve upon it, see 'Maddison Historical Statistics' in https://www.rug.nl/ggdc/historicaldevelopment/maddison/ (accessed 24 February 2020).

[3] For a study of 'labour tenancy' system in Nyasaland, or Malawi, see Mandala (2018).

[4] An influential statement of the view says that the imperialists in much of Africa ruled over the countryside using a recreated notion of tribal authority and customary law (Mamdani 1996). Critics of the view say that Mamdani overstated the power of the colonialists to manipulate indigenous institutions (see, for example, the survey by Spear 2003).

8

Colonialism and the Environment

There are many reasons to be interested in the link between colonialism and the environment in Asia and Africa. During colonial rule, the commercial value of land, minerals and forests increased along with export production. It was in the states' interest to promote exports and make resource extraction sustainable. The attraction of 'ghost acreage' or the availability of colonial resources to relieve the pressure of overpopulation in Europe made colonial resources vital to Europe's wellbeing. Railways and other technological advances improved the capacity of the states and private businesses to exploit resources. New laws strengthened the idea of private property, and some colonial regimes established state or private property rights on the commons, disenfranchizing the indigenous population from the right to use and sometimes conserve trees and water. Alongside sponsoring policies that entailed damage to the environment, colonial states collected a lot more information about the natural world than regimes before. They did this because they needed the data to govern. Moreover, inherited ideas and technologies sometimes clashed with indigenous ideas about nature.

But there is a lot that we do not know about the link between colonialism and the environment. We do not know in precise terms what environmental management before colonial rule looked like. Some of these same processes had been in existence from a long time past. The precolonial era was hardly a changeless one. Despite such ignorance about the prehistory, it would be safe to say that the scale of the impact of colonial states on the environment was unprecedented.

The state is central to the whole story, and its motivations varied. A large scholarship – often tagged as 'postcolonial' – using evidence from South and Southeast Asia claimed that these states invented the very concept of regulation over the forests and the commons.

Whereas the administrators justified the regulation as a measure against unchecked commercial exploitation, historians inspired by Michel Foucault and Edward Said read the regulation as a measure to extend state power over indigenous peoples. In another approach, called colonial environmentalism, state regulation stemmed from theories about ecological balance, and how human action could upset the balance. Testing such theories required data, and therefore, environmentalism led to the collection of novel kinds of data on nature.

Both these approaches presume that the states had a lot of power and freedom to take actions. Did they really have so much power? Elsewhere in this book, we show that most colonial states were poorly funded. The desperate need to raise revenue from land, trade or from commercial contracts could equally well produce the drive to exploit resources as well as the drive to conserve their use. In this sense, regulation was a cautionary and exploratory reaction to the fear that resources of potential value to the state might otherwise be lost.

This chapter does not try to settle these areas of potential dispute. It shows instead what economic history can learn from such discussions on the nature of the colonial legacy on the environment. The chapter surveys six themes that have figured prominently in the environmental history of the tropical and equatorial regions. These are: the precolonial baseline, commercialization, state intervention in forests, water, public health, and environmentalism.

The precolonial baseline

To what extent did the colonial period alter the landscapes of resource use and environmental regulation? The scholarship on British India has shaped the discussion on this question to a significant degree. India, therefore, is a good place to start. Conceptual frameworks developed in India in the 1980s, especially through the work of Madhav Gadgil and Ramachandra Guha, suggested that, before colonialism, collective bodies such as village communities negotiated right of access to common property including forests, and designated castes specialized in the maintenance of forest resources (Guha 1989; Gadgil and Guha 1992). This specialization in resource use made some of them take care of the resource responsibly. The forests of the western Himalayas were previously used by a large migratory pastoralist population, as well as by the peasants who lived on small plots of hillside lands between the forests. As the elevation increased, agriculture alone became insufficient to sustain a living, and had to be combined with animal husbandry, mining, trade and extraction of diverse resources from the forests. Village communities decided on access to and usage of these forests.

Against this precolonial equilibrium, the colonial era was a huge disruption. The regime recognized only one kind of property right – ownership. Therefore, in an indirect way, it weakened the community by empowering owners of land, undermined traditional conservation practices by reserving forests for the use of the state, and in these ways destroyed an indigenous moral economy about responsible use of nature. Projects, often state-sponsored, to exploit and extract commercially valuable resources from the commons made for a revolutionary change in ecological balance, and possibly destroyed forever a more harmonious relationship between humans and their habitats that had existed in the past.

In the 1990s, environmental history modified the model of a precolonial equilibrium upset by colonial intrusion quite substantially. New research showed that the precolonial India was a bundle of experiences rather than a uniform picture. The so-called harmony of precolonial India was vulnerable to agricultural expansion and political actions to capture resources (essays in Rangarajan and Sivaramakrishnan, 2012). Further, it is not clear how far the village community or traditional communities were pre-existing or recreated by the colonial state while trying to define customary property rights (Singh 1998; Grove et al 1989). Sumit Guha (2006), among others, disputes the notion of a precolonial equilibrium marked by a separation between agriculture and forest-dependency into distinct fields of specialization. Forests, instead, were tied to the agrarian landscape through a set of dynamic relationships. People combined livelihoods and identities, and peasants used forests as a resource as well as a political domain. In many regions, dominant peasant clans had superior rights to the forests and retained these rights in the colonial regime. Others criticized the image of the forest dweller as a relic from times before agricultural civilization, or attempts to 'essentialize' the original dweller as 'tribe' and helped blur the boundary between farms and forests (Das Gupta 2011). Present-day scholarship on nomadism confirms that agrarian and nomadic environments can co-exist and exchange people between them (Robbins 1998).

The scholarship on Africa and Southeast Asia since the 1990s has seen a similar shift. The environmental history of Indonesia before Dutch colonization tells us that precolonial Indonesia was not immune to humanmade changes acting on the natural environment, some of it seriously disruptive.[1] '[M]uch environmental research on Africa,' writes a paper on the environmental history of Tanzania, 'treats the pre-colonial period as a baseline in which farmers were engaged only in subsistence production and natural environments were literally "undisturbed"' (Håkansson et al 2008). Questioning this assumption, the authors suggest that the Indian Ocean trade and caravan trades in export goods wrought significant changes, though a lack of data does not permit a precise account of what the changes were. We do know that one of the transmission channels was food production along trade and settlement routes. The growth of early-modern trade would require such expansion of local food production, which sometimes occurred on marginal soils. The South Asia scholarship too acknowledges that in precolonial times, expansion of the cultivation frontier was often active in shaping ecological change.

Whereas the assumption of a changeless precolonial is a simplification, there is little dispute that the colonial marked an ecological watershed. It was a colossal disruption in two ways. First, the colonial era saw the state taking a range of actions to promote commercial exploitation of flora (and destruction of fauna) and at times protect resources such as the forests. This role of law and bureaucratic-administrative intervention had no precedence. We may think that these interventions were a specifically colonial and European implant. Second, colonial states encouraged or permitted the economic exploitation of natural resources on a much larger scale from before, to promote trade, to collect taxes, or via concessions offered to expatriate businesses to encourage them to invest in the colonies. The role of the state, therefore, needs a fuller discussion.

State and environmental decline

Science and technology allowed for deeper penetration of capitalist and commercial interests and industrialization increased the demand for tropical resources. While these effects, being parts of a globalization process, would possibly have happened without the agency of European states, European power did play a critical intermediary role. The enormously greater military (if not fiscal) power of the colonial states facilitated the unilateral imposition of economic ideology on regions and localities. Resource exploitation was a part of that ideology, though mixed up with a conservationist tendency.

Colonialism shaped the environment indirectly by enabling commercialization of resources and expansion in agriculture. Where nature would permit it, the states encouraged changes in crop mix in tune with changes in consumption. Thus, coffee, cocoa and tea plantations received favourable interventions in property rights.

Definition of plantation rights sometimes discriminated against the indigenous smallholders. In South Asia, the state invested in the railways and canal irrigation to promote extension of cultivation.

States also shaped the environment directly by acting as vehicles for the transmission of western science to the tropical regions. Whereas western science was a tool for the colonizer to extract resources, science enabled the administration to claim that they offered a beneficent rule. The rulers cultivated the notion that European rule was distinct because it took knowledge seriously, leading to advances in medicine, research of tropical diseases and conservation of nature. The decline in mortality rates and epidemics from the end of the 19th century gave some credibility to this claim. As a justification for the continuation of colonial rule, the claim ultimately failed. Still, for a considerable period, science served as a justification for colonialism, and science delivered results, good or bad (Goss 2009).

Colonialism, technological change and globalization led to huge pressure upon forests in some regions. In the 19th century, the demand for railway sleepers, fuel for railway locomotives, and timber for shipbuilding enormously increased the use of forest resources in India. Private contractors took forest patches on lease and cut down trees in large numbers. In several parts of India, the destruction upset the pattern of vegetation and wildlife. From the late 19th century, laws regulated the process of exploitation of forest resources, whereas, as we have seen, the laws also entailed exclusion of indigenous people from access to the forest resources.

In 18th-century Java, Dutch colonization accelerated the exploitation of timber for ships. Overexploitation of forests induced some form of state regulation. After 1830, growth of sugar and coffee industries under active support of the state again gave a new impetus to the destruction of forests. 'Thus, though the foundations were being laid for state forest management in this early period, the power of other government sectors was sufficient to make the state itself the forests' major enemy' (Peluso 1991). Laws regulating access to forest resources did come into place and, in the process, a great deal of knowledge was created on customary uses of forest resources and the value of the forests themselves. However, the bureaucratic management of forests continued to be driven by the sense that forests were to be preserved for profit.

John MacKenzie shows that a cult of hunting, originating in Britain, spread to the British possessions overseas. Expansion of farming, especially when done by European settlers, brought armed farmers into conflict with wildlife. These processes had consequences not only for the animals slaughtered but also the people who depended on forests. A conservationist impulse took shape within the same elite that enjoyed hunting, out of anxiety over depleting 'game'. The sentiment led to the creation of nature reserves (Mackenzie 1988; see also Beinart 1990). Conservationism, in another view, had origin in a radically different ecological sensibility, one that extended into hunting bans. No matter the ideological root of the hunting ban, the fact that wild animals were not a productive resource helped them to survive.

Alfred Crosby (1986) suggests that the environmental impact of colonialism did not stem from technology or control alone, but also a 'biotic' package consisting of crops, animals and disease organisms transported from Europe to very different ecological settings. At the same time, colonialism also brought face to face European people and their medical knowledge on one side and tropical diseases and epidemics on the other. Economic policy contributed to new epidemics, or created winners and losers as colonial governments attempted to manage endemic diseases. For example, the link between the population of game and the prevalence of tsetse fly set up conflicts between settlers interested in the expansion of the cattle industry and those wishing to preserve game stocks (Gargallo 2009).

The epistemic and survival crises led to a lot of research on the causation of human and veterinary diseases that Europeans had not seen before, such as malaria or rinderpest. The research was bearing results in the interwar period. Food production and railways contributed to better nutritional conditions overall. General mortality rates started to fall rapidly, in South Asia from 1921, and in most regions of Africa from the 1940s. As population pressure on limited resources began to grow, concerns over degradation of land and fragility of ecosystems emerged, now informed by the effects of a demographic rather than a colonial agency.

Agricultural expansion

An almost universal priority for colonial states was to encourage a shift from pastoralism and transhumance to settled agriculture, which had environmental consequences. Population pressure was one contributor. The state was also an active agent in the process. Its motivation was partly fiscal, partly regulatory, and partly scientific and conservationist. Premodern states, if they could, would encourage economic change which would allow them to collect more taxes. However, their options were limited. Modern and colonial rules had better hardware (armed power to enforce writs) and software (institutional ideas) at their disposal to extract more taxes.

In some places, the land was an easier asset to tax than livestock. Colonial states also extended rights over forests and pastures, either to convert some of it to farmlands, or collect a rent by asserting ownership rights over them. Doing so could speed up the commercialization of forest resources like timber. Eventually, there was also a drive to regulate the exploitation of forests.

By all accounts, the biggest impact of the emergence of the British Indian state on the use of natural resources fell on the land, mainly through the redefinition of legal rights to land. The colonial rulers defined private property in land differently from previous regimes. They defined it as an ownership right rather than as a right to use the produce of the land. Access to village grazing land, 'waste' land, and forests, however, required setting out rules of use rather than of ownership, and this task was left incomplete. A variety of consequences followed from the anomaly. Commons rights were eroded, and sharp divisions came into being between nomads, pastoralists, and forest-dependent peoples on the one hand, and the peasants, planters and landlords on the other, the last-mentioned being the more favoured by the new institutional regime and able to take away lands the pastoralists and nomads had rights over in earlier times.

Large parts of the tropical world specialized in the production and export of primary commodities in the 19th century. Global demand and the Industrial Revolution jointly pushed such expansion. The agriculture-manufacturing terms-of-trade rose steadily between 1870 and 1920, as technology cheapened manufactured goods and the demand for industrial materials and food rose. To this market process, the poverty of the colonial states added an impetus. Land revenue was the main source of tax in British India. Therefore, for a considerable time, the only instrument the state had to raise finances locally was to encourage the expansion of cultivation. Agricultural growth, in turn, put pressure on other livelihoods as well as the environment.

In India in the first half of the 19th century, expansion of cultivation made fuel such as straw or charcoal expensive, which hurt certain traditional industries. Salt production in Bengal was one such industry (Kanda 2010). Several attempts to start iron smelting on a large scale by European artisans failed to make profits among other reasons because of charcoal shortages due to the retreat of the forests. After 1870, with state investment in canals, agricultural expansion in British India became a pan-regional process. Cultivated area increased by 50–70 per cent between 1870 and 1920, including in regions where little land had initially been available for exploitation. Agricultural growth led to deforestation, changes in river morphology, imposed pressure on soil quality, and converted the common lands into farmlands. Canals occasionally had adverse effects on the environment. The railway boom in the late 19th century led to deforestation and extraction of timber on an extensive scale, especially in the foothills of the Himalayas (Das 2011).

Agricultural expansion intensified competition for land and water. In land, rising rents reflected the scarcity value and competition for land. In irrigation water, where the supply was limited and confined to specific sources, there were conflicts over distribution. With canals and tanks, 'head-reach' and 'tail-end' farmers faced different supply situations and levels of water security during scarcities. The inequality, if not redressed by collective action or state intervention, would induce one group of farmers to overuse water and switch to water-intensive crops, and another group to seek alternative sources and other livelihoods.[2]

Europeans, by and large, took a dim view of Asian and African agricultural practices. Administrators often emphasized the difference between indigenous and western knowledge of resource conservation, management and exploitation. They criticized swidden or slash-and-burn techniques and extensive farming. These techniques, however, were usually responses to water scarcity or poor soil. Swidden involved long fallow, which regenerated fertility with the action of time. In colonial thinking, any form of intensive cultivation was the mark of progressive farming. Such a strategy would invariably use more water than otherwise, and place enormous pressure on the soil. Water was an extremely scarce resource in the tropics, as was rich loamy soil. Where intensive cultivation did emerge, there was considerable potential for overuse or depletion of water and loss of soil fertility. These effects became serious issues in the wake of the 1970s Green Revolution in much of the tropics, but they had a beginning in the colonial times.

A precolonial state would perhaps be happy to pursue intensive cultivation, only they did not have the right technology nor the geographical scale to do so. European rulers had more engineering capacity and ruled over larger territories like British India. The large size of the territory in command made thinking about large-scale projects like an extensive canal network possible. India was an exception in this regard: in only a few regions were large territory and the supply of perennial river water combined on this scale. The general tendency of a push for more intensive agriculture, however, existed everywhere, and in the arid zones it involved a redistribution of water rights.

A study of late colonial Senegal shows that the changeover from transhumance to settlement in the Sahel increased the pressure on the boreholes around which the settlements appeared. 'Pastoralists settled around permanent water sites but (rightly, as it turned out) with no intention of giving up their potential for mobility, which is one of their principal ways of managing climatic and ecological risks' (Toure 1988). This increased pressures on the boreholes and had the curious effect of making the maintenance of herds increasingly difficult.

In Kenya, colonial ideology started to support the small farmer emphatically in the interwar period. Commercialization of agriculture, laws restricting the farming population to designated areas, and increasing pressure on these lands in the 20th century meant that some traditional practices protecting land quality – rotation and fallow especially – were being given up. From the 1930s, fears of soil erosion and land degradation with the spread of farming in the Kenyan Highlands drove the state to step into conservation in Kikuyu reserves. The move turned political. Resistance to the move reflected the sentiment that 'environmental concerns [were] a weapon used by the settler to legitimate security of title to the land and to persuade the colonial government in Nairobi to continue to support settler agriculture' (Mackenzie 1991).

The colonial conservation policy in the East African highlands focused on terracing.[3] Later assessment showed that the policy was based on a misreading of the cause of land degradation. The rainfall and topographical features of the regions had made 'rain splash' or dislodging of soil particles during a rainstorm more of a problem than water run-off. The solution would be increasing tree cover and revival of traditional practices of rotation rather than terracing. However, the state insisted on terracing, which was both a labour-intensive and land-intensive process. The state assessed the quality of authority of the chiefs against this benchmark. In post-war Tanganyikan highlands, a push for radical shifts in land-use policy stemmed from a belief that the region had 'suffered from severe soil erosion caused by human and livestock overpopulation and inappropriate husbandry methods' (Conte 1999: 237). Even when the diagnosis was correct, solutions to an unsustainable cycle of population growth, commercialization and intensive agriculture in fragile environments were not easy to come by.

Regulation of forests

Like agricultural expansion, forest regulation was a major focus of colonial policy. Forest history is a site for testing four different theories of state intervention under colonialism. Almost everywhere in the colonial world, laws about access and usage of forests, and along with these, definition and classification of forests emerged during European rule. According to one story, state regulation of forests shows the colonial state's desire to control populations on the margins of the economic and political systems that lived on settled agriculture. In a second story, the state was anxious to regulate forests from fears that commercial resources valuable to the state would otherwise be depleted. In a third narrative, state regulation had an older and apolitical origin, in the ideas of scientific forestry or silviculture that originated in late 18th-century observations about vulnerable environments. In a yet fourth account, called 'declensionist', colonial explorers, scientists and officers created a narrative of environmental decline caused by indigenous actions, implicitly justifying colonialism and reallocation of natural resources to European settlers (Davis 2007). Forests are not the main or the only example of this tendency, but one example.

Whatever the origin, the degree of state intervention varied according to the local political setup in place and the commercial value of the forests. In India, princely states and landlord estates (*zamindar*) followed their own rules. Although many of the forest regulations in British East Africa were borrowed from India, those forests were not as profitable except for a short period around the Second World War (Anderson 2002).

In India, colonial officers and local myths represented nature as a wild space occupied by tribes and located on the margins of settled agricultural society. Such a vision of nature made it likely that laws would be devised to improve the state's oversight of these marginal regions (Sivaramakrishnan 2000). Among the policymakers, however, there was little agreement over whether the rights of forest-dependent people over forest resources should be protected or replaced. In some cases, regulation accommodated within itself efforts to preserve some form of access of indigenous people to the forests. Thus, even as the state's right to regulate forests was defined, customary usage was documented and 'customary rights' over the use of forests were defined at the same time (Peluso and Vandergeest 2011).

Richard Grove, in *Green Imperialism* (1995), showed that the rise of a conservationist ideology had its roots in colonial rule, especially in the island colonies like St Helena and Mauritius in the 17th and 18th centuries, where natural resource conditions were especially vulnerable to forest felling. In a follow-up work, Grove (1997) showed how fears of human-induced climate change led to actions directed at state control over forest resources, often at the risk of conflicts both with the indigenous users of forest resources and colonists and settlers. Grove influenced a series of works that explored the origins of scientific forestry in the colonized territories (Rajan 2006).

In 1864, the establishment of the Forest Department, and the Indian Forest Act the next year, were the first steps towards formal legal restraints on access to forest resources in India. A more comprehensive and powerful act was passed in 1878. Research on the history of colonial forestry has investigated the roots of state control and ownership of Indian forests through these centralizing acts. Commercial overexploitation was one motivation. A better assessment of the commercial value of forests, in which non-timber resources such as medicinal plants figured in an increasingly important way, also strengthened conservationism.

In German East Africa (Tanzania) around 1900, forest reserve policy 'severed the peasant economy from forests, making them virtually off-limits to African use, often requiring people to relocate villages and farms and to abandon fruit trees, ancestral shrines, and hunting frontiers' (Sunseri 2003: 431). The reservation also adversely affected trade and Indo-African trading networks engaged in the produce from the commons, including ivory. In French Indochina, '[t]he extension of colonial interest and control into the remoter forest areas of the territory increasingly brought [hunters and shifting cultivators] into contact and conflict with the nascent forestry service' (Cleary 2005: 263).

Hydrology

Like forests, rivers became a field of state intervention, a field to test inherited European knowledge about institutions and technologies, and a field where different ideas about state intervention were discussed and contested. Rivers in the arid tropics were a more vital ingredient of life than they were in the temperate zones. Rivers provided drinking water, enabled multiple cropping or any cropping at all. They were often the only available transport routes. And from the interwar period, rivers were a potential source for electricity. To harness these potentials for irrigation or power, big projects were needed. In other words, the state was needed. Big projects disrupted local usage of water and involved setting up a new legal regime defining private property in water. In short, the state doing all this might empower itself and serve commercialization, but at a political cost.

In India, the state did build large canals, mainly using the perennial rivers of the Indo-Gangetic Basin fed by Himalayan snowmelt water. British engineering modified the project design to suit the terrain, enabled such projects and made the irrigation advisers valuable to the state. Canal projects became for some time the stone that would kill three birds at once: pacification of a potentially restless peasantry, increased taxation for the state, and reduced risk of famines. Punjab, with its network of five huge rivers, was geographically suitable for canal projects. The fact that Punjab's troops, local princely states and farmers did not join the rebels during the Indian Mutiny, though some of them came close to doing so, made the region a suitable ground for recruitment of soldiers for the British Indian army. The Punjab countryside, it was felt, deserved this reward. In British-ruled West Africa, the engineering paradigm was different in content but aimed to serve some of the same purposes as in India (Hoag 2013).

This was colonial hydrology. As with forestry and public health, it was a technological paradigm of European origin, implemented with political backing and sometimes with an explicit political aim. We should not, however, overemphasize the political dimension. If we concentrate on the political axis, colonial hydrology would merely appear as an instrument to enhance the authority of the state (Gilmartin 2003). Technology and power, control over water and control over people, thus reinforced one another.[4] We would go too far to see all big water projects as a symbol of power and authority. They entailed significant economic gains and costs and, therefore, offer a diverse range of lessons for the economic historian.

First, colonial revenue policy and property rights regime weakened and eventually destroyed local small-scale systems of irrigation that relied on community management (Sengupta 1980). Thus, before new hydraulic knowledge established itself as the best option, old local knowledge had to retreat and be forgotten. Many local systems of water recycling did indeed disappear in this way. The extent of the economic loss, however, is uncertain. Accounts of precolonial water systems tend to exaggerate the capacity of local systems and underestimate the choices and agency of the farmer in switching to newer systems capable of supplying bigger volumes of water more cheaply. The literature sometimes hints at a golden age of community control that may never have existed.

Second, geography imposed severe limits on the application of colonial hydrology. The proportion of irrigated land was about 20 per cent overall at the end of colonial rule in India, and considerably smaller in the water-scarce Deccan Plateau. In the arid tropics with rainfed rivers, the problem of water distribution was far too big for the engineers to solve. Systems of mining underground water did exist in the early 20th century, but this was a private good and needed access to capital. Colonial hydrology symbolized power in some regions; it symbolized a weak state elsewhere. The idea of the fragility of environments emerged soon after some of these exploitative processes did, and pushed states or some parts of colonial administrations in different directions.

Environmentalism

The tropics challenged European notions of nature. For example, the Indian climate, the geology, the quality of land and the germs that caused diseases were very different from those regions that Europeans had left behind. The numerous attempts that followed from the late 18th century to gather data and discuss these in an emerging Indo-European public sphere, in such platforms as the Asiatic Society or the Royal Society of Arts, can be seen alternatively as helping efficient exploitation of resources, or helping 'environmentalism'.

Broadly, environmentalism is an acknowledgement that humans have agency in changing nature permanently, and the follow-up idea that the state should manage the environment to protect it from disruptive human action.[5] Underlying the latter notion, there was another developing idea – that human welfare depended on sustaining the environment. Studies of environmentalism using colonial India have been influenced by Grove's work (1995) showing how European thinking on nature was influenced by meeting non-European environments. The birth of scientific forestry is traced to ideas called 'desiccationist', held together by the belief that there was a link between tree cover and soil erosion and drought. Later studies on scientific forestry also emphasized the training of the participants and the intellectual exchanges they took part in (Rajan 2006).

All this is not to suggest that environmentalist notions did not exist in indigenous societies before, but they did not form part of public intellectual discourse with political effect, to the extent the colonial-era environmentalism did. The anxiety that human action could, in fact, damage nature was also a modern one and reinforced by deforestation and agricultural intensification. Nevertheless, the application of resource management ideas derived from environmentalist impulses often came in conflict with existing practices, resistance by locals who lost access to resources, and sheer impracticality, a friction that Guha demonstrates well (Guha 1985). And there were many disagreements and differences within environmentalism over the channels through which human action left a footprint.

The systematic study of nature was a 19th-century enterprise. By systematic study we mean an attempt to construct theoretical models of climate, geology, and ecology, or attempts to derive propositional knowledge (statements telling why a phenomenon happened) and prescriptive knowledge (statements telling what can be done) from raw data, and recognizing feedbacks between these types of knowledge

(Mokyr 2004). A systematic study of nature in this sense had significant implications for material life, livelihoods and economic history.

The scholarship on environmentalism tends to be preoccupied with forests. Disasters were another area that saw data collection and efforts to build explanatory theories. South Asia faces a significantly higher-than-world-average risk of occurrence of natural disasters like earthquakes and coastal storms. These events interested amateur geologists, ship captains, port assessors and weather scientists from the early 19th century, because they were often directly affected by such events. Well before the state had created institutions where geographical research would take place, research papers began to be published, often using limited quantities of data, on the nature of these events.

Every earthquake confronted the 19th century geologist in India with a set of 'baffling phenomena'. While meeting these challenges, geologists enriched the understanding of Himalayan plate tectonics. The great Bay of Bengal storms of the 19th century led to the formation of a theory of cyclones in the region. Initially, the data gathered to study these phenomena were random, being gathered from ships' logbooks. In the long run, the scientific enterprise led to the creation of a meteorological department, and of geographical information systems that could predict the occurrence of major climatic events (Roy 2012).

The challenge that pathogens posed to life was mentioned before. That tropical and equatorial diseases killed Europeans is well known, but that legacy can be exaggerated. The threat of tropical pathogens to indigenous people posed a political challenge to European rule over these regions, as we now see.

Disease and public health

European expansion in the New World destroyed native ecosystems and population through new diseases, plants and animals, enabling the creation of neo-Europes in these regions. In equatorial Africa, the effect was rather similar if on a more modest scale and over a shorter period. European soldiers and explorers introduced new diseases. Mining, farming and the destruction of forests forced migration and resettlement, and spread these diseases. Between 1900 and 1914, one study suggests, these humanmade factors disrupted population growth, possibly causing depopulation over a vast region in equatorial and tropical Africa (Headrick 1994).

In the Old World of Asia, the impact was of a different order from that of the 'Columbian exchange'. The existence of developed agricultural civilizations, dense settlements and, therefore, greater disease resistance enabled these populations to withstand the disease organisms that came with the Europeans. Indeed, tropical Asia had more to offer by way of the disease organism. The demographic balance of payments was against the Europeans in this case. Nevertheless, in Asia, too, during a peak period of colonial rule, a demographic shock did occur. In colonial India, the population did not grow and life expectancy fell between 1881 and 1901 due to repeated famines and the epidemic diseases that these famines brought in their wake. The diseases themselves were caused by bacilli and parasites that were indigenous rather than transplanted.

Famines and epidemics posed the most serious ideological threat to British imperialism in India. Between 1876 and 1899, three famines in the Deccan Plateau of southern India killed several million people. Indian nationalists and British critics of the empire zeroed in on the famines to suggest that British rule, while encouraging capitalistic businesses in the region, compromised welfare and increased poverty of the ordinary people. The administrators knew that the only effective way to prevent famines was to secure water during dry seasons. There was no affordable or easy mechanism to do this in the arid regions of India. The major focus of irrigation canal construction fell on relatively water-abundant floodplains of large rivers, not the dry areas. And in those zones, canals produced benefits as well as environmental costs in the shape of waterlogging and obstruction of natural drainage.

If prevention was difficult, could cure work better? Cure would mean railways to transport food quickly. Railways did become a priority. Faster cure of famine conditions would also mean strengthening public health, and control of the epidemic diseases that spread in the wake of famines. These areas needed to become a target of state intervention. In equatorial Africa, too, diseases induced the state to act in a similar fashion.

In none of these fields did state intervention follow a set pattern or an announced policy. In Africa, Rita Headrick (1994) showed, European medical professionals and service were ineffective for a variety of reasons, including under-funding. Mark Harrison (1994) has shown for India that the rhetoric of public health intervention and the realities did not match, in part, because the state accorded a lower priority to welfare than defence. There was discord within the medical system about the ideal form of intervention. One historian calls the discord one between the professionals and the populists: the former upheld western standards, top-down and curative remedies. The latter favoured reliance on indigenous knowledge and institutions as well as western ones and believed in preventive action rather than curative remedies.

It is likely that in areas indirectly ruled the colonial state would side relatively more with the populist brand of intervention. In Punjab, where a distinctly Punjab 'school' of administration advocated rule by customary law, the support for populism was strong. For practical reasons, doctors and medical officers in the employ of the government often leaned towards the populist prescription.

The long-term effect of the disjointed efforts to control epidemics and improve life expectancy was nevertheless a positive one. In nearly all regions under colonialism, basic demographic indicators improved in the early 20th century. Dryland famines disappeared in India after 1900. Urban sanitation improved. Epidemics were brought under control. The theory that malaria was a mosquito-borne disease led to efforts to clear mosquito breeding areas and distribution of quinine. The research and observational data collected by the medical service professionals made for better causal models for epidemics and, thus, more effective prevention. Infant mortality implied in an 1850 report on Calcutta city was around 250 per 1000. It was about 200 in 1900. From 1921, the infant mortality rate began to fall rapidly, in all regions, reaching 146 in 1947. Science, the state and taxpayers' money did confer a great benefit on the colonial population: longer life. This demographic transition put pressure on limited land and water, as it did in India too.

In India, public health intervention was shaped by politics and disputes within medical ideology between western models and indigenous ones. In Africa, the same tensions appeared in a different way. The measures to cut off infections during a plague epidemic involved forced resettlement and segregation of the poorer residents of a city, feeding into resentment about colonial rule, and as David Arnold has shown, eventually leading to a change in strategy (Arnold 1993). This was the case in Bombay around 1900. A study of the return of the bubonic plague in Dakar (Senegal) in the interwar period shows that even as the measures did not change, the resentment and resistance became more muted in the 1940s compared with the 1910s, because influential members of the indigenous population had come round to accepting the logic of infection control (Echenberg 2002). The disappearance of the plague, however, had owed less to direct state interventions whether in Bombay or Dakar and more to better sanitation practices, nutrition and probably antibiotics.

In livestock-intensive economies, animal diseases could produce devastating effects. At the turn of the 20th century, tropical Africa experienced a series of natural disasters. Locust attacks and loss of livestock due to rinderpest and theileriosis (East Coast Fever) from

Somaliland to Tanganyika to the Cape Colony disrupted farming. Animal farming was a substantial source of income in some of these regions. Animal wealth facilitated credit markets, and cattle carried goods overland. The sudden fall in cattle population, therefore, was a devastating shock to trade and a variety of livelihoods. The initial reaction to rinderpest (in Natal) was to enforce segregation of cattle zones to cut off the infection, followed by more drastic measures like shooting infected cattle before inoculation began to produce results. As in plague control, the measures led to political unrest for the targets were African cattle owners. The long-term legacy of the disasters, therefore, was an economic structural shift with racial implications: the 'demise of an older agricultural system in favour of a new one that was more intensive, commercial, and better equipped to withstand [the] vagaries of South Africa's climate and ecology' (Ballard 1986: 450). The economy of Natal's African farmers declined under these pressures.

Conclusion

This chapter has shown why imperial history and environmental history overlap so much. Whether by design or accident, the colonial states unleashed forces that acted on the natural world more extensively and more deeply than before. These forces ranged from commercialization and institutional reform to conservation, accumulation of knowledge and information, and the transplantation of scientific paradigms.

The overlap between the two fields makes for a distorted type of environmental history. Within 'postcolonial' historiography, environmental history has developed as an offshoot of imperial history. In this paradigm all environmental changes followed from the empires' desire to extend power. This is an unhelpful and narrow model from an economic history perspective. The state, of course, had more power and more desire to intervene in the environment. Quite often it did so on behalf of businesses and farmers. In public health, the state moved to avoid the political embarrassment that famines and epidemics might cause. The preoccupation with colonialism also leads to an overemphasis on the commons and the village. By contrast with the over-researched forests, urbanization, population growth and technology remain under-researched.

In another way, the scholarship remains incomplete. The environmental history of the colonial territories has developed by describing conditions before and after European intrusion. This method obscures from view the regions where the European influence was indirect and limited. Alongside directly ruled territories, there were territories indirectly ruled by chiefs and landlords. Independent Siam was located next to British and French colonies in Southeast Asia. Did independence or indirect rule make for a substantially different environmental history? Did these other zones escape environmental decline because these were independent? What was colonial about the environmental history of colonial territories? So far, no one has insisted that independence did make for a different history. If indeed the whole world, colonial or not, experienced an environmental decline, that should tell us that European rule was not an exceptionally intrusive or disruptive force. It was a passive facilitator of globalization, not an active agent of environmental change.

Notes

[1] For example, several essays in Boomgaard et al (1998).
[2] For a discussion of distributional conflicts, and a case study, see Saravanan (2001).
[3] There were other examples of conservation campaigns which provoked political reactions, such as destocking in Kenya inspired by anxieties over the livestock-carrying capacity of the land (Anderson 2002; Tignor 1976: 12–13), and destruction of cocoa trees during the swollen shoot epidemic.
[4] For a survey and the phrase colonial hydrology, see D'Souza (2006).
[5] On environmentalism, see Barton (2002).

9

Business and Empires

Until recently, global business history existed mainly as an extension of the business history of Western Europe and North America. The assumption was that modern business emerged in Europe first, and travelled to the tropical world via European expansion and colonialism. Colonists needed the colonies to find markets for goods produced at home. Colonialism created fields of investment of surplus capital that earned too little return in Europe. The value of overseas territories as fields of employment was also considerable. In turn, the beneficiaries of the system, be they industrialists or bankers in the free regions, backed colonial rule.

There are two problems with this narrative. First, whereas the theory of capital or commodity export presumed that the return to investment in the colonies was necessarily high, the risks were high, too. In the 19th century, investors often had exaggerated and ill-informed ideas about the profitability of projects in the tropics. Governments sometimes helped firms to manage risks. They gave concessions and monopolies to companies in southern Africa, guaranteed profits of railway companies in India, gave profitable or subsidized contracts to shipping lines, and regulated markets in post-Depression West Africa. But they also sometimes refused to help. Rival businesses resented subsidies, and governments lost money or legitimacy in the process. The firms themselves had to devise ways to manage risk. This process was locally variable because the nature of the risk varied. To sum up, the notion that colonialism pushed global capitalism overestimates colonial power, and underestimates risks and the local context that shaped these risks.

A second problem with a West-centric historiography is that it says little about indigenous enterprise in the colonized regions. There is yet no general model, or indeed any model at all, of how indigenous enterprise evolved under colonialism. To write the business history of the tropics, in the West-centric approach, we need to understand colonial politics first. Indigenous enterprise did exist but functioned in niche areas. If one were a Marxist of the 1970s vintage, indigenous business necessarily functioned in a dependent relationship or in niches in which metropolitan capital did not enter. Because it did, indigenous business also struggled to shake off the burden of dependence, eventually succeeding in the mid-20th century. The left-of-centre historiography of decolonization in India pushes for such an interpretation of the Indian role in the movement for independence (Mukherjee 2002, for example).

The West-centric business history should be discarded, and is being discarded, not because it is wrong, but because it makes a business history of indigenous enterprise impossible without the reference to colonial power, and that is limiting. But what could be an alternative way to write the business history of Asia and Africa? Two useful concepts are specialization, and the nature of productive capital.

Colonialism aided the export of tropical produce, but not necessarily with the same tools or capacity everywhere. Exploiting the marketable surplus in most cases required *both* indigenous and expatriate entrepreneurs, for their interests were often compatible, but their skills different. Europeans had access to cheaper capital thanks to a head start in financial development, but indigenous actors knew the producers of tropical export commodities better. This is how specialization mattered.

The nature of capital mattered too. If the main productive capital was plantation land and diamond mines, who had the property rights to these assets would matter to indigenous enterprise. In some of the settler colonies exporting plantation crops and minerals, Europeans, aided by colonial power, were the wealthiest capitalists, leaving little room for growth to the indigenous capitalists. If the main capital was money funding commodity trade, as in West Africa or India or Indonesia, indigenous enterprise and foreign enterprise would differ depending on where they got the money from and at what cost. British trading firms in Asia and Africa obtained it from the cheaper financial market of Britain. Indian or Chinese businesses relied on indigenous bankers or their own profits. That financial market was efficient but costlier. And yet, when money circulated within known social networks, finance became more affordable. Such a pattern of financing cemented community ties.

European rule reshaped these worlds by opening markets and reducing trade costs, via the creation of settler power over some types of assets, and via institutional change like the transplantation of the joint-stock limited liability company from Europe to Asia and Africa.

Institutional transplants like the corporate form or contract law did help business raise money, sometimes stimulated the stock markets, but were rarely revolutionary in effect. Most trading firms remained under partnerships and family-owned. Even when subject to the same law, an Indian or a Chinese company differed operationally from European ones (see also Box 9.1).

Box 9.1: Trading firms and the British Empire

Once the royal and chartered companies had established secured bases in Asia and Africa, British merchants followed them. In the 19th century, many of these private enterprises took a corporate form. They represented what S.D. Chapman called 'diversification and redeployment of merchant capital'. Adoption of a formal legal identity by these trading firms allowed them to make fuller use of the commercial laws operating in the wide geographical space ruled over by the European empires. In turn, their presence encouraged quick transplantation of corporate laws from Europe to the colonies.

These firms, though multinational in operation, were not like the modern multinational nor were they like their partner firms at home. They were not because they needed to solve a special problem with more limited resources than the modern multinational: how to contain the principal-agent problems that were bound to arise in the presence of long-distance transactions with poor transportation and communication systems in place. Research shows that the adoption of a combination of family proprietorship and corporate identity enabled some of the trading houses to use flexible strategies, conserve limited managerial resources, and mitigate the transaction costs that remote management entailed.

British trading companies sustained the empire in many ways. Their owners and partners were a political lobby backing economic liberalism, they led the commodity trade boom that sustained Britain's industrialization and its economic and political power worldwide, they contributed to industrialization in the colonized zones, which came in handy when Britain fought in the world wars, and they were a source of information for the political class usually more ignorant of local conditions.

Further reading

Geoffrey Jones (2000) *Merchants to Multinationals: British Trading Companies in the Nineteenth and Twentieth Centuries*, Oxford: Oxford University Press.

Michael Aldous (2019) 'From traders to planters: the evolving role and importance of trading companies in the 19th century Anglo-Indian indigo trade,' *Business History* [online].

S.D. Chapman (1985) 'British-based investment groups before 1914', *Economic History Review*, 38(2): 230–47.

These observations help us set out a framework for this chapter. Big business in the colonized regions was not alike just because these regions had been under some form of European rule. There was no such thing as *colonial* capitalism. Colonial power intruded, but not in the same way or similar degree everywhere. The experience of firms differed over time, over geographies, between types of enterprise (agriculture, trading, banking, mining), between types of colony, and according to the prehistory of indigenous entrepreneurship. These differentiations are fundamental to understanding the long-term legacy of business development in these regions. How different were these regions in the pattern of development of private enterprise in modern times? What was different? And what was colonial about this history?

The global drivers

Factors that were at work in forging globalization in the 19th century – technology, military power, financial development, expansionist states and institutional change – were present with force in the colonized territories (see also Chapter 3). Europeans imported modern transportation and communication technologies to the tropics. Railways and steamboats in India and Africa greatly reduced the costs of bringing goods from the interior to the ports, and thus made for closer integration of agriculture, mining and manufacturing interests. 'The impact of the telegraph,' Jones (2002: 49) writes, 'was more radical.' Information was a key ingredient in capitalism at any time. As capitalism spread worldwide and included more goods and services, information costs became critical to the success of the business enterprise. In economies where agricultural commodity trades dominated private capitalistic enterprise, telegraphs acted as a tool of business development. After 1860 in India, 'English and Indian businessmen now had a source of almost instantaneous information concerning shipping, weather, and the prices of commodities' (Gorman, 1971: 601). The telegraph massively reduced the costs of transmitting information.

A second factor was military power. Colonialism did not usually lead to big governments but did invariably lead to the spread of military power over territories controlled by local rulers. The latter had neither the interest nor the capacity to regulate movements of cargo through their regions. Most independent or princely states in India were land locked, whereas the major ports were in British India. Both, therefore, shared an interest in railway development.

A third factor was capital export from the metropolitan countries to the colonies. Britain was the largest capital exporter of the 19th century. British capital went to different parts of the British Empire, and different types of enterprise, from commodity trade in the Indian Ocean, to the Indian railways, East African plantations, South African mining and Indian manufacturing. Other European regions had a more local but equally significant role. For example, companies from Belgium and the Netherlands were dominant in equatorial Africa until the Second World War. American money moved into the colonies in the interwar period. An example was J.P. Morgan's investment in the diamond company De Beers in the Cape Province (see 'Other private investment' in Table 9.1).

European enterprise and European states were mutually dependent spheres. State intervention shaped the pattern of capitalist development. For example, colonial rulers often tried to redirect trade away from traditional routes towards routes managed by them. To encourage trade, customs tariffs were kept low, as in the Congo free trade zone, or within the British Empire. In parts of precolonial Africa, states had devised efficient tax assessment systems (Heywood and Thornton

Table 9.1: Industrial composition of British capital exports to selected countries, 1865–1914 (percentages, total in billion pounds)

	USA, Canada, Australia, Argentina	India	South Africa
Government	17	46	51
Railways	41	41	2
Other private investment	22	14	47
Share of regions in total British investment to these areas	81	8	6
Total	2.49	0.32	0.26

Source: Stone (1999).

1988). However, the weakening of state power in both India and Africa also weakened some of these institutions, leaving the states poorer than they needed to be, as in British India, or providing extraordinary levels of power and concessions to the companies in return for money, as in equatorial Africa. The compliance of peasants and labourers with trading arrangements often involved compulsion in various forms.

Seeing how close and yet unusual the link between the colonial power and expatriate business was, we may ask whether capitalism was driven mainly by interests that formed in the colonist countries. Marxist theories of imperialism suggested that this was the case. More recently, the notion of 'extractive' colonialism again emphasized metropolitan interest as the main driver behind the emergence of new economic systems in the wake of colonial rules. However, research done in business history and the colonized regions disputes this approach. The state was not necessarily an ally of business. Local states sometimes allied with those actors that businesses tried to coerce. Companies were complex entities and not merely appendages of the extractive state. They processed novel information, took risks, raised capital in the market, developed partnerships with banks and trading firms, and circulated competent and experienced personnel among them. Politics might have helped them, but they were entrepreneurial too. It is an open question to which one of the two things more of their profits had owed.

It has long been recognized that the expansion of British power overseas and the export of British capital were interlinked processes. 'The surplus of capital in the most advanced industrial countries,' writes a Marxist account of imperialism, 'led to the search for new profitable opportunities for accumulation overseas' (Barratt-Brown, 1974: 170). In turn, the accent on capital export revised a classic interpretation of imperialism in Karl Marx's own writings, that had emphasized trade instead. P.J. Cain and A.G. Hopkins (1993) show that from the mid-19th century, the axis of the British economy and society was shifting. As the landed aristocracy declined in economic and political influence, and industrialization in the rest of the world limited the industrial bourgeoisie, the service sector forged ahead. Cain and Hopkins call this softer type of capitalists 'gentlemanly'. London was the centre of international banking. Debts of governments worldwide were raised in London through the intermediation of a small set of banks. Their field was global. While they operated both in colonial and independent territories, colonialism made their business safer in some cases. 'The gentlemanly class,' Cain and Hopkins write, 'formed the backbone of the Colonial Office' (124).

The Cain-Hopkins thesis accents the supply side. From the colonial side, the demand for money was very great. Most colonial governments in the tropics were underfunded, poor and dependent on public debt raised in London. The spread of colonial power reduced investment risks and made governments in distant lands more creditworthy. One of the poorest governments in the world, British India – poor in revenue per head – was also one of the most trusted borrowers in London. Colonialism explains the paradox. Recent scholarship has shed much light on this fiscal drive sustaining capital export and Britain's transition to gentlemanly capitalism (Accominotti et al, 2011; Gardner, 2017).

Geoffrey Jones adds to this story of service-sector growth the continuing prominence of merchant firms in Britain's globalization. With roots in the so-called East India trade in textiles and indigo, as well as the Atlantic slave trade, Europeans in the mid-19th century had established their presence in the trading ports all over the world. These networks exchanged information, managers and increasingly money so well that it was not too difficult for parts of the system to move to new trades when the old ones became obsolete. The networks also allowed them to access considerable economies of scope to diversify and backward-integrate, when possible. The business conglomerates that emerged from the process, Jones (2002) shows, were comparable in size to the largest industrial firms of the time. Although they were often managed by partnerships and families and used informal 'socialization' methods to make a decision and communicate, they displayed remarkable staying power. British capital export through the stock exchange or banks gave a huge boost to that staying power.

Exported capital and mobile firms did not move along primarily colonial channels. Nor was Britain exceptional in exporting capital and managerial capitalism overseas. Similar dynamics can be found in France, Holland, Belgium and Japan. Neither capital nor managerial skill had a bias for specific borders. Britain and the City of London were exceptional in the scale of these transactions, and the British Empire was a bigger field of operation than its counterparts.

Finally, European rule contributed to institutional development in the colonies. The French transplanted French commercial laws abroad, the British transplanted British laws of company and contract to India, and via India, to East Africa and Southeast Asia. The transmission was very fast and complete with Britain and India, and slower and more incomplete in many other regions.

We must be careful in assessing how big this contribution was. Any presumption that the non-European world lacked sophisticated commercial institutions and secure property rights before the Europeans came to the scene must be avoided. Most societies that engaged in trade before colonialism had also developed the institutions to deal with credit risks, weak states and multiple currencies. The presence of rich merchants shows that property was secure. In precolonial India, the trade-bill-cum-remittance-instrument called *hundi* was a widely used institution (Martin 2012). Overland trade in Africa too was characterized by well-developed commercial systems (Stiansen and Guyer 1999).

But if these institutions were adequate to serve commodity trade on a small scale, they could not supply capital at low enough cost on the large scale demanded by industrialization and transcontinental trade. Instruments like the *hundi* were used extensively by big banking firms in India, but they were not acceptable beyond a limited network of exchange. Large-scale deployment of capital could not rely on such local instruments nor networks of personal reputation and needed limited liability, banks, stock markets and companies, laws and organizations which came from Europe to the colonies. These global drivers did not always work with the same force everywhere. There was a chronological difference in the pattern of business development, as well as distinctions based on the type of enterprise and geographies, which subsequent sections explore in greater detail.

Chronology

The transition from 1650 to 1750, when enterprise existed without even the distant prospect of empires, to full-fledged colonies of the 19th century raises a puzzling set of questions. In the earlier set of years, far from colonialism aiding capitalism, capitalism created the promise of colonial rule. Why did trade make a political transition likely? From the 1600s if not earlier, slaves, spices and textiles were being procured from Africa and Asia on an ever-increasing scale. Europeans who conducted these trades bought and shipped the goods but did not dominate the supply zones, or the states that ruled these zones. How did they manage to extend political domination? What, if anything, did these trades have to do with the rise of imperialism?

There are perhaps three models of history now available to think about this question. With Indian textiles, a promising hypothesis emerged from the writings of C.A. Bayly.[1] Centuries of trade consolidated an indigenous bourgeoisie. Facing a collapse of political power in the interior in the 1740s, this class saw the East India Company as an ally sharing compatible interests.[2] And therefore, an unusual and precocious European state emerged in 18th-century India from origins in trade.

All of this is sketchy, but it has not been proven wrong. However we qualify the thesis, it remains a useful model.

West Africa, by contrast, supplies a second model that has some elements in common with the Indianist one. The common factor is that 'Africans were beginning to create their bourgeoisie and were establishing significant contacts with European businesspersons and financial houses' from long before the late 19th century partition of Africa.[3] The role played by this class in shaping politics or business after abolition is speculative. The generally accepted view is that by the 1880s when the partition happened, colonizing states were inspired by the prospect of grabbing natural resources rather than promoting trade.

The third model takes the resource-grabbing impulse as the main driver and eliminates the indigenous bourgeoisie from the scene. East and South Africa, where settlers controlled access to mineral and plantation resources, were similar examples. The businesses that this story draws our attention to were, in the more extreme cases, partners of a brutal state that claimed ownership of resources by using force; and in the more benign ones, trading firms with exceptional access to capital and information thanks to their European origin.

The business history of equatorial Africa makes a distinction between two types of state-business interdependence, one that lasted from the Berlin Conference to the first decade of the 20th century, and the second that followed this episode. The first phase of 'robber colonialism' led by white 'hunters and gatherers' saw forced extraction of resources on an extensive scale (Hopkins 1987: 129). These agents knew that Africa had resources and scrambled to get their hands on them somehow. Their actions and strategies were opportunistic and did not leave much of a legacy for a business enterprise. Governments stood at a distance. The second type, called 'mature colonialism', saw states focus more on governance, and companies invest more money in the territories they operated in. 'The firms which survived to the 1920s and beyond grew to appreciate the advantages of size, capital, and organization' (Hopkins 1976: 280). Elements of managerial capitalism took shape, and firm strategies covered the long term better. There was more of a shared interest in the former phase, and a parting of the ways in the second (Clarence-Smith 1983).

The most famous example of robber colonialism was the Belgian Congo between 1890 and 1909. History seems undecided on whether the Congo Free State was a state, a firm, or a fief of King Leopold II (1835–1909, reign 1865–1909). The Berlin Conference (1884–85) treated it as a state. The king ruled it like a landlord, with the help of mercenary soldiers and two companies, the Anglo–Belgian Rubber

Co. (1892) and Société Anversoise de Commerce au Congo (1892). In 1901, the king entered a contract with the Compagnie du Kasai for the exploitation of the resources of the Katanga region. This was driven largely by the fact that Leopold could not afford to administer the Congo with his own resources, as he had claimed he could. The setup laid claim first to ivory and then to the hugely lucrative supply of wild rubber, causing death to rubber tappers on a large scale. The regime formally ended with Belgian takeover of Congo from the king in 1908, the outcome of a combination of international outrage and the fact that Leopold kept asking for money. For about ten years until that happened, Leopold dismissed worldwide outrage at the brutal treatment of rubber tappers in Congo.

After government takeover, open coercion ceased, but tacit extortion and bullying continued. In 1911 the government entered a contract with the British soap company Lever Brothers delivering monopoly and concessional rights to procure and export palm oil. The procurement of oil and kernel involved forms of forced labour. The popular history of the region tends to be preoccupied with the unusual reign of Leopold II. Economic history also considers its varied legacy. The regime's steadfast pursuit of natural resources revealed the enormous natural wealth that existed here and attracted Belgian capital and enterprise on a large scale, mainly into mining and railways. A study of this investment shows that the companies made enormous profits from the mineral trade (Buelens and Marysse 2009). Little of that profit was taxed and invested in public goods.

The shift in the trajectory in Congo suggests that once colonial rule began, the robber-type and the mature-type of colonialism converged to some extent. As market integration proceeded, new types of foreign investment flowed in, and new non–European and local actors built a stake in the globalization process and its imperialist sponsors. The migration of Indian merchants to East and South Africa, for example, contributed to the consolidation of capitalism irrespective of European agency.

Such a sequence from robbery to mature colonialism is rare in West Africa or South Asia. European firms in West Africa or India did not extract forest resources but needed to rely on indigenous cultivators, intermediaries and firms for access to commodities for export to Europe. The colonial state had emerged from such trades and was aware of the level of interdependence between domestic and foreign actors in making the economy work. In parts of West Africa, concessions given to large companies like the Royal Niger Company brought governance and trading into an interdependence, though this experiment did not last. The main contribution of the state, from the start, was indirect and institutional. Throughout the Empire, and especially in India, the government reformed and made laws. Company and contract laws were a product of a late 19th century legal activism. One of the other products of that time, contractual labour act in India (1859), indirectly sanctioned employer coercion, but following the British legal precedents.

In all regions and types of colonialism, the interwar period and the Great Depression shook up business. The First World War in India, for example, weakened the metropolitan state and business enterprise, while leaving indigenous enterprise intact or stronger than before. At the same time, the event made some of the big Indian business interests more politically ambitious than before. The extremely limited avenues for self-government and representation that the despotic state had permitted so far clashed with this tendency, making way for businesses funding the nationalist movement.

Whether the business world saw more coercion or more collaboration depended partly on the types of enterprise. A.G. Hopkins distinguishes between immobile and mobile enterprises (1976: 277), the most immobile being settler-agriculture, in contrast to trading and banking. Being rooted and being tied to a resource, Hopkins implies, might make the companies more anxious to remain in control of the resource and obstruct others' access to it. Bankers and merchants were less worried about excluding access. Still, when expatriates dominated agriculture, trade and banking together, the concentration of economic and political power and the association between race and capital accumulation increased manifold. This was the case in East Africa, where white planters dominated commercial agriculture, and expatriate firms dominated the trade in these goods. In West Africa (and India) by contrast, expatriate interests were barred or discouraged from competing with cultivators. European capitalists, therefore, faced different situations in their places of business. Equally diverse was the manner of their entry into these places.

Metropolitan capital

On two occasions in the early 19th century, European (mainly British) firms needed to change their stake in India and Africa. In 1813, the end of the East India Company's monopoly legitimized private investment into fields that were previously formally restricted by the royal charter. The monopoly existed only in name at the time, so the move was not a big deal for private enterprise. Its formal abolition ended a conflict of interest between running a government and running a business, and allowed the Company to focus more attention on developing infrastructure and institutions.

In 1807, the abolition of the British slave trade in West Africa forced numerous firms and individuals with interest in the trade to find 'legitimate' alternatives. The transition was more traumatic in this case. In one respect, both these occasions were similar in their effect: private capital needed the colonial state more, if differently from before. While the slave trade had occurred based on local collaboration, commodity trades depended on safe trade routes, ports and harbours and laws. The state was needed to create them. More business firms needed more of that kind of indirect support.

In the 1830s, trade between Britain and West Africa came to be based on palm oil exports, though many other commodities such as ivory, gum, beeswax and timber also figured in the trade. Palm oil had a variety of uses as an ingredient in soap and as an industrial lubricant. Initially exported from Old Calabar in the Niger Delta, palm oil production and trade spread widely. Between 1785 and 1851, palm oil imported into Liverpool increased from 55 to 30,000 tons.

The commercial network in the British Empire that traded in colonial goods centred in London, Liverpool and Glasgow. Having one foot in one of these ports and another in the colonies made for a significant advantage. A base in the British city made it easier to form partnership with a bank or a trading firm, circulate partners and managers better, and manage re-export trade. European traders enjoyed that advantage.

Most European firms in colonial Africa around 1900 were commodity traders. Their origin and business strategies were diverse. By the mid-19th century, British power had consolidated along the West African coast. From then until the end of the century, 'the expatriate merchants … operated on a very modest scale' (Davies 1977 : 10). But there was a growing number of them, from Liverpool, Bristol and Glasgow. Liverpool was the main port conducting trade, both before and after the rise of legitimate commerce.

The risk of the trade was high, and mergers were common. A study of the Liverpool traders John and Thomas Tobin, and Charles Horsfall, shows that trading firms in the mid-19th century faced risks of losing money (or 'trust') in failed contracts with local agents (Lynn 1992). From the 1860s, risks increased. Hydrocarbons and tallow oils from Asia and America reduced the demand for palm oil in Britain. Although the shift from sail to steam reduced costs of palm oil transport, the competition was intense. Smaller firms did not disappear but were under pressure to reconstitute as companies or form consortia. With the expansion of French and German control in Africa, inter-imperial rivalry increased. Trading needed more capital as well as territorial control.

Partly in response to this need, the British Crown restarted the practice of issuing monopoly charters. The short-lived Royal Niger Company (1886–1900) was formed with a royal charter, and controlled land (lower Nigeria), as the East India Company had in Bengal. The company was the outcome of George Goldie's efforts to monopolize the palm oil trade. Goldie persuaded the government that succeeding in the trade required a command of military and governance power as well. Being the single largest buyer of commercial produce helped the company to repress prices, and being the government allowed it to earn revenue. The company, however, faced powerful opposition from Liverpool merchants, and it had stretched its resources too much. In 1900, its career ended (Pearson 1971).

Shipping, a capital-intensive activity, attracted large-scale enterprise in the 19th century. The shipbuilder of Liverpool and Birkenhead, Macgregor Laird, started the African Steamship Co. Alexander Elder, an engineer in Laird's firm, set up the main rival to the company, British and African Steam Navigation Co. As in the Indian Ocean, the big transoceanic shipping companies of West Africa sometimes cooperated, especially when there was a threat of entry locally, and sometimes competed (Davies 1977). Steam shipping encouraged the entry of a 'new class' of small-scale merchants, indigenous and European, in the late 19th century (Lynn 1989).

After 1900, cocoa was the main export from West Africa. The new players were of a different type from their predecessors. Some, like Lever Brothers and Cadbury, moved into Africa trade from a base in manufacturing industry in Britain. Lever had purchased the assets of several 19th-century firms whose fortunes rose and fell with the palm oil trade. The United Africa Company of the Lever Brothers achieved extraordinary integration of import, export and shipping. That level of integration enabled the firm to cut costs and cut competition; it also allowed the Company to control re-export trade. European companies operating in a single area, such as cocoa in West Africa or jute and tea in India, tended to form cartels, which were used to overcome an increasingly strong challenge from small-scale traders (Fieldhouse 1994). Around the mid-20th century, the Lever Brothers (Unilever from 1930) invested in industrial production in Ghana, in fields related to its trading expertise.

In southern Africa, Cecil Rhodes led the British South Africa Company, an indirect result of the partition of Africa. The company received a royal charter, and was expected to colonize, rule and develop regions, and exploit resources at the same time. Others, like Rhodes' rival in diamond mining in Kimberley, Barney Barnato, were adventurers who happened to be at the right place at the right time. Rhodes' firm and Barnato's eventually amalgamated to form De Beers. The Bristol trading firm Kings moved into palm oil soon after legitimate commerce took off. The Eastern European Jewish business family Susman diversified from cattle ranching to trade and transport in early 20th century Zambia (Macmillan 2005).

In India, European trading firms conducted a part of the overseas trade in the main export commodities, cotton, wheat, rice, jute and tea. British firms or those with strong links to Britain, such as Sassoon and Ralli, were the main players. Their British partners and subsidiaries took care of sale abroad, supplied capital, and sent managers to work in India. Some like Charles Forbes, Thomas Parry (1768–1824) and James Finlay (1727–92) emerged around 1800. Others arrived in the 1850s and the 1860s. The partners of Greaves Cotton started as a trader in cotton and textile machinery around 1850. The family of David Sassoon (1792–1864) were Turkish Jews who shifted base to Bombay around 1840. Sassoon inherited his father's trading firm. It carried on business in Persian, Indian and British goods, and later moved to China to trade Indian goods there. In Cochin in Kerala, Robert H. Peirce and Patrick Leslie formed Peirce, Leslie, and Co in 1862 to trade in Malabar spices. A few years later, John Aspinwall set up a trading and shipping firm in Cochin. In the 1840s, the Wallace family entered the India trade in Burma teak. In 1851, Salomon Volkart (1816–93), a commodity trader, moved from the Mediterranean to Bombay, and the Greek merchant Pantia Ralli (1793–1865) set up an operation in Calcutta. Volkart dominated Indian cotton export and Ralli wheat export.

The Great Depression disrupted a long period of commercialization in Asia and Africa. The most affected businesses were the European firms engaged in exports. These included traders of cocoa or palm oil and manufacturers of tea or jute in India. The crisis led to mergers through which Unilever emerged as the largest firm operating in West Africa. Colonialism was still going strong in Africa, though it was on the defensive in India. Across this front, European firms sought government help to fix prices. The effort largely failed in India, because the state had no stomach for bullying Indian rivals of these firms. The lobbying succeeded for cocoa exports in West Africa, where a government-sponsored marketing board emerged to set prices. During good demand conditions, the move helped the major buyers of cocoa – Unilever and

Cadbury – and short-changed smaller African-owned export firms (Meredith 1988). Shortly after the Second World War, the idea of a government monopoly in export commodities extended to a range of goods made in British West Africa (Bauer 1954).

Although in specific territories discriminatory policies against domestic enterprise were in force, the 'global drivers' were neutral concerning the ethnicity of the capitalist. Local players and Europeans were distinct more in terms of their access to cheaper capital markets than that of political patronage received.

Indigenous business

A coherent account of how globalization led to the consolidation of an indigenous bourgeoisie comes from colonial India. Colonial India was mainly a trading economy. The Indian mercantile marine had owed its prominence to the huge scale and antiquity of the Indian Ocean trade. Europeans like the East India Companies used this strength by developing collaborative ties with local players. Long after the Industrial Revolution and vast changes in the composition of world trade, which consolidated the position of Europeans and British firms in Asian trade, trade remained in the hands of Indians in South Asia.

In the 19th century, transoceanic trade and overland trade expanded. Coastal and river-borne trade possibly grew, since all other types of network did too. Europeans dominated transoceanic shipping, but not coastal shipping and overland transport. The volume of cargo carried by the railways and the ports increased from roughly 1 million tons in 1840 to well over a hundred times that in the next century. At its peak, 80–90 per cent of the volume consisted of rail-borne trade, where Indians dominated, and 10–15 per cent seaborne trade, where the Europeans dominated. No good estimates exist yet of coast-to-coast trade and river-borne trade within India, in which again Indian merchants and shippers were the dominant players.

The Indian merchants of the western coast especially – like the Chinese in Southeast Asia – entered the colonial-era trading from a prehistory of maritime trading. They had multiple bases and presence in the littoral regions of the Indian Ocean. The expansion of British power in the entire region strengthened this process of commercial expansion in Africa and Southeast Asia. What historians now call 'diaspora' was something else in the 19th century. Gujarati trading firms in Natal or Aden or Zanzibar were extensions and branches of trading firms in Gujarat, and not exactly migrants into a foreign land. Their continued success depended on imperialism, but not on imperialism alone. Gijsbert Oonk's (2009) fascinating study of the Bohra 'merchant prince' Karimjee Jivanjee of Zanzibar shows how closely their success and survival power depended on engaging with administrators, politicians, local commerce, and India-based networks.

Colonialism reinforced that transoceanic network. Indians always dominated short-haul and coastal shipping, as well as overland trade. In the early 19th century, this dominance saw them make a lot of money in opium, indigo and cotton trades. The Parsis of Bombay and Calcutta and the Marwari merchants involved in the inland trade made money in central Indian opium. The Parsis were a small community settled mainly in Bombay and Surat. Some of them partnered with the East India Company and private traders in the 18th century, and when the Company's monopoly ended, took over a part of the shipping and timber business. Thanks to this advantage they dominated Indochina and coastal shipping, the big names being Wadia, Readymoney, Banaji, Hormusjee Dorabjee Lascari, Dady Sett, Seth Dada Nusserwanjee and Cama. A few Bohra firms of Bombay also owned ships. A similar efflorescence of indigenous business occurred in Calcutta in Eastern India, and Madras in South India. In all of these places, local players and professional merchants accumulated capital by forming partnerships with European traders. Some of these partnerships did not last into the late 19th century because of a weak financial system and the commodities these actors specialized in lost their market.

Was this a decline-and-fall story? Probably not; several families had already begun to diversify their investment towards financial services and industry. A subset of these merchants and shippers set up cotton mills in Bombay and Ahmedabad from the 1870s. The early pioneers were a few Parsi individuals of Bombay. Several other merchant communities joined them in the late 19th century, including Bohras, Khojas, Kachchhi Bhatia and Marwaris from western India. The Bengali merchants suffered a setback but invested heavily in education. So did the Parsis. Both communities dominated the cultural and intellectual life of the port cities in the late 19th century.

The port city merchants and transoceanic networks account for one advantage the Indians had. Their other advantage was in overland trade and stemmed from knowing the producers of traded goods. Mature colonialism in India coincided with an enormous rise in demand for cotton from India. European merchants rarely ventured into the trade in the interior of the country. Poor transport links, the fear of insecurity, and the fear of diseases inhibited them from going inland. A further obstacle was the institutional complexity of agricultural trade. For example, finding out who was creditworthy in the countryside was difficult for an outsider. The trade, therefore, was in the hands of the Indians. Gujarati merchants and bankers in Bombay dominated the trade. A lot of good cotton grew in the South Gujarat coast. The trade interlinked Bombay, Broach (Bharuch) and Ahmedabad. In towns along the coast, merchants invested in gins and spinning mills. Grain trade was spread out more, penetrated most villages in India, and involved a more varied set of actors. A hierarchy of agents lived in the railway towns and went into the village markets to buy grain or cotton on behalf of bigger merchants.

These examples confirm the generalization made in the introduction to the chapter, that indigenous capital operated in fields where it enjoyed certain advantages, and which fields grew in the wake of colonialism. This interpretation supports and modifies the views of other readings of colonial commercialism. Rajat Ray suggests that indigenous trading-cum-banking firms (the 'bazaar') occupied an 'intermediate space' between European capital serving overseas trade and the Indian peasant (Ray 1988, 1995). Claude Markovits (2007: 122) stresses 'the ability of South Asian merchants to maintain significant areas of independent international operations throughout European economic and political domination'. Markovits' examples come from fields where Europeans were not present at all, such as mobile merchants and bankers in central Asia.

Theories which label Asian and African merchants as middlemen of some sort implicitly assume that Europeans were naturally dominant because of colonialism, leaving only a junior partnership role available to the locals. That framework is not necessarily helpful because it undervalues risks and limited information in doing any kind of business. The Europeans did not just permit the locals to find their niche but needed the locals because they understood and dominated some forms of market exchange. In Southeast Asia, a similar 'middlemen paradigm' applied to Chinese business has faced criticism (Post 2002).

Like the Indian Ocean trade, the commercial complexes that developed as parts of the trans-Saharan trade carried many goods the Europeans wanted – slaves, gold, ivory, among others – but could not get access to without local intermediaries. After the abolition of slave trading in 1807, new goods were made and traded in West Africa, all of which involved indigenous enterprise. The supply of palm oil and kernel involved such actors. 'One of the most significant factors' behind the growth of groundnut exports from the Guinea coast 'was the pioneering role of Senegalese Eurafricans and Africans whose trading enterprise stimulated African production in the 1830s and 1840s' (Brooks 1975: 42). Economic historians of West Africa observe a great deal of entrepreneurship among the smallholder cultivators who sustained a cash crop boom in the early 20th century (Austin 2005). In Ghana and Nigeria, urbanization encouraged private enterprise in trading.[4]

One of the world's largest gold mining corporations emerged from the explorations of two merchants, Joseph Etruson Ellis and 'Chief' Joseph Edward Biney, in the 1890s.[5] They followed a European-led gold rush in the Cape Coast. In the same broad region, coastal trading flourished in the late 19th century on the strength of local demand. Salt trade on the Volta estuary, the import of manufactured consumer goods from Europe, and an agency of the European companies in the palm oil trade, timber and rubber expanded the 'entrepreneurial niche' in which African merchants operated (Dumett 1983).

'Before the nineteenth century,' Carl Trocki (2002) writes, 'it is no exaggeration to say that capitalism did not exist in Southeast Asia.' Capitalism in the specific sense implied in this statement, large-scale export-oriented production backed by capital and new institutions, grew with the expansion of European power in the region, and the growth of trades in tea, opium, rubber, gambier, pepper, coffee and sugar (many of which had their main markets in Europe). Reforms in landed property rights helped plantations to develop. Although European capital then came into the export processing industries, European capital did not dominate the business world in Southeast Asia. Chinese enterprise in opium and tin mining in Indonesia and Malaya, sugar in Indonesia, and Japanese investment in rubber estates in British Malaya show that more Asians than Europeans made use of the opportunities.

Opium is a good example. Opium commerce in wider Asia gained from British and Indian trade in the article in the 19th century, and in turn, from the British Indian government's sponsorship of the trade. Opium revenue sustained the governments in India and British territories in Southeast Asia. Asians controlled the trade, and Asians were the main consumers of opium. Colonialism helped the trade grow if the governments shared an interest in the trade. When they did not, colonialism killed the trade. By the end of the 19th century, the international campaign against opium smoking had become intense, and the Dutch in Indonesia, the French in Indochina and the British in India did what they could to suppress the trade. By then opium profits had moved into other channels, including cotton mills in India and tin mining in Malaya.

Although most Chinese enterprises in Southeast Asia remained small in scale, a few exceptional firms emerged to compete with the Dutch and British companies operating in the area. They grew bigger by combining modern methods of raising capital, traditional networks, a fluid ethnic identity and multinational operation. 'Pre-war ethnic Chinese business in Southeast Asia was to a large extent transnational; it crossed colonial boundaries and did not limit itself to one particular colony' (Post 2002: 296).

Asian and African traders did not usually step out of known niche areas. Some did invest in manufacturing industry, but they were a small minority among the trading class. In explaining this reservation, just one factor is enough: the high cost of capital. 'The merchants' central financial problem,' writes a study of entrepreneurs of Ghana, 'was an inability to maintain sufficient liquidity to expand even ordinary trading operations, let alone to diversify into new forms of enterprise' (Dumett 1983). A book on India builds around this central problem, and suggests why explaining any investment at all in such a milieu is a worthy task for the business historian (Roy 2018).

The cost of capital and limits of indigenous business

If the success of expatriate trading firms can be at least partly explained by their access to the British capital, the shallow capital markets of the colonies would have handicapped indigenous business. Although capital did travel from the capital markets of the West via stock markets and business investment, little of it financed local production and exchange in the tropics. Corporate banking was slow to develop in these regions, and when it did exist, it proved too conservative in dealing with indigenous businesses. Why was that the case?

Corporate banks with British shareholding were engaged mainly in trade financing. Overall, these banks had a deeper impact on the payments systems linked to international trade, that is, on the bills discounting business than on funding capital formation. This was true of India. It was also the case in the Cape Province in South Africa after the entry of 'imperial banks' in the region from the 1860s (Jones 1998). In Nigeria at the turn of the 20th century, the formation of new banks made for collusion rather than competition (Uche 1999). In India, the biggest of the corporate banks did not easily lend to Indians, even though it did accept bills issued by the reputed Indian banking firms (Bagchi 1997).

As agricultural production and mining expanded, the need for credit grew too. Financial systems caught up slowly and imperfectly with the rise in demand. What was the problem with credit development in the colonies? Sometimes legally acceptable collateral for a mortgage was missing, for example, when the land was jointly held rather than individually owned. However, not all debt needs to be mortgage-backed. Often, foreign bankers did not understand bookkeeping done in the local tradition. Bankers in these times preferred to lend to clients they knew personally. Most foreign banks in the colonies knew the wealthier clients who lived in the port city and engaged in overseas trade. Few of them knew the potential clients engaged in domestic trade. In West Africa, the big banks believed that the credit market was too small to sustain competition among banks. Along with these structural problems, there was also the attraction of anti-competitive actions like price-fixing, collusion, rent-seeking and insider lending, possibly just because the banks were so few.

With some exceptions, local corporate banks were of small means and failed often. In India, if the European banks were accused of client selection, the Indian-origin banks practised insider lending on a large scale and had higher mortality as a result. The absence of adequate regulation and supervision made things worse. In the Cape Province in South Africa, British-style local banks declined when imperial banks entered the scene.

Did insufficient credit supply from banking companies constrain investment by domestic businesses? Not necessarily. There were escape routes from this constraint. Accumulation of profits in trade gave merchants an escape route. Despite there being few banks and the rate of interest high by any standard, enough capital moved into the cotton textile industry to create the world's fourth-largest cotton mill complex in Bombay and Ahmedabad. The missing link was trading profit. By fostering trade, the colonial system could still make savings available for investment. There was a difference between capital sourced from the market and capital sourced from the pockets of merchant families. The former allowed for wider participation and ownership of large companies. The latter made for closely held companies and firms, owned by castes and communities long engaged in trading. Capital scarcity did not pose an obstacle to investment but increased the role of business groups, castes and ethnic combines.

Conclusion

This chapter has shown that colonialism and capitalism interacted deeply, mainly because administrators and businesspeople shared the desire to exploit tropical natural resources. As some of these resources rose in value – like rubber – so did the intensity of the desire. Colonial states rarely intervened directly to make exports happen. Rather, they acted indirectly to strengthen the drivers of globalization, such as technology, law, encouragement to migration, or military power. A variety of actors made use of the opportunities, from companies that set their own rules, to companies that functioned by the rule of law. The attitude of the states towards indigenous entrepreneurs varied from repression to laissez-faire. Therefore, the form of the interaction varied over time and place.

Much of the story is about trade. Business history and globalization overlap in this narrative. However, making money from trade sometimes drove the capitalists to start production. In mining and plantations, the inducement was strong. In agricultural commodities, the ability of merchants to control producers or production was limited, and entrepreneurship involved the cultivators as much as 'big' business. Trade generated huge externalities – banks and factories were the most obvious ones. The port cities in the tropical colonized regions originated in trade in the early modern times, transformed into administrative centres, and reinvented as trading-manufacturing hubs in the early 20th century.

European and indigenous enterprise tended to specialize. That the Europeans had easier access to the cheaper capital markets of the West differentiated the two fields. Indigenous actors had access to information and community capital or trading profits and operated differently. These indigenous actors were not bound by national borders. Empires were collections of territorial units, and Indian and Chinese businesses crossed over these units often.

From the interwar period, European business faced difficulties. More businesses were started to serve the home market rather than exports, and reformed policy removed discrimination or offered protection, from which domestic groups benefited. Japanese and American capital moved into Asia and Africa on a large scale. This shifting balance of economic power influenced the course of decolonization, in South and Southeast Asia especially.

Notes

[1] See Roy (2013) for a discussion of this scholarship.
[2] See discussion in Roy (2013).
[3] Cited in Tignor (2007).
[4] See, for example, Gertzel (1962).
[5] Explaining this entrepreneurial venture, a study of the Ashanti Goldfields Corporation writes: 'the Fantes had closer language and cultural affinities with the Asantes than Europeans had and these advantages no doubt enabled them to discover the location of Asante's richest mines' (Taylor 2006: 64). See also Dumett (1998).

10

Decolonization and the
End of Empire

Histories of formerly colonized countries written in the immediate aftermath of the transfer of power often stressed how short the colonial period actually was, particularly when set in the context of the longer histories of these countries. One reason for this was the relatively rapid dismantling of the European empires which occurred in the 20 years or so after the end of the Second World War. This was contrary to the expectations of many people at the time, who expected the transition to independence to be gradual, and hoped to retain strong relationships with their colonial territories going forward.

There are two contrasting perspectives on why the empires collapsed relatively suddenly. One, which might be termed the imperial perspective, argues that the colonizing powers saw the economic benefits of their empires decline as economic links within Europe became more important (Feinstein 1997). This narrative is challenged by voices from imperial governments which showed little sign until late in the day that decolonization was an intended or desired outcome. Particularly in the immediate aftermath of the war, colonies were important sources of both raw materials and foreign exchange, and thus the intention of many imperial governments was to strengthen rather than weaken their ties to their colonies (White 2011). The second explanation turns to the colonies themselves. Economic instability and hardships during the Depression and then the war led to considerable social unrest and demands from people in the colonies for more comprehensive public service provision, and according to this view it was these developments which forced the hand of the imperial powers and made it impossible for them to retain their hold. A third perspective, which might be described as the neocolonial perspective, argues that full decolonization never really occurred at all but rather that 'American capitalist imperialism swallowed up' what had been the European empires (Louis and Robinson 1994: 462).

Changes related to the upheaval of the war and the economic recovery that followed were common to all empires, but responses to them varied. One important influence on the future economic condition of the former colonies was the way in which political independence was achieved. In some, the process was peaceful and relatively orderly, while in others it resulted in protracted conflict. Limited investment in human capital in some colonies made it difficult to build up effective independent governments without being dependent on retained expatriates. Fragmentation among nationalist groups increased risks of political frictions after the transfer of power was achieved.

The transfer of power offered both opportunities and risks to the former colonies. They had the opportunity to address the development gaps left by imperial policies focused on maximizing of primary exports, and to re-imagine the structure and future of their economies. However, exercising their new sovereignty to implement these visions was not always straightforward. Some chose to retain comparatively close ties to imperial businesses and governments, while others looked to rival powers – notably the Soviet Union and China – for trade and investment. In the middle of these different forces were imperial business interests which had to find ways of building relationships with post-independence governments (Schenk 2008; Stockwell 2000; Tignor 1998).

This chapter examines how colonial policies and economic change paved the way for the end of empire, and shaped the process of decolonization. It focuses particularly on the role of economic change – for colonies and metropolitan states – in shaping the timing of decolonization. It also examines the process of decolonization and the ways in which various actors in the colonies attempted to forge new economic paths after the transfer of power.

Why did empires end?

In 1945, many observers probably would not have predicted that the majority of European colonies would be independent within 20 years. True, Indian independence followed almost immediately after the end of the war in 1947, but this built on a process of constitutional change which had begun much earlier. India also had a much larger and more active political class than many other colonies, which had been making the case for independence since before colonial rule was firmly established in, for example, much of Africa. There were economic reasons which also potentially explained its separation from the empire. But what about others? Did metropolitan governments plan to cede power to their colonies? Or were they forced to withdraw, either by growing nationalist pressure or the external efforts of, for example, the American government?

The idea that metropolitan powers might have planned for the transfer of power is not, perhaps, as far-fetched as it might seem. Even the victorious Allies emerged from the war weakened, both financially and militarily, and with crippling reconstruction needs at home. In much of Southeast Asia, colonies had been – albeit temporarily – taken over by Japan. The British, Dutch and the French governments would discover that bringing these colonies back under their control would not be as simple as they anticipated. Flint (1983) makes the argument that the reforms to colonial rule from the 1930s were part of a planned process by which the British government, in particular, intended to transition crown colonies to the system of self-rule under which the dominions had operated in previous decades. In the Dutch Empire, as well, there had been proposals as early as the 1930s for a Commonwealth-like relationship between the Netherlands and the Dutch East Indies (Foray 2013).

Further evidence to bolster this claim might be found in the gradual constitutional changes which, at least in retrospect, appear to have paved the way for full independence. In India, these had begun as early as 1892, when the Raj acceded to demands by the nascent Indian National Congress for greater Indian representation on provincial legislatures and the Imperial Legislative Council (Kulke and Rothermund 2004: 278–9). Further changes followed the First World War. Indian contributions to the war effort – in both manpower and money – illustrated the 'fragility of the Raj' and gave the nationalists considerable bargaining power in pressing for political change (Brown 1999: 429). In 1917, the Secretary of State for India declared that the goal of the British Raj was responsible governance for India, and the so-called Montagu-Chelmsford reforms of 1919 expanded Indian representation and granted Indian members on the executive control of the 'transferred subjects' such as education, health and local government. After the passage of the Government of India Act in 1935, this system was replaced by one of provincial autonomy (Kulke and Rothermund 2004: 281–4).

While India's was perhaps the most protracted process of constitutional reform, other colonies also proceeded to independence via a series of stages. In the Gold Coast, the first direct general election with full adult suffrage was held in 1954, with the government elected 'to enjoy something very close to full internal self-government' (Rathbone 2008: 709). In Nigeria, Governor John Macpherson, appointed in 1948, initiated conversations with what he saw as moderate nationalists which resulted in the adoption of a new constitution in 1951, known as the 'Macpherson constitution'. Like the 1935 Government of India Act, it also expanded the powers of regional governments and increased African representation. It was subsequently revised by the Lyttleton constitution of 1954, which strengthened the federal structure of Nigerian institutions ahead of independence in 1960 (Lawal 2010).

In retrospect, these policies might seem part of a broader plan for decolonization, as suggested by Flint for Africa. However, Frederick Cooper (2002: 38) cautions against the risks of viewing history backwards. Most of these changes were concessions offered to nationalist groups in the colonies when imperial governments felt they were about to lose control. In that context, ceding some, but not all, authority was considered a necessary evil rather than part of a coordinated plan. As Kulke and Rothermund (2004: 279) write with regard to India, 'as long as such constitutional reforms did not lead to the control of the British executive by a legislative dominated by a non-official Indian majority, the association of Indians with the legislative process could only enhance the legitimacy of British rule without diminishing the authority of British administrators'. The 1919 and 1935 acts retained British control over government finances and other key government services. Hopkins (2008: 216) argues that the view of decolonization as 'a continuous process that accelerated after the Second World War and became irreversible with the loss of India in 1947' may have merit 'when placed in the longest perspective, but it misses important discontinuities that have led to a reappraisal of the causes as well as the timing of the end of empire'.

The other reason for reassessing discussions of planned decolonization was the perceived economic importance of colonies to metropolitan states after the end of the Second World War (White 2011). By the end of the war, Allied governments were heavily in debt and dependent on aid from the United States. Colonial economies, if developed, could serve as important markets for metropolitan exports, potentially offsetting the declining competitiveness of European industry relative to the United States. Further, the raw materials colonies produced could be exported to metropolitan countries without draining scarce foreign exchange reserves. Colonial exports to the United States could actually contribute to dollar earnings in the respective metropolitan currency areas.

For colonies to play this role in metropolitan economic recovery required the retention (or, in the case of Southeast Asian colonies, the reassertion) of imperial control over the monetary and economic policies of their colonies. Trade policies needed to restrict imports by colonies from outside the sterling or franc areas, which often meant an increase in the cost of living for colonial consumers. It also meant continuing wartime interventions in the production and marketing of exports, including mandatory state purchase through marketing boards and other institutions, and the bulk buying of minerals like copper. White (2011) argues that these factors help explain both the efforts by European states to strengthen colonial relationships after the end of the war as well as the variance in timing between parts of the empire. By 1947, he argues, India was no longer a net contributor to the sterling area dollar pool. Similarly, in the French Empire, the importance of dollar earnings shifted the attention of the French government from Indochina and North Africa to sub-Saharan Africa. Even this, however, did not last forever. After the immediate post-war years, the possession of colonies offered few benefits to the British economy as a whole, and the loss of the colonies coincided with a global 'golden age' of growth and greater integration with Europe (Feinstein 1997).

This kind of explanation accords much of the agency in determining the timing and nature of decolonization to metropolitan states. However, it glosses over the role of people in the colonies, and in particular increasingly vocal nationalist movements which had been empowered by international rhetoric on freedom and self-determination. Often it was pressure from below which provided the immediate cause for such reforms. Organized activism expanded during and after the war, partly as a result of the economic impacts of global shifts and colonial development policies (see Box 10.1 on the Second World War). Nationalist leaders often emerged from the ranks of labour unions and welfare associations, which showed their strengths through strikes and protests. These began during the Great Depression in the 1930s, when a wave of labour unrest swept through British colonies in the Caribbean as well as in parts of Asia and Africa. This trend accelerated in the years after the end of the war, threatening the post-war development of the colonies.

A further catalyst was the external pressure on imperial governments from the United States and from the newly established United Nations. Since the First World War, the rhetoric of international politics had shifted. During and after the war, there were proposals from various quarters for a peace settlement based on the principal

Box 10.1: The Second World War

The Second World War was the biggest, and most expensive, conflict in the history of the world. It was also complex – its origins, execution and legacies are all the subject of voluminous historical studies. As a result it is perhaps not surprising that wider histories of the war tend to neglect both the involvement of colonized territories in the war effort, as well as the significant impacts of the war on the future of the European empires.

As in the First World War, colonies helped turn what was initially a conflict between European nations into a global war. For the combatant countries, victory depended on maintaining supplies of raw materials, food and labour. Colonies provided materials, locations for the staging of military operations, and, crucially, troops – 2.5 million from India alone. Within the colonies, the mobilization of both goods and people required a rapid expansion in both the scale and scope of state involvement in colonial economies, which was not fully reversed once the war ended.

The war created considerable hardships, and not only for those on active service. In Southeast Asia, the invasion of Japanese forces temporarily replaced European colonial rulers with another colonial regime equally desperate for raw materials. Outside active combat, there were significant economic hardships. Even as they were being pressed to increase production for the war effort, people in the colonies had to endure sharp increases in the price of imported goods. Inflation became a major problem in many colonial cities.

Together, the struggles of the war along with the return of troops contributed to the rapid growth of what had in many colonies been nascent nationalist movements during the interwar period. In Southeast Asia this was further exacerbated by the often violent attempts by European governments – such as the Dutch in Indonesia or, more famously, the French in Indochina – to restore their control over their colonies.

The complexities of the period make it difficult to say to what extent the war created new pressures for decolonization or merely accelerated the growth of those that existed already. However, it is clear that the Second World War was a transformative period for the colonies as well as for their European colonizers, in part due to the impact of the war on colonial economies. The economic impact of the war tends, however, to be neglected in favour of political histories, and thus remains an area which would richly repay future research.

Further reading

Mark Harrison (2008) 'The economics of World War II: an overview', in *The Economics of World War II: Six Great Powers in International Comparison*, Cambridge: Cambridge University Press.

Judith A. Byfield, Carolyn A. Brown, Timothy Parsons and Ahmad Alawad Sikainga (eds) (2015) *Africa and World War II*, Cambridge: Cambridge University Press.

of self-determination, encapsulated by Woodrow Wilson's '14 points' speech of January 1918. Colonized people around the world hoped that this shift would lead to a change in power relations in the aftermath of the war, and the end of colonial empires. These hopes were quickly dashed, and Erez Manela (2007) argues that the disappointments of this period helped fuel the anticolonial nationalism of the 1930s and 1940s. The failure of the 'Wilsonian moment' to lead to any fundamental change in the relationship between European countries and their colonies foreshadowed the later ambivalence of the United States in the end of empires. Given the importance of American aid in European reconstruction after the Second World War, the United States was, if anything, in a stronger position to press for the end of empires than it had been in 1918. However, as in 1918, the interests of the American government in 1945 pulled in different directions. While there was an economic interest in ending imperial preferences that made it more difficult for American companies to access colonial markets, it was often dominated by concerns about the potential for instability and the expanding influence of the Soviet Union. It thus supported the continuation of European rule in the colonies even while American officials spoke out against colonialism. American aid to colonies 'was rarely articulated because explicit support for the revival of European colonialism sat uncomfortably with the rhetoric of the Atlantic Charter or the Truman Doctrine' (White 2011: 220).

The United Nations played a different role. Jessica Pearson (2017) argues that the threat of international oversight by the UN and other new international organizations prompted both changes in colonial policy as well as diplomatic efforts by the imperial powers to defend their stewardship of their colonies. However, this became increasingly difficult as more and more newly independent countries joined the UN as members in their own right. There was something of a 'snowball' effect in the history of decolonization. Much like the economic growth of Japan during the late 19th and early 20th centuries had provided Asian colonies with an example of an independent country, the progressive decolonization of individual countries in all regions paved the way for others. Judith Brown (1999: 422) writes of Indian independence that 'independence for the oldest and most prestigious Asian part of the empire was to be a beacon for nationalists in other parts of the empire'.

Of course not all colonial powers responded to these global changes in the same way. After resisting pressure for the transfer of power for much of the post-war period, the Belgians proceeded rapidly once the decision to decolonize was made, aware that they could rely on neither volunteer Belgian troops nor the colonial Force Publique which had mutinied during the war. Compared to the gradual process of constitutional change described for India, Ghana and Nigeria, the transfer of power in the Congo happened very quickly. The first local elections were held in 1957. In January 1960, the Belgian government convened a conference in Brussels with the various nationalist groups. By May of the same year a new constitution was adopted. Formal independence was declared by the end of June, with few transitional arrangements in place.

Others continued to resist, with often tragic consequences. Attempts by the Dutch and French governments to reconquer their Southeast Asian colonies led to years of conflict after 1945, and in the case of Vietnam set the stage for the Vietnam War when the French government framed the battle against Ho Chi Minh in Cold War terms. Under the dictatorship of Salazar, Portugal attempted to strengthen its links with its African colonies in a manner similar to that of the French Empire, declaring colonies to be overseas provinces in 1951. Thousands of Portuguese migrated to the newly declared provinces, exacerbating racial tensions. The Portuguese had been the first colonial power but became the last to agree to a transfer of power, when the Estado Novo established by Salazar was overthrown in 1974 (Rothermund 2006: 81–5, 223).

'A changing definition of the possible'

> Independence days are intended to be joyful occasions and, like Tolstoy's happy families, they resemble one another; all of them appear to share similar quotients of military display, fireworks, pious sentimentality at midnight, and the profoundly implausible pledges of eternal friendship between long-term antagonists. (Rathbone 2008: 705)

'The moment of decolonization,' according to Tony Hopkins (2008: 11) 'is recorded to dates and signalled by ceremony: the guard, political as well as military, is changed, anthems are composed; flags are redesigned.' However, these 'moments' of ceremony were just one part of a long process of political, economic and administrative disentanglement which at times began years before and continued years after one flag was replaced with another. One part of this process was a phase of re imagining the states that would become independent. Frederick Cooper notes that decolonization seemed to herald 'a changing definition of the possible' (1996: 1). Much of the stability in boundaries and institutions taken for granted today was seen as malleable at the time, and debates between different proposals brought out tensions between rival factions within both metropolitan and indigenous societies.

From the European side, one such proposal was the federation or amalgamation of smaller or poorer colonies into larger units which might be more economically sustainable in the future. As early as 1922, Lord Lugard (1922: 97) had written that

> there are in British tropical Africa several blocks of territory under the separate administrations which are contiguous to each other, and the question arises whether it would be more advantageous that they should be placed under a single directing authority, with a single fiscal system, a common railway policy and identical laws.

In the post-war years, such proposals developed a new momentum as colonial governments demanded increasing financial autonomy. In both East and Central Africa, the British government supported schemes for closer regional coordination, as a result of which the Federation of Rhodesia and Nyasaland was established in 1953. While an East African Federation never came into being, regional coordination in economic and other policies expanded. Similarly, in the West Indies, older proposals for federation were brought back to life as 'the best means of a joint decolonization of the Caribbean' (Rothermund 2006: 213).

The reasons given for these proposals would be familiar to proponents of federation in other contexts. It was argued that larger political units would increase fiscal stability and allow poorer colonies to be subsidized by wealthier ones, reducing potential metropolitan liabilities. Larger units would be better able to bear the costs of new state functions devolved from the metropole, including defence and foreign policy.

Finally, larger political units meant larger domestic markets and potentially more sustainable economic development.

At the same time, nationalist leaders had their own proposals and discussions about the shapes that nations should take after the end of the colonial period. Several future presidents of independent African states, including Sekou Toure of Guinea and Kwame Nkrumah, supported the creation of a 'United States of Africa', which would integrate the countries of the continent in a single political and economic union, following proposals made by Nkrumah in his *Africa Must Unite* (1963). Others, like Jomo Kenyatta of Kenya and Julius Nyerere of Tanzania, supported a more gradual, measured form of African integration.

There were also proposals for territorial integration linked to locally specific concerns rather than broader Pan-Africanist agendas. For example, Senegal, a former French colony, pressed for a political and economic union with the Gambia, which was a British colony until its independence in 1965. During the colonial period, higher tariffs in the French territory had made the Gambia, which cut directly into Senegal along the banks of the Gambia River, a hub for smuggling of both imports and exports. The loss of revenue from trade taxes to the Senegalese government made this the subject of persistent political tensions, which prompted Senegal to threaten an invasion. However, proposals for a union between the two territories encountered resistance from elites who gained from the arrangement (Golub and Mbaye 2009).

In the end, neither imperial nor nationalist proposals for regional integration accomplished many of their aims. Proposals from both sources often foundered on suspicions that some groups would gain more from federation than others. In the Caribbean, Jamaican officials did not want to subsidize its poorer neighbours, while other colonies feared Jamaican dominance. The Central African Federation was seen by nationalists in both Northern Rhodesia and Nyasaland as serving the interests of European settlers concentrated in Southern Rhodesia, and thus likely to result in the extension of the racially restrictive policies of the latter. In East Africa, federation proposals were seen in a similar light, and Kenya's dominance in even the limited regional bureaucracy that was established generated resentment in Uganda and Tanganyika, which doomed proposals for post-independence regional coordination.

Another failed attempt at political union after decolonization was the inclusion of Singapore in the Federation of Malaysia in 1963. British officials had initially left Singapore out of the Malaysian Union when it became independent in 1959, owing to demographic differences, in particular the dominance of Chinese migrants and their descendants in Singapore, and the importance to Singapore of maintaining its free port status and trade with Indonesia. However, the People's Action Party led by Lee Kuan Yew believed that Singapore could not be self-sufficient outside Malaysia. A political compromise which allowed Singapore to have special economic status while being underrepresented politically brought the two countries together, but the Federation was short lived. Economic retaliation by the Indonesian government exacerbated existing tensions, and by 1965 Singapore was independent (Huff 1994: 29–30).

Other re-imaginings of the post-independence state involved fragmentation rather than integration. The most notable split was the partition of British India into three territories (India, Pakistan and Bangladesh). This was intended to address religious tensions between Hindu and Muslim communities, but the boundaries between the territories were hastily drawn and left a lasting set of resentments in the region. Elsewhere, there were numerous secession campaigns, for example in Katanga in the Congo (1960–63) and Biafra in Nigeria (1967–70). Both of these cases involved the attempted secession of mineral-rich regions (oil in Biafra and copper in Katanga) from countries which relied heavily on the revenue they generated. In the case of Katanga, Belgian investment in the mining areas had generated significant regional inequalities. Neither effort was successful, but the Biafran conflict inflicted a sharp shock on the Nigerian economy in the immediate aftermath of independence, and the Katangan secession contributed to the political instability of newly independent Congo.

Within all colonies, there were extensive debates about the policies new states should adopt, and in particular how they should address the shortcomings of colonial policies, which included both the excessive dependence of many colonial economies on a narrow range of primary exports as well as minimal investments in human and social capital. In the early Cold War era, what still appeared to be a successful Soviet Union offered a credible alternative, and many newly independent governments adopted aspects of communism or socialism in their economic planning. Their discussions also followed prevailing ideas about state-led development policies, which had informed many of the more expansive colonial programmes. It was thus common across newly independent countries to adopt strategies for state-led development and structural change. However, the precise forms that these policies took varied.

In India, for example, the economic policy of the 1950s had much in common with that of many other developing economies, with a strategy of protectionist or import–substituting industrialization. By 1956, Indian leaders decided that capital–intensive industry – metals, chemicals and machines – should take priority over traditional sectors like textiles, minerals or tea. Protectionist industrialization meant, for India, building capability in an area where there was little in–house expertise and which was too expensive for domestic capital market to finance. Therefore, the Indian pathway came to depend on the state, which negotiated foreign aid and technology transfer, and regulated investment and financial markets to supply capital to the capital–intensive sectors.

In Africa, post–independence economic policies were often described as 'African socialism', even though the plans of individual countries encompassed a range of ideas from across the spectrum from capitalist to socialist. Emmanuel Akyeampong (2018: 70) argues that each represented 'a search for an indigenous model of economic development that would be revolutionary both in time and scale'. For many African leaders, 'capitalism ... often smacked of "neo–colonialism" because, by putting them back in the arms of Western expatriate capital, it would seem to subvert the achievement and purpose of political independence'. At the same time, the lack of industrialization and limited urbanization meant that Marxist theories were not immediately applicable in many African contexts. So they took, as Cooper writes 'the best of what Europe and Africa had to offer'. Similarly, Lee Kuan Yew said of Singapore that 'we borrowed in an eclectic fashion, elements of what Hong Kong was doing, what Switzerland was doing, what Israel was doing, and we improvised. I also went down to Malta to see how they ran the dry docks' (quoted in Huff 1994: 40).

Capacities and constraints

Newly independent governments faced a range of difficulties in implementing new ideas and building new institutions, which influenced later economic outcomes. First, they needed to take over many of the government functions previously controlled by metropolitan governments, including foreign affairs, monetary policy and defence. Second, most came to power having been elected by newly enfranchised voters who had high expectations of the economic fruits that independence would deliver. Precisely how to do this required these new governments to design development plans of their own. Finally, they needed to cope with internal divisions which had been masked by the shared goal of achieving independence.

In taking over responsibility for these services, independent governments had to make sometimes difficult and complicated choices regarding their future relationships with their former colonizers, which often pitted stability against a decisive and visible break with the past. One example is in the area of monetary policy. During the colonial period, most colonies had currencies tied in some fixed way to the metropolitan currency. This helped reduce transaction costs for trade and government transfers within each empire (Helleiner 2002). Such arrangements were often criticized for favouring metropolitan interests ahead of those of the colonies, by not allowing colonial governments to use monetary policy to adjust for local shocks. Huff (2003) attributes the limited financial development of Southeast Asia to the colonial currency board system along with the dominance of European banks.

At independence, therefore, there was often pressure at least in some quarters for the creation of new national currencies, both for economic purposes and as a symbol of political sovereignty. However, levels of financial development were often low. Independent governments thus adopted different strategies. Many, though not all, of the Francophone countries in Africa opted to remain within what had been the former colonial monetary system, based on the CFA franc, which was pegged to the French franc. Most former British colonies, on the other hand, established new national currencies issued by national central banks. Stasavage (2003) attributes this difference to the closer ties that elites in Francophone Africa had with the metropolitan country. Whatever the cause, this decision had significant economic consequences moving forward. In the 1970s, CFA franc countries avoided much of the exchange rate instability and inflation that affected countries which had issued their own currency. However, by the 1980s, the overvaluation of the CFA franc had become a drag on growth for members of the currency union.

Such decisions about the direction of monetary policy as well as other areas of governance newly under indigenous control were not made easier by the limited investments in human capital made until very late in the colonial period. India was an exception, given the expansion of secondary and tertiary education and the pathway that had existed during the Raj for Indians to enter the civil service. In many other colonies, colonial administrations had not been open to indigenous staff beyond the lowest levels. Particularly in Africa, colonial public services were comprised of a very small number of highly-paid European officials and a larger number of Africans in low-paid posts (Simson 2019: 82). Rothermund (2006: 156) notes with regard to the

Belgian Congo that 'at the time of independence about 10,000 Belgians were serving as officers, judges and administrators in the Congo. They had been promised equivalent positions at home if the situation in the Congo deteriorated. Now they all left at once and the Congo was bereft of all administrative personnel.' With the departure of Belgian administrators, there remained just three university graduates in the country (Akyeampong 2018).

One implication of this was that the staffing of government departments such as the judiciary or the treasury continued to depend on expatriates for some time. This was also true of the military – the first Zambian commanding officer of the Zambian military was not appointed until 1970, six years after independence (Gardner 2012: 230). Often, the foreign officials hired were the same officials who had done these jobs during the colonial period, either hired directly by the post-independence governments or more often reappearing as 'technical assistance' granted by the former colonizers or new international organizations like the World Bank.

Indigenization and political readjustment were not only challenges faced by governments. In the context of these larger political developments, metropolitan businesses operating in the colonies had difficult choices to make. On the one hand, they often relied on colonial governments for security and policies which supported the profitability of their enterprises. The revenue imperative discussed in Chapter 6 had led to close, if not always symbiotic, relationships between imperial businesses and colonial administrations, and employees of both moved in relatively small social circles in colonial capitals. During the early 1930s, for example, the colonial administration of Northern Rhodesia was able to ask the two copper mining companies operating in the colony for an advance on their income tax payments, to blunt the impact that the declining price of copper had on the public treasury (Pim and Milligan 1938: 133). Further, staffing of expatriate enterprises resembled that of the colonial government. Barclays DCO, for example, retained certain positions for Europeans at their African branches and some had distinct pay scales by ethnic group (Ackrill and Hannah 2001: 273).

Even before independence, businesses realized that their close association with the colonial establishment could be a liability with ascendant nationalist groups. Businesses that wished to continue doing business in former colonies and avoid nationalization needed to show that they were equally willing to cooperate with newly independent governments. Barclays, for example, began to expand services beyond its traditionally expatriate customer base as well as to indigenize its staff (Decker 2005). At the same time, indigenous businesses often hoped to gain many of the advantages they perceived imperial businesses to have had during the colonial period, setting up political competition between the two.

A further obstacle to the implementation of post-independence policies was the extent of internal divisions. Nationalist groups included a diverse set of actors representing a range of interests. In Rathbone's (2008: 13) account of Ghanaian independence, he describes images from the celebrations as 'somewhat reminiscent of wedding photographs: large numbers of people who loathe one another can be forced to smile when faced by a camera and the implications of a permanent record'. Julius Nyerere of Tanzania acknowledged these differences in a speech to the Uganda People's Congress (1974: 16):

> the job of our political parties is much more difficult now than it was when we were struggling for independence. Then, we called mass meetings; we shouted "Uhuru"; we abused the colonists – who, I may add, richly deserved it! But now we are building nations. If we have mass meetings we cannot abuse the government, for we are the government.

Such divisions dominate the political histories of former colonies after independence. Omar Garcia-Ponce and Leonard Wantchekon (2013) argue that the nature of the nationalist pressure, and whether it manifested itself in urban protests or rural insurgencies, influenced the structure of political institutions after independence, with urban protest better able to build more democratic norms and institutions. Overcoming these internal divisions in many cases proved to be too much for newly formed democracies, and the decades after independence saw coups d'état in some countries and a general drift towards single-party rule and other forms of authoritarianism in others. While this might have overcome some of the barriers to achieving disputed policy changes in a democratic country, it also increased political instability, which was further exacerbated by the global economic challenges of the 1970s.

Despite the 'pomp and partying' of celebrations marking the transfer of power, the leaders of newly independent nations were aware that the path towards exercising their hard-won sovereignty would be difficult. How binding those constraints were, however, depended both on the economic and political institutions that had emerged during the colonial period, and on the political settlements between diverse groups of nationalists that formed the political coalitions which ruled new states. The next section considers the diverse economic legacies of these events as revealed in a widening divergence between colonies in the decades following decolonization.

Legacies

In 1957, the leaders of two newly independent nations – Ghana and Cote d'Ivoire – placed a good-natured bet on which set of choices would be the most successful: Ghana's shift towards socialism, or Cote d'Ivoire's strategy of retaining strong links to France and encouraging export agriculture under expatriate management. In neither country did things go entirely to plan. When the ten years were up in 1967, Nkrumah had been overthrown in a coup d'état in 1966, after a decade of lacklustre economic performance. Cote d'Ivoire had enjoyed impressive growth, but this was followed from 1980 by 15 years of negative growth which eliminated the gains it had made previously (Nugent 2004: 166–7). Neither, in other words, had found the path to sustained economic growth. However, other former colonies did, and have seen significant improvements in standards of living in the years since the end of colonial rule.

One puzzle in understanding the economic legacies of colonialism is the varied histories of the formerly colonized regions since independence. Figure 10.1 shows GDP per capita in five formerly colonized countries since 1950. While not necessarily representative of their regions as a whole, they illustrate something of the diversity of experience across the former colonies. At independence, there were only relatively small gaps between the levels of per capita incomes of many countries in Africa and Asia, as shown here for Nigeria, Zambia, India and Vietnam. Jamaica began the post-war period with a higher level of GDP per capita than the others. However, steady and rapid growth in the two Asian countries since the 1970s has widened this gap significantly, and allowed them to overtake Jamaica as well.

It is notable that many of the Asian countries that achieved independence not long before Africa became major sources of foreign investment in the region in the 21st century. There are of course outliers in each of these regions. Some countries in South Asia, for example Bangladesh and Pakistan, remain comparatively poor, with per capita incomes in 2016 lower than those of Nigeria. At the same time, some African countries, including Botswana and South Africa, had comparatively high per capita incomes. Overall, however, Africa in general has experienced less growth than Asia.

Figure 10.1: GDP per capita since independence, 1950–2016 (1990 international dollars)

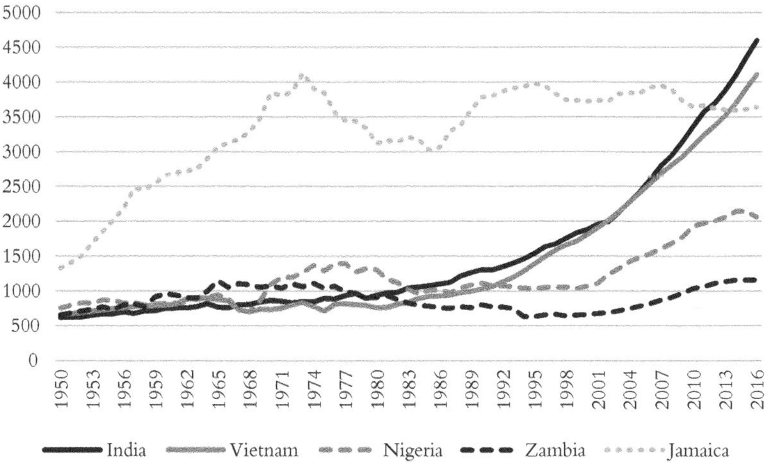

Source: Bolt and van Zanden (2014)

In some respects, this might be surprising from the perspective of the immediate post-war decades. In a comparison of West Africa and Southeast Asia, Booth (2008) notes that on most economic indicators there were few differences between the two regions during the interwar period. While both suffered from the decline in prices for primary commodities during the Great Depression, West African colonies seemed somewhat more resilient. Further, colonies in Southeast Asia suffered extensive damage due to the invasion of Japan and subsequent European efforts to regain control. In attempting to explain Africa's relative poverty later on, Englebert (2000a) turns to the limited legitimacy of states inherited from the colonial period which, in his words, led post-independence states 'to resort instead with greater frequency to redistributive policies which retard or hinder growth'.

Englebert does not attempt to extend his argument to other regions, but to do so raises further questions. The vast majority of post-independence states were creations of the colonial period, with limited links to precolonial political units, and Africa was far from the only region where the control of the central state was contested. Studies of the post-independence policies of countries in other regions also tended to focus on policies without searching for the deeper historical influences constraining policy choices. According to one economic history of India,

185

> post-colonial development in South Asia is often analyzed by economists exclusively in terms of state policy and ideology, a practice that risks overlooking the institutional and other forms of continuity that shaped state capacity. The practice risks misreading factors that helped or impeded development as right or wrong decisions that the state took. (Roy 2011: 288)

However, there were also other differences, some highlighted in the previous section, which may help explain the different experiences of Asia, the Caribbean and Africa in the post-independence period. One is the duration of colonial rule, which was much longer in Asia and the Americas than it was in Africa. In a comparative study of islands, James Feyrer and Bruce Sacerdote (2009) find that countries colonized earlier, with a longer history of colonial rule, have higher levels of per capita income after independence, on the basis that 'longer colonial rule might have left islands with a more stable or better structured government'. While this argument is only speculative and does not detail what this might mean for colonial institutions, the comparison of the two regions suggests some possible mechanisms. The first is that, as mentioned earlier, the expansion in education enrolments began earlier in many Asian colonies than in Africa, leaving a greater stock of human capital at the post-independence period (Booth 2008). This allowed, in part, for greater indigenous presence in colonial business and civil service, as well as a larger indigenous political and entrepreneurial class. Many Asian colonies had a larger industrial base during the colonial period on which to build after independence, a fact not unrelated to the greater influence of indigenous entrepreneurs. There were exceptions to this – in colonial Burma, for example, Burmese staff played only a marginal role in business and government and the economy remained largely agricultural (Fenichel and Huff 1975: 322). However, across most of South and Southeast Asia, the economic structures which had emerged (either because or in spite of colonial policies) provided a better foundation for the export-led industrial policies which helped pave the way for sustained economic growth.

Conclusion

Contributions in economics on the legacies of colonial rule often ignore the era of decolonization, focusing instead on 'high points' of colonial rule before the First World War or during the interwar period. However, this chapter has argued that the end of empire, as much as the beginning, was the product of interactions between indigenous actors and European officials and institutions in a context of rapid economic and political change. The economic legacies of colonial rule, then, were as much an outcome of those interactions as of decisions made by Europeans in the relatively short period of colonial rule.

The process of decolonization has often been neglected by economic historians. While it is sometimes included in explicitly national economic histories, there are few comparative works on the economic origins and implications of the transfer of power. The focus of national histories on fine-grained political detail makes such comparative work difficult. However, this period should be regarded as a formative one in shaping the economic legacies of colonial rule. Economic shifts during the colonial period, driven from below as much as from above, influenced the structure of the collective groups – whether unions, cooperatives, or welfare societies – which ultimately formed the foundations of nationalist movements. The response of colonial powers to pressure from those groups similarly depended on the incentives of that government, and the economic and political importance to it of retaining its colonies.

Once independence was achieved, the capacity of new national governments depended on a host of factors directly linked to the historical legacies of colonial rule. Stocks of human and social capital, geography and economic structure, and the role of outside pressures, all played a role in helping determine which former colonies have seen sustained improvements in living standards since the colonial period ended.

11

Summary and Conclusion

In recent years, economic historians have developed an interest in the legacies of colonialism, as new arguments emerged about the origins of international economic inequality from the mid-19th century (see Chapter 1). The interest has generated a great deal of debate, discussion, statistical research and data reconstruction. A part of this scholarship conducts empirical tests, correlating economic growth outcomes with the presence or absence of characteristics expected to produce long-run economic growth. Another set of writings cautions that the processes of colonization and state construction were too diverse for the world to be divided in this way, and that this diversity needs to be taken into account in considering the ways in which colonialism shaped patterns of growth. This book is inspired by the second approach, and illustrates that process matters, and matters differently from one colony to another.

Claims about the diversity of experience raise questions about whether there can ever be a general account of colonialism. This book has argued that there can, but that such an account needs to include the relationship between 'European expansion', the meaning of which shifted somewhat between the 18th and the 19th centuries, and political and economic transformation of Asian and African societies. That broad basket includes a wide variety of changes, from imperial decline, to commercialization in the seaboard, to the rise and fall of slave trade, to the growing global knowledge of tropical resources and commodities (Chapter 2). Some of these changes are called early-modern globalization, though the term takes on a more substantial meaning moving on to the 19th century (Chapter 3).

The combination of these forces operated in quite different ways between, say, West, North and East Africa, South and Southeast Asia, and the Pacific and Atlantic islands, because the conditions on the ground varied a lot. Once colonial states were established, governance needed to adapt to these conditions, which again was a diverse process because resources and polities were not at all similar. The presence of settlers adds a complication to the story, but this was only one of several things that the colonial states needed to worry about.

How did this combination of factors influence the development of the global economy in the 19th century? Economic historians have tried to answer the question with a battery of measures of standards of living. Reviewing this material, it becomes clear that there was a relationship between government policies and living standards (Chapter 4), but the states alone did not shape living standards. Their influence changed over time, and it was not uniformly and everywhere a negative one. Colonial states did not exist merely to exploit or benefit the local population and, therefore, the nature of their impact was more mixed than we may imagine.

Why, then, did colonies exist at all? In a much older economic history of colonialism, the answer was obvious: these rules existed for the colonists to extract surplus value from their colonies and become rich in the process. The claim was not seriously tested until the 1980s and 1990s, but even then the outcome was confusingly open-ended. Still, the scholarship enabled a more nuanced understanding of 'the imperial experience' (Chapter 5). The inconclusive outcome underscored another point: these states existed to serve power and prestige in the first place, but their economic legacies were not always a direct consequence of their actions.

The ultimate test of the power of a state is a fiscal system that is sustainable, and that can raise enough money to fund public goods such as defence, education, healthcare and transport. Fiscal histories of the empires had long remained a dry technical subject. Recently, economic historians have infused new life into this topic, in two ways. A literature on state formation in Europe showing how warfare induced some 18th century states to take control of the fiscal system raised the question of how the same states managed the military-fiscal challenge outside Europe. And the interest in living standards drove some scholars to examine the capacity of states to fund public goods. Chapter 6 shows that this was everywhere constrained by a variety of factors, including limited taxable resources, power of the elite, limited administrative capacity, and the desire to keep trade as free as possible, among others. Colonial states were far from readymade states, let alone European transplantations. They were a work in progress, and a rather imperfect work at best.

If colonial states were not copies of European states, they could still act as a conduit for the transplantation of European institutions like laws of property and contract. This, recent writings suggest, was a significant factor behind comparative economic growth and inequality. Rather like the fiscal story, the institutional one too shows that the transmission of institutions was constrained by limited state capacity and the authority of indigenous institutions (Chapter 7). Thus, colonial laws had to make compromises with local laws in the matter of property rights, whereas colonial laws could more freely borrow commercial law from home. And no matter how the states made laws, the states had little ability to make enforcement, or systems of justice, accessible to all.

The rest of the book (Chapters 8, 9, and 10) moved into areas which have not featured as prominently in economic history debates, namely environment, business history and decolonization, which are intricately bound to the book's main themes of state capacity and globalization. Chapter 8 shows that colonial states had ambiguous effects on the environment, but both the good and the bad effects were quite unprecedented in their power to change local societies. Chapter 9 questions a tendency to identify business in colonial situations with the history of European firms. European enterprise cannot be understood without reference to indigenous enterprise, nor the other way around. Thus, the chapter does more than survey the history of firms, it also asks: how should we write the business history of Asia and Africa in those times?

Perhaps curiously, economic historians who have emphasized the importance of colonialism for patterns of development have not engaged much with the reasons for and manner of its decline. The political narrative of decolonization that the defenders of empires would favour was a story that went like this. Nineteenth-century liberals assumed that the western civilization had a mission to improve the lives of the backward Africans and the moribund Indians, a view that made denial of liberty to these people a good deed. The mission succeeded so well that after a century of British imperial rule, the Asians and the Africans had found the voice to challenge the rule. The imperialists knew all along that a handover of power when the subjects were ready for self-rule was inevitable. The question was, were they ready now? Around the mid-20th century, the answer was, they were. Such a view, which presumes that imperialism was founded on goodwill, is effectively challenged by the 'postcolonial' historiography that has shown that imperialism was also founded on violence and racism. In this approach, decolonization became inevitable when protest and criticism of the system became too much for the European states to withstand.

Between goodwill and violence, there was another thing that these regimes relied on: economic interest. An empire made some people rich, and their support sustained it. An empire might make the imperialists rich, which again would be a reason to hold on to it. Economic interest is the realm of economic history, though the field has been strangely indifferent to that crucial period of the 20th century when the empires ended one after the other. Chapter 10 shows that big shifts in global economic environment influenced the structure of the collective groups that eventually formed the foundations of nationalist movements.

Former colonies are home to a majority of the world's poor people, but they also include most of the world's fastest-growing economies. Growth, in turn, has brought in its wake environmental challenges, often addressed by laws that were colonial in origin. The task for a book like this one is to explain the historical roots of poverty, growth, challenges, and the means to cope with them. Historians of empire, no matter which road one takes to enter the field, will find useful material here. Historians apart, anyone with a serious interest in the great drama of our times – economic emergence of Asia and Africa – will find this book relevant.

Until recently, the economic history of colonialism was too preoccupied with showing how European rules wanted to exploit Asia and Africa, to be up to that task. For some time, a new perspective has suggested that by moving away from European intentions to exploit and by paying more attention to the tropical societies it is possible to understand the historical processes that emerged during colonialism better. This book is a synthesis of this new understanding of the economic history of colonialism. It brings together scholarship from both economics and history to show how a complex interaction between European ideas and institutions and tropical societies and geographies shaped poverty as well as prosperity in these regions.

References

Accominotti, O., Flandreau, M. and Rezzik, R. (2011) 'The spread of empire: Clio and the measurement of colonial borrowing costs', *Economic History Review*, 64(2): 385–407.

Acemoglu, D. and Johnson, S. (2005) 'Unbundling institutions', *Journal of Political Economy*, 113(5): 949–95.

Acemoglu, D., Johnson, S. and Robinson, J.A. (2001) 'The colonial origins of comparative development: an empirical investigation', *American Economic Review*, 91(5): 1369–401.

Acemoglu, D., Johnson, S. and Robinson, J.A. (2002) 'Reversal of fortune: geography and institutions in the making of the modern world income distribution', *Quarterly Journal of Economics*, 117(4): 1231–94.

Ackrill, M. and Hannah, L. (2001) *Barclays: the business of banking 1690–1996*, London: Barclays Bank.

Adas, M. (ed) (1999) *Islamic and European expansion: the forging of a global order*, Philadelphia, MA: Temple University Press.

Ade Ajayi, J.K. (1968) 'The continuity of African institutions under colonialism', in T.O. Ranger (ed), *Emerging Themes in African History*, Nairobi: East Africa Publishing House, pp 169–200.

Akyeampong, E. (2018) 'African socialism; or, the search for an indigenous model of economic development?', *Economic History of Developing Regions*, 33(1): 69–87.

Akyeampong, E. and Fofack, H. (2014) 'The contribution of African women to economic growth and development in the pre-colonial and colonial periods: historical perspectives and policy implications', *Economic History of Developing Regions* 29(1): 42–73.

Albouy, D.Y. (2012) 'The colonial origins of comparative development: an empirical investigation: comment', *American Economic Review*, 102(6): 3059–76.

Alexopoulou, K. (2018) 'An anatomy of colonial states and fiscal regimes in Portuguese Africa: long-term transformations in Angola and Mozambique, 1850–1970', PhD thesis, Wageningen University.

Alpers, E. (1975) *Ivory and slaves in Central Africa*, Berkeley and Los Angeles, CA: University of California Press.

Amin, S. (1973) 'Underdevelopment and dependence in Black Africa', *Social and Economic Studies*, 22(1): 177–196.

Anderson, D. (2005) *Histories of the hanged: the dirty war in Kenya and the end of empire*, London: Weidenfeld and Nicolson.

Anderson, D.M. (2002) *Eroding the commons: the politics of ecology in Baringo, Kenya 1890–1963*, Athens: Ohio University Press.

Anderson, D.M. (2015) 'Guilty secrets: deceit, denial and the discovery of Kenya's "migrated archive"', *History Workshop Journal*, 80(1): 142–160.

Anon (1953) 'Cecil Rhodes', *British Medical Journal*, 2(4826): 29–30.

Arnold, D. (1993) *Colonizing the body: state medicine and epidemic disease in nineteenth century India*, Berkeley, CA: University of California Press.

Arroyo Abad, L. and van Zanden, J.L. (2016) 'Growth under extractive institutions? Latin American per capita GDP in colonial times', *Journal of Economic History* 76(4): 1182–215.

Austin, G. (2005) *Labour, land and capital in Ghana: from slavery to free labour in Asante, 1807–1956*, Rochester, NY: University of Rochester Press.

Austin, G. (2008) 'The "reversal of fortune" thesis and the compression of history: perspectives from African and comparative economic history', *Journal of International Development*, 20(8): 996–1027.

Austin, G. (2009) 'Cash crops and freedom: export agriculture and the decline of slavery in colonial West Africa', *International Review of Social History*, 54(1): 1–37.

Austin, G., Baten, J. and van Leeuwen, B. (2012) 'The biological standard of living in nineteenth-century West Africa: new anthropometric evidence for Northern Ghana and Burkina Faso', *Economic History Review*, 65(4): 1280–302.

Bagchi, A.K. (1997) *The evolution of the state bank of India. Volume 2: The era of the Presidency banks 1876–1920*, New Delhi: State Bank of India and Sage Publications.

Bairoch, P. (1988) *Cities and economic development: from the dawn of history to the present*, Chicago: Chicago University Press.

Ballard, C. (1986) 'The repercussions of rinderpest: cattle plague and peasant decline in colonial Natal', *International Journal of African Historical Studies*, 19(3): 421–50.

Bandyopadhyay, S. and Green, E. (2016) 'Precolonial political centralization and contemporary development in Uganda', *Economic Development and Cultural Change*, 64(3): 471–508.

Banerjee, A. and Iyer, L. (2005) 'History, institutions and economic performance: the legacy of colonial land tenure systems in India', *American Economic Review*, 95(4): 1190–213.

Barratt-Brown, M. (1974) *The economics of imperialism*, Harmondsworth: Penguin.

Barro, R.J. (1991) 'Economic growth in a cross section of countries', *Quarterly Journal of Economics*, 106(2): 407–43.

Barton, G.A. (2002) *Empire forestry and the origins of environmentalism,* Cambridge: Cambridge University Press.

Bassino, J.-P. and Coclanis, P.A. (2008) 'Economic transformation in biological warfare in colonial Burma: regional differentiation of average height', *Economics and Human Biology*, 6(2): 212–27.

Baten, J., Stegl, M. and van der Eng, P. (2013) 'The biological standard of living and body height in colonial and post-colonial Indonesia, 1770–2000', *Journal of Bioeconomics*, 15: 103–22.

Bauer, P.T. (1954) 'Origins of the statutory export monopolies of British West Africa', *Business History Review*, 28(3): 197–213.

Bayly, C.A. (2008) 'Indigenous and colonial origins of comparative economic development: the case of colonial India and Africa', World Bank Policy Research Working Paper, 4474.

Beinart, W. (1990) 'Empire, hunting and ecological change in southern and central Africa', *Past and Present*, 128(1): 162–86.

Belmessous, S. (ed) (2015) *Empire by treaty: negotiating European expansion, 1600–1900*, Oxford: Oxford University Press.

Bentley, J.H. (1997) 'Revisiting the expansion of Europe: a review article', *Sixteenth Century Journal*, 28(2): 503–10.

Benton, L. and Ross, R.J. (eds) (2013) *Legal pluralism and empires, 1500–1850*, New York: New York University Press.

Bertocchi, G. and Canova, F. (2002) 'Did colonization matter for growth? An empirical exploration into the historical causes of Africa's underdevelopment', *European Economic Review*, 46: 1851–71.

Bhacker, M.R. (1992) *Trade and empire in Muscat and Zanzibar: roots of British domination*, London: Routledge.

Bigsten, A. (1986) 'Welfare and economic growth in Kenya, 1814–1976', *World Development*, 14(9): 1151–60.

Blackburn, R. (2006) 'Haiti, slavery and the age of democratic revolution', *William and Mary Quarterly*, 63(4): 643–74.

Bloom, D.E. and Sachs, J.D. (1998) 'Geography, demography and economic growth in Africa', *Brookings Papers on Economic Activity*, 2: 207–73.

Bolt, J. and Gardner, L. (forthcoming) 'How Africa shaped British colonial institutions: evidence from local taxation', *Journal of Economic History.*

Bolt, J. and Hillbom, E. (2016) 'Long-term trends in economic inequality: lessons from colonial Botswana, 1921–74', *Economic History Review*, 69(4): 1255–84.

Bolt, J. and van Zanden, J.L. (2014) 'The Maddison Project: collaborative research on historical national accounts', *Economic History Review*, 67(3): 617–51.

Boomgaard, P., Colombijn, F. and Henley, D. (eds.) (1998) *Paper landscapes: explorations in the environmental history of Indonesia*, Leiden: KITLV Press.

Booth, A. (2007a) 'Night watchman, extractive or developmental states? Some evidence from late colonial south-east Asia', *Economic History Review*, 60(2): 241–66.

Booth, A. (2007b) *Colonial Legacies: Economic and Social Development in East and Southeast Asia*, Hawai'i: University of Hawai'i Press.

Booth, A. (2008) 'West Africa and the Southeast Asian mirror: the historical origins of the post-1960 divergence', *Itinerario*, XXXII(3): 61–90.

Booth, A. (2012) 'Measuring living standards in different colonial systems: some evidence from South East Asia 1900–1942', *Modern Asian Studies*, 46(5): 1145–81.

Bourguignon, F. and Scott-Railton, T. (2015) *The globalization of inequality*, Princeton: Princeton University Press.

Bowden, S., Chiripanhura, B. and Mosley, P. (2008) 'Measuring and explaining poverty in six African countries: A long-period approach', *Journal of International Development*, 20(8): 1049–79.

Brennan, L., McDonald, J. and Shlomowitz (1994) 'The heights and economic well-being of north Indians under British rule', *Social Science History*, 43(4): 578–608.

Brereton, B. (2007) 'Contesting the past: narratives of Trinidad and Tobago history', *New West Indian Guide*, 81(3/4): 169–96.

Broadberry, S. and Gupta, B. (2015) 'Indian economic performance and living standards 1600–2000', in L. Chaudhary (ed), *A new economic history of colonial India*, London: Routledge, pp 15–32.

Broadberry, S. and Gardner, L. (2019) 'Economic growth in sub-Saharan Africa, 1885– 2008', LSE Economic History Working Papers 296.

Broadberry, S., Custodis, J. and Gupta, B. (2015) 'India and the great divergence: An Anglo-Indian comparison of GDP per capita, 1600–1871', *Explorations in Economic History*, 55: 58–75.

Broadberry, S., Guan, H. and Li, D.D. (2018) 'China, Europe, and the Great Divergence: A Study in Historical National Accounting, 980–1850', *The Journal of Economic History*, 78(4): 955–1000.

Brooks, G.E. (1975) 'Peanuts and colonialism: consequences of the commercialization of peanuts in West Africa, 1830–70', *Journal of African History*, 16(1): 29–54.

Brown, J. (1999) 'India', in J. Brown and W.R. Louis (eds), *The Oxford History of the British Empire, Volume IV: The Twentieth Century*, Oxford: Oxford University Press, pp 421–46.

Brown, K. (2006) 'Trees, forests and communities: some historiographical approaches to environmental history on Africa', *Area*, 35(4): 343–56.

Buelens, F. and Marysse, S. (2009) 'Returns on investments during the colonial era: the case of the Belgian Congo', *Economic History Review*, 62(S1): 135–66.

Burnard, T. (1996) 'European migration to Jamaica, 1655–1780', *William and Mary Quarterly*, 53(4): 769–96.

Butter, J.H. (1955) 'Problems of colonial financial policy', *East African Economics Review* 2: 24–38.

Cain, P. (2010) 'Was it worth having? The British Empire 1850–1950', *Revista de Historia Económica/Journal of Iberian and Latin American Economic History*, 16(1): 351–76.

Cain, P. and Hopkins, A.G. (1993) *British imperialism*, London: Longman.

Cappelli, G. and Baten, J. (2017) 'European trade, colonialism, and human capital accumulation in Senegal, Gambia and Western Mali, 1770–1900', *The Journal of Economic History*, 77(3): 920–51.

Carey-Jones, N.S. (2017) *Make way for the auditor: memoirs of a colonial civil servant Part 3 – British Honduras (Belize)*, Independently published.

Chang, S.-D. (1968) 'The Distribution and Occupations of Overseas Chinese,' *Geographical Review*, 58(1): 89–107.

Chapman, S.D. (1985) 'Rhodes and the city of London: another view of imperialism', *The Historical Journal*, 28(3): 647–66.

Chaudhary, L. (2015) 'Caste, colonialism and schooling: education in British India', in L. Chaudhary, B. Gupta, T. Roy and A. V. Swamy (eds), *A new economic history of colonial India*, London: Routledge, pp 161–78.

Chaudhary, L. and Garg, M. (2015) 'Does history matter? Colonial education investments in India', *Economic History Review*, 68(3): 937–61.

Chaudhary, L. and Swamy, A. (2017) 'Protecting the borrower: an experiment in colonial India', *Explorations in Economic History*, 65(1): 36–54.

Chaves, I., Engerman, S.L. and Robinson, J.A. (2014) 'Reinventing the wheel: the economic benefits of wheeled transportation in early colonial British West Africa', in E. Akyeampong, R.H. Bates, N. Nunn and J. Robinson (eds), *Africa's Development in Historical Perspective*, Cambridge: Cambridge University Press, pp 321–65.

Chelliah, R.J. (1971) 'Trends in taxation in developing countries', *IMF Staff Papers,* 18(2): 254–325.

Clarence-Smith, W.G. (1976) 'Slavery in coastal Southern Angola, 1875–1913', *Journal of Southern African Studies,* 2(2): 214–23.

Clarence-Smith, W.G. (1983) 'Business empires in equatorial Africa', *African Economic History,* 12(1): 3–11.

Cleary, M. (2005) 'Managing the forest in colonial Indochina, c. 1990–1940', *Modern Asian Studies,* 39(2): 257–83.

Cleveland, T. (2018) 'Feeding the aversion: agriculture and mining technology on Angola's colonial-era diamond mines, 1917–1975', *Agricultural History,* 92(3): 328–50.

Coatsworth, J.H. (2008) 'Inequality, institutions and economic growth in Latin America', *Journal of Latin American Studies,* 40(3): 545–69.

Cogneau, D., Dupraz, Y. and Mesple-Somps, S. (2018) 'Fiscal capacity and dualism in colonial states: the French Empire 1830–1962', Paris School of Economics Working Paper 27.

Collier, P. and Gunning, J.W. (1999) 'Explaining African economic performance', *Journal of Economic Literature,* XXXVII: 64–111.

Conte, C.A. (1999) 'Colonial science and ecological change: Tanzania's Mlalo Basin, 1888–1946', *Environmental History,* 4(2): 220–44.

Cooper, F. (1996) *Decolonization and African society: the labor question in French and British Africa,* Cambridge: Cambridge University Press.

Cooper, F. (2002) *Africa since 1940: The Past of the Present,* Cambridge: Cambridge University Press.

Cooper, F. (2005) *Colonialism in question: theory, knowledge, history,* Los Angeles: University of California Press.

Crosby, A. (1986) *Ecological imperialism: the biological expansion of Europe 900–1900,* Cambridge: Cambridge University Press.

D'Souza, R. (2006) 'Water in British India: the making of a "colonial hydrology"', *History Compass,* 4(4): 621–8.

Darwin, J. (2009) *The empire project: the rise and fall of the British world system,* Cambridge: Cambridge University Press.

Das Gupta, S. (2011) *Adivasis and the Raj: socio-economic transition of the Hos, 1820–1932,* Hyderabad: Orient Blackswan.

Das, P. (2011) 'Colonialism and the environment in India: railways and deforestation in 19th century Punjab', *Journal of Asian and African Studies,* 46(1): 38–53.

Davies, P.N. (1977) 'The impact of the expatriate shipping lines on the economic development of British West Africa', *Business History,* 19(1): 3–17.

Davis, D.K. (2007) *Resurrecting the granary of Rome: environmental history and French colonial expansion in North Africa,* Athens: Ohio University Press.

Davis, L.E. and Huttenback, R.A. (1986) *Mammon and the pursuit of empire: the political economy of British imperialism, 1860–1912*, Cambridge: Cambridge University Press.

de Haas, M. (2017) 'Measuring rural welfare in colonial Africa: did Uganda's smallholders thrive?', *Economic History Review*, 70(2): 605–31.

de Haas, M. and Frankema, E. (2018) 'Gender, ethnicity and unequal opportunity in colonial Uganda: European influences, African realities, and the pitfalls of parish register data', *Economic History Review*, 71(3): 965–94.

de Roo, B. (2016) 'Colonial taxation in Africa: a fiscal history of the Congo through the lens of customs (1886–1914)', PhD thesis, Ghent University.

de Roo, B. (2017) 'Taxation in the Congo Free State, an exceptional case? (1885–1908)', *Economic History of Developing Regions*, 32(2): 97–126.

De Vries, J. (2010) 'The limits of globalization in the early modern world', *Economic History Review*, 63(3): 710–33.

de Zwart, P. and van Zanden, J.L. (2015) 'Labor, wages and living standards in Java, 1680–1914', *European Review of Economic History*, 19: 215–34.

de Zwart, P. and van Zanden, J.L. (2018) *The origins of globalization: world trade in the making of the global economy, 1500–1800*, Cambridge: Cambridge University Press.

Deane, P. (1953) *Colonial Social Accounting*, Cambridge: Cambridge University Press.

Decker, S. (2005) 'Decolonising Barclays Bank DCO? Corporate Africanisation in Nigeria, 1945–69', *Journal of Imperial and Commonwealth History*, 33(3): 419–40.

Dell, M. and Olken, B.A. (2020) 'The development effects of the extractive colonial economy: the Dutch cultivation system in Java', *The Review of Economic Studies*, 87(1): 164–203.

Dincecco, M. (2011) *Political transformations and public finances: Europe, 1650–1913*, Cambridge: Cambridge University Press.

Donaldson, D. (2018) 'Railroads of the Raj: Estimating the impact of transportation infrastructure', *American Economic Review*, 108(4–5): 899–934.

Dormois, J.-P. and Crouzet, F. (1998) 'The significance of the French colonial empire for French economic development (1815–1960)', *Revista de Historia Económica/Journal of Iberian and Latin American Economic History*, 16(1): 323–49.

Drake, P.J. (1979) 'The economic development of British Malaya to 1914: an essay in historiography with some questions for historians', *Journal of Southeast Asian Studies*, 10(2): 262–90.

Dumett, R.E. (1983) 'African merchants of the Gold Coast 1860–1905: dynamics of indigenous entrepreneurship', *Comparative Studies in Society and History*, 25(4): 661–93.

Dumett, R.E. (1998) *El Dorado in West Africa: The gold-mining frontier, African labor and colonial capitalism in the Gold Coast, 1875–1900*, Athens, OH: Ohio University Press.

Dyson, T. (2018) *A population history of India: from the first modern people to the present day*, Oxford: Oxford University Press.

Easterly, W. and Levine, R. (2016) 'The European origins of economic development', *Journal of Economic Growth*, 21(3): 225–57.

Echenberg, M. (2002) *Black death, white medicine: bubonic plague and the politics of public health in colonial Senegal, 1914–1945*, Portsmouth, NH: Heinemann.

Edelstein, M. (1982) *Overseas investment in the age of high imperialism: the United Kingdom, 1850–1914*, New York: Columbia University Press.

Engerman, S.L. and Sokoloff, K.L. (2013) 'Five hundred years of European colonization: inequality and paths of development', in C. Lloyd, J. Metzer and R. Sutch (eds), *Settler economies in world history*, Leiden: Brill, pp 65–103.

Englebert, P. (2000a) 'Pre-colonial institutions, post-colonial states, and economic development in tropical Africa', *Political Research Quarterly*, 53(1): 7–36.

Englebert, P. (2000b) 'Solving the mystery of the AFRICA dummy', *World Development*, 28(10): 1821–35.

Epstein, S.R. (2000) *Freedom and growth: the rise of states and markets in Europe 1300–1750*, London: Routledge.

Federico, G. (1998) 'Italy's late and unprofitable forays into empire', *Revista de Historia Económica*, 16(1): 377–402.

Feinstein, C. (1997) 'The end of empire and the golden age', in P. Clarke and B. Supple (eds), *Understanding decline: perceptions and realities of British economic performance*, Cambridge: Cambridge University Press, pp 212–33.

Fenichel, A. and Huff, G. (1974) 'Colonialism and the economic system of an independent Burma', *Modern Asian Studies*, 9(3): 321–35.

Fenske, J. (2013) 'Does land abundance explain African institutions?', *Economic Journal*, 123(573): 1363–90.

Fenske, J. (2014) 'Ecology, trade and states in pre-colonial Africa', *Journal of the European Economics Association*, 12(3): 612–40.

Ferguson, N. (1999) *The house of Rothschild: the world's banker, 1849–1999*, New York: Viking.

Ferguson, N. and Schularick, M. (2006) 'The empire effect: the determinants of country risk in the first age of globalization, 1880–1913', *Journal of Economic History*, 66(2): 283–312.

Feyrer, J. and Sacerdote, B. (2009) 'Colonialism and modern income: islands as natural experiments', *Review of Economics and Statistics*, 9(12): 245–62.

Fibaek, M. and Green, E. (2019) 'Labour control and the establishment of profitable settler agriculture in colonial Kenya, c 1920–45', *Economic History of Developing Regions*, 34(1): 72–110.

Fieldhouse, D.K. (1994) *Merchant capital and economic decolonization: the United Africa Company 1929–1987*, Oxford: Clarendon Press.

Firmin-Sellers, K. (2000) 'Institutions, context and outcomes: explaining French and British rule in West Africa', *Comparative Politics*, 32(3): 253–72.

Flandreau, M. and Flores, J.H. (2009) 'Bonds and brands: foundations of sovereign debt markets, 1820–1830', *Journal of Economic History*, 69(3): 646–84.

Flint, J. (1983) 'Planned decolonization and its failure in British Africa', *African Affairs*, 82(328): 389–411.

Foldvari, P., van Leeuwen, V., Marks, D. and Gall, J. (2013) 'Indonesia regional welfare development, 1900–1990s: new anthropometric evidence', *Economics and Human Biology*, 11: 78–89.

Foray, J.L. (2013) 'A unified empire of equal parts: The Dutch Commonwealth schemes of the 1920s–40s', *The Journal of Imperial and Commonwealth History*, 41(2): 259–84.

Forbes Munro, J. (1976) *Africa and the international economy, 1800–1960: an introduction to the modern economic history of Africa south of the Sahara*, London: J.M. Dent.

Fourie, J. (2016) 'The data revolution in African economic history', *Journal of Interdisciplinary History*, 47(2): 193–212.

Fourie, J. and van Zanden, J.L. (2013) 'GDP in the Dutch Cape Colony: The national accounts of a slave-based society', *South African Journal of Economics*, 81(4): 467–90.

Frankel, S.H. (1938) *Capital investment in Africa: its course and effects*, Oxford: Oxford University Press.

Frankema, E. (2010a) 'Raising revenue in the British empire, 1870–1940: how 'extractive' were colonial taxes?', *Journal of Global History*, 5(3): 447–77.

Frankema, E. (2010b) 'The colonial roots of land inequality: geography, factor endowments, or institutions?', *Economic History Review*, 63(2): 418–51.

Frankema, E. (2011) 'Colonial taxation and government spending in British Africa, 1880–1940: Maximizing revenue or minimizing effort?', *Explorations in Economic History*, 48(1): 136–49.

Frankema, E. (2012) 'The origins of formal education in sub-Saharan Africa: was British rule more benign?', *European Review of Economic History*, 16(4): 335–55.

Frankema, E. (2015) 'The biogeographic roots of world inequality: animals, disease and human settlement patterns in Africa and the Americas before 1492', *World Development*, 70: 274–85.

Frankema, E. and van Waijenburg, M. (2012) 'Structural impediments to African growth? New evidence from real wages in British Africa, 1880–1965', *Journal of Economic History*, 72(4): 895–926.

Frankema, E. and van Waijenburg, M. (2014) 'Metropolitan blueprints of colonial taxation? Lessons from fiscal capacity building in British and French Africa, c. 1880–1940', *Journal of African History*, 55(3): 371–400.

Frankema, W. and Jerven, M. (2014) 'Writing history backwards or sideways: toward a consensus on African population 1850–2010', *Economic History Review* 67(4): 907–31.

Frankema, E., Green, E. and Hillbom, E. (2016) 'Endogenous processes of colonial settlement: the success and failure of European settler farming in sub-Saharan Africa', *Revista de Historia Económica/Journal of Iberian and Latin American Economic History*, 34(2): 237–65.

Frankema, E., Williamson, J. and Woltjer, P. (2018) 'An economic rationale for the West African scramble? The commercial transition and the commodity price boom of 1835–1885', *Journal of Economic History*, 78(1): 231–67.

Gadgil, M. and Guha, R. (1992) *This fissured land: an ecological history of India*, Berkeley and Los Angeles, CA: University of California Press.

Gallup, J.L., Meilinger, A.D. and Sachs, J.D. (1998) 'Geography and economic development', NBER Working Paper 6849.

Galor, O., Moav, O. and Vollrath, D. (2009) 'Inequality in landownership, the emergence of human-capital promoting institutions, and the Great Divergence', *Review of Economic Studies*, 76(1): 143–79.

Gardner, L. (2010) 'An unstable foundation: taxation and development in Kenya 1945–63', in D. Branch, N. Cheeseman and L. Gardner (eds), *Our turn to eat: politics in Kenya since 1950*. Berlin: Lit Verlag, pp 53–76.

Gardner, L. (2012) *Taxing colonial Africa: the political economy of British imperialism*, Oxford: Oxford University Press.

Gardner, L. (2013) 'The fiscal history of the Belgian Congo in comparative perspective', in F. Buelens and E. Frankema (eds.) *Colonial Exploitation and Economic Development: The Belgian Congo and the Netherlands Indies Compared*. London: Routledge, pp 130–52.

Gardner, L. (2015) 'The curious incident of the franc in the Gambia: exchange rate instability and imperial monetary systems in the 1920s', *Financial History Review*, 22: 291–314.

Gardner, L. (2017) 'Colonialism or supersanctions: sovereignty and debt in West Africa 1871–1914', *European Review of Economic History*, 21(3): 236–57.

Gardner, L.A. (2019) 'New colonies, old tools: building fiscal systems in east and central Africa', in E. Frankema and A. Booth, *Fiscal capacity in the colonial state in Asia and Africa, c. 1850–1960*, Cambridge: Cambridge University Press, pp 193–229.

Gargallo, E. (2009) 'A question of game or cattle? The fight against trypanosomiasis in Southern Rhodesia (1898–1914)', *Journal of Southern African Studies*, 35(3), 737–53.

Gerring, J., Ziblatt, D., Van Gorp, J. and Arevalo, J. (2011) 'An institutional theory of direct and indirect rule', *World Politics*, 63(3): 377–433.

Gertzel, C. (1962) 'Relations between African and European traders in the Niger Delta 1880–1896', *Journal of African History*, 3(2): 361–6.

Gilmartin, D. (2003) 'Water and waste: nature, productivity and colonialism in the Indus Basin', *Economic and Political Weekly*, 38(48): 5057–65.

Golub, S.S. and Mbaye, A.A. (2009) 'National trade policies and smuggling in Africa: the case of the Gambia and Senegal', *World Development*, 37(30): 595–606.

Good, K. (1974) 'Settler colonialism in Rhodesia', *African Affairs*, 73(290): 10–36.

Gorman, M. (1971) 'Sir William O'Shaughnessy, Lord Dalhousie and the establishment of the telegraph system in India', *Technology and Culture*, 12(4): 581–601.

Goscha, C.L. (2009) 'Widening the colonial encounter: Asian connections inside French Indochina during the Interwar Period', *Modern Asian Studies*, 43(5): 1189–228.

Goss, A. (2009) 'Decent colonialism? Pure science and colonial ideology in the Netherlands East Indies, 1910–1929', *Journal of Southeast Asian Studies*, 40(1): 187–214.

Grafe, R. and Irigoin, A. (2012) 'A stakeholder empire: the political economy of Spanish imperial rule in America', *Economic History Review*, 65(2): 609–51.

Grier, R.M. (1999) 'Colonial legacies and economic growth', *Public Choice*, 98: 317–335.

Grove, R.H. (1995) *Green imperialism: colonial expansion, tropical island edens and the origins of environmentalism, 1600–1860*, New York: Cambridge University Press.

Grove, R.H., Damodoran, V. and Sangwan, S. (1989) 'Introduction', in R.H. Grove, V. Damodoran and S. Sangwan (eds) *Nature and the Orient*, New Delhi: Oxford University Press, pp 1–28.

Guha, R. (1985) 'Scientific forestry and social change in Uttarakhand', *Economic and Political Weekly*, 20(45–47): 1939–52.

Guha, R. (1989) *The unquiet woods: ecological change and peasant resistance in the Himalaya*, New Delhi: Oxford University Press.

Guha, S. (2006) *Environment and ethnicity in India 1200–1991*, Cambridge: Cambridge University Press.

Guntupalli, A.M. and Baten, J. (2006) 'The development and inequality of heights in North, West and East India 1915–1944', *Explorations in Economic History*, 43: 578–608.

Gupta, B. and Swamy, A. (2017) 'Reputational consequences of labor coercion: evidence from Assam's tea plantations', *Journal of Development Economics*, 127(C): 431–9.

Hailey, M. (1942) *Native Administration in British Tropical Africa*, London: HMSO.

Håkansson, N.T., Widgren, M. and Borjeson, L. (2008) 'Introduction: historical and regional perspectives on landscape transformations in Northeastern Tanzania, 1850–2000', *International Journal of African Historical Studies*, 41(3): 369–82.

Hargreaves, J.D. (1956) 'The establishment of the Sierra Leone Protectorate and the Insurrection of 1898', *Cambridge Historical Journal* 12(1): 56–80.

Harris, C. (2004) 'How did colonialism dispossess? Comments from an edge of empire', *Annals of the Association of American Geographers*, 94(1): 165–82.

Harrison, M. (1994) *Public health in British India: Anglo-Indian preventative medicine, 1858–1914*, Cambridge: Cambridge University Press.

Hatton, T.J. and Williamson, J.G. (eds) (1994) *Migration and the international labor market, 1850–1939*, London and New York: Routledge.

Havinden, M. and Meredith, D. (1996) *Colonialism and development: Britain and its tropical colonies 1850–1960*, London: Routledge.

Headrick, R. (1994) *Colonialism, health and illness in French Equatorial Africa, 1885–1935*, Atlanta, GA: African Studies Association Press.

Heldring, L. and Robinson, J.A. (2012) 'Colonialism and economic development in Africa', NBER Working Paper 18566.

Helleiner, E. (2002) 'The monetary dimensions of colonialism: why did imperial powers create currency blocs?' *Geopolitics*, 7(1): 5–30.

Henderson, M. and Whatley, W. (2014) 'Pacification and gender in colonial Africa: evidence from the Ethnographic Atlas', MPRA Paper 61203.

Herbst, J.I. (2000) *States and power in Africa: comparative lessons in authority and control*, Princeton: Princeton University Press.

Herranz-Loncan, A. and Fourie, J. (2018) ' "For the public benefit?" Railways in the British Cape colony', *European Review of Economic History*, 22: 73–100.

Heston, A. (1983) 'National income', in D. Kumar and M. Desai (eds), *The Cambridge Economic History of India, Volume 2: c.1757–c.1970*, Cambridge: Cambridge University Press.

Heywood, L. and Thornton, J. (1988) 'African fiscal systems as sources for demographic history: the case of central Angola, 1799–1920', *Journal of African History*, 28(2): 119–40.

Hoag, H. (2013) *Developing the rivers of east and west Africa: an environmental history*, New York: Bloomsbury.

Hoffman, P.T. (2015) *Why did Europe conquer the world?* Princeton: Princeton University Press.

Hoffman, P.T. and Roy, T. (2021) 'Wars and empires', in S. Broadberry and K. Fukao (eds), *The Cambridge Economic History of the Modern World*, Cambridge: Cambridge University Press, forthcoming.

Hogendorn, J.S. (1978) *Nigerian groundnut exports: origins and early development*, Ibadan: Oxford University Press.

Hopkins, A.G. (1973) *An Economic History of West Africa*, London: Longman.

Hopkins, A.G. (1976) 'Imperial business in Africa, Part II: Interpretations', *Journal of African History*, 17(2): 267–90.

Hopkins, A.G. (1978) 'Innovation in a colonial context: African origins of the Nigerian cocoa farming industry, 1880-1920s', in C. Dewey and A.G. Hopkins (eds), *The imperial impact: studies in the economic history of Africa and India*, London: Athlone Press, pp 83–96.

Hopkins, A.G. (1987) 'Big business in African studies', *Journal of African History*, 28(2): 119–40.

Hopkins, A.G. (1988) 'Accounting for the British Empire', *Journal of Imperial and Commonwealth History* 16: 234–47.

Hopkins, A.G. (2008) 'Rethinking decolonization', *Past and Present*, 200(1): 211–47.

Huff, G. (1994) *The economic growth of Singapore: trade and development in the twentieth century*, Cambridge: Cambridge University Press.

Huff, W.G. (1993) 'The development of the rubber market in pre-World War II Singapore', *Journal of Southeast Asian Studies*, 24(2), 85–306.

Huff, W.G. (2003) 'Monetization and financial development in Southeast Asia before the Second World War', *Economic History Review* 56(2): 300–45.

Huillery, E. (2014) 'The black man's burden: the cost of colonization of French West Africa, *Journal of Economic History* 74(1): 1–38.

Hurd, J.M. (1983) 'Railways', in D. Kumar and M. Desai (eds), *The Cambridge Economic History of India*, Cambridge: Cambridge University Press, pp 737–61.

Iliffe, J. (2007) *Africans: The History of a Continent*, Cambridge: Cambridge University Press.

Institute for Commonwealth Studies (2013) 'Indirect rule – right or wrong?' A transcript of the proceedings of a seminar held on 29 March 2012, Occasional Paper of the OSPA Research Project 6.

Isaacman, A. and Isaacman, B. (1983) *Mozambique: from colonialism to revolution, 1900–1982*, Boulder, CO: Westview Press.

Iyer, L. (2010) 'Direct versus indirect colonial rule in India: long-term consequences', *Review of Economics and Statistics*, XCII(4): 693–713.

Jasanoff, M. (2012) *Liberty's exiles: the loss of America and the remaking of the British Empire*, London: HarperPress.

Jedwab, R. and Moradi, A. (2016) 'The permanent effects of transportation revolutions in poor countries: evidence from Africa', *Review of Economics and Statistics*, 98(2): 268–84.

Jedwab, R., Kerby, E., and Moradi, A. (2016) 'History, path dependence and development: evidence from colonial railways, settlers and cities in Kenya', *The Economic Journal*, 127(603): 1467–494.

Jedwab, R., Meier zu Selhausen, F. and Moradi, A. (2019) 'The economics of missionary expansion: evidence from Africa and implications for development', University of Sussex Economics Working Paper Series 10-2019, pp 1–43.

Jennings, E.T. (2014) *Free French Africa in World War II: The African Resistance*, Oxford: Oxford University Press.

Jones, F.S. (1998) 'Business imperialism and the imperial banks in South Africa', *South African Journal of Economics*, 66(1): 30–42.

Jones, G. (2002) *Merchants to multinational: British trading companies in the nineteenth and twentieth centuries*, Oxford and New York: Oxford University Press.

Kanda, S. (2010) 'Environmental changes, the emergence of a fuel market and the working conditions of salt makers in Bengal, c. 1780–1845', *International Review of Social History*, 55(S18): 123–51.

Karaman, K.K. and Pamuk, S. (2013) 'Different paths to the modern state in Europe: the interaction between warfare, economic structure, and political regime', *American Political Science Review*, 107(3): 603–26.

Keagy, T.J. (1972) 'The poor whites of Barbados', *Revista de Historia de America*, 73: 749–52.

Ken, W.L. (1979) 'Twentieth-century Malayan economic history: a select bibliographic survey', *Journal of Southeast Asian Studies*, 10(1): 1–24.

Kennedy, P. (1989) 'The costs and benefits of British imperialism 1846–1914', *Past and Present*, 125(1): 186–92.

Kesner, R.M. (1981) *Economic control and colonial development: crown colony financial management in the age of Joseph Chamberlain*, Westport, CT: Greenwood Press.

Kirk-Greene, A.H.M. (1980) 'The Thin White Line: The size of the British Colonial Service in Africa', *African Affairs*, 79(314): 25–44.

Klerman, D.M., Mahoney, P.G., Spamann, H. and Weinstein, M.I. (2011) 'Legal origin or colonial history?', *Journal of Legal Analysis*, 3(2): 379–409.

Knapman, B. (1985) 'Capitalism's economic impact in colonial Fiji, 1874–1939: development or underdevelopment?', *Journal of Pacific History*, 20(2): 66–83.

Krebs, P.M. (1999) *Gender, race and the writing of empire: public discourse and the Boer War*, Cambridge: Cambridge University Press.

Kulke, H. and Rothermund, D. (2004) *A history of India*, London: Routledge.

La Porta, R., Lopez-de-Silanes, F., Shleifer, A. and Vishny, R. (1999) 'The quality of government', *Journal of Law, Economics, and Organization*, 15(1), 222–79.

Laidlaw, Z. (2005) *Colonial connections, 1815–45: patronage, the information revolution and colonial government*, Manchester: Manchester University Press.

Lains, P. (1998) 'An account of the Portuguese African empire 1885–1975', *Revista de Historia Económica*, 16(1): 235–63.

Lal, B.V. (2012) *Intersections: history, memory, discipline*, Canberra: ANU Press.

Law, R. (2009) 'Introduction', in *From slave trade to 'legitimate commerce': the commercial transition in nineteenth-century West Africa*, Cambridge: Cambridge University Press, pp 1–31.

Lawal, O.A. (2010) 'From colonial reforms to decolonization: Britain and the transfer of power in Nigeria 1947–1960', *Journal of the Historical Society of Nigeria*, 19: 39–62.

Leunig, T. (2010) 'Social savings', *Journal of Economic Surveys*, 24(5): 775–800.

Lonsdale, J. and Berman, B. (1979) 'Coping with the contradictions: the development of the colonial state in Kenya, 1895–1914', *Journal of African History*, 20(4): 487–505.

Louis, W.R. (2006) *Ends of British Imperialism: the scramble for Empire, Suez and decolonization*, London: IB Tauris.

Louis, W.R. and Robinson, R. (1994) 'The imperialism of decolonization', *Journal of Imperial and Commonwealth History*, 22(3): 462–511.

Low, D.A. and Lonsdale, J.M. (1976) 'Introduction: Towards a new order 1945–63', in D.A. Low and A. Smith (eds), *Oxford History of East Africa*, Vol. 3 (Oxford, 1976).

Lowes, S. and Montero, E. (2018) 'The legacy of colonial medicine in Central Africa', CEPR Discussion Paper 12772.

Lugard, F.D. (1922) *The dual mandate in British tropical Africa*, London: W. Blackwood and Sons.

Lynn, M. (1989) 'From sail to steam: the impact of the steamship services on the British palm oil trade with West Africa, 1850–1890', *Journal of African History*, 30(3): 227–45.

Lynn, M. (1992) 'British business and the African trade: Richard and William King Ltd of Bristol and West Africa, 1833–1918', *Business History*, 34(4): 20–34.

Mackenzie, F. (1991) 'Political economy of the environment, gender and resistance under colonialism: Murang'a District, Kenya, 1910–1950', *Canadian Journal of African Studies*, 25(2): 226–56.

Mackenzie, J.M. (1988) *The empire of nature: hunting, conservation and British Imperialism*, Manchester and New York: Manchester University Press.

Macmillan, H. (2005) *An African trading empire: the story of Susman Brothers and Wulfsohn, 1901–2005*, London: I. B. Tauris.

Maddison, A. (2010) 'Statistics on world population, GDP and per capita GDP 1–2008 AD', Groningen Growth and Development Center (http://www.ggdc.net/maddison/oriindec.htm)

Madhavan, M.C. (1985) 'Indian emigrants: numbers, characteristics, and economic impact', *Population and Development Review*, 11(3): 457–81.

Magee, G. B., Greyling, L, and Verhoef, G. (2016) 'South Africa in the Australian mirror: per capita real GDP in the Cape Colony, Natal, Victoria and New South Wales, 1861–1909', *Economic History Review* 69(3): 893–914.

Mamdani, M. (1996) *Citizen and subject*, Princeton, NJ: Princeton University Press.

Mandala, E. C. (2018) 'The triumph of the peasant option and the parasitic cotton sector in Malawi, 1891 to 1995', in K. Hofmeester and P. de Zwart (eds), *Colonialism, institutional change and shifts in global labour relations*, Amsterdam: Amsterdam University Press, pp 173–203.

Manela, E. (2007) *The Wilsonian moment: self-determination and the international origins of anticolonial nationalism*, Oxford: Oxford University Press.

Mann, G. (2009) 'What was the 'Indigenat'? The 'empire of law' in French West Africa', *Journal of African History*, 50(3): 331–53.

Manning, P. (2004) *Slavery, colonialism and economic growth in Dahomey, 1640–1960*, Cambridge: Cambridge University Press.

Maravall Buckwalter, L. (2019) 'The impact of a 'colonizing river': colonial railways and the indigenous population in French Algeria at the turn of the century', *Economic History of Developing Regions*, 34(1): 16–47.

Markovits, C. (2003) *The global world of Indian merchants, 1750–1947: traders of sind from Bukhara to Panama*, Cambridge: Cambridge University Press.

Markovits, C. (2007) 'Structure and agency in the world of Asian commerce during the era of European colonial domination (c. 1750–1950)', *Journal of the Economic and Social History of the Orient*, 50(2/3): 106–23.

Martin, M. (2012) 'An economic history of the Hundi, 1858–1978', PhD thesis, London School of Economics.

McKeown, A. (2010) 'Chinese emigration in global context, 1850–1940', *Journal of Global History*, 5(1): 95–124.

McPhee, A. (1926) *The economic revolution in British West Africa*, London: Routledge.

Meier zu Selhausen, F., van Leeuwen, M.H.D. and Weisdorf, J. (2018) 'Social mobility among Christian Africans: evidence from Anglican marriage registers in Uganda, 1895–2011', *Economic History Review*, 71(4): 1291–321.

Meredith, D. (1988) 'The colonial office, British business interests and the reform of cocoa marketing in West Africa, 1937–1945', *Journal of African History*, 29(3): 285–300.

Metzer, J. and Engerman, S.L. (eds) (2004) *Land rights, ethno-nationality and sovereignty in history*, London: Routledge.

Michalopoulos, S. and Papaioannou, E. (2013) 'Pre-colonial ethnic institutions and contemporary African development', *Econometrica*, 81(1): 113–52.

Mitchener, K.J. and Weidenmier, M. (2008) 'Trade and empire', *Economic Journal*, 118(533): 1805–34.

Mokyr, J. (2004) *The gifts of Athena: historical origins of the knowledge economy*, Princeton, NJ: Princeton University Press.

Mollan, S. and Michie, R. (2012) 'The City of London as an international commercial and financial center since 1900', *Enterprise and Society*, 13(3): 538–87.

Moradi, A. (2008) 'Confronting colonial legacies – lessons from human development in Ghana and Kenya, 1880–2000', *Journal of International Development*, 20(8): 1107–21.

Moradi, A. (2009) 'Toward an objective account of nutrition and health in colonial Kenya: a study of stature in African army recruits and civilians 1880–1980', *Journal of Economic History*, 96(3): 720–55.

Morris, M.D. (1963) 'Towards a reinterpretation of nineteenth-century Indian economic history', *Journal of Economic History*, 23(4): 606–18.

Mosley, P. (1983) *The settler economies: studies in the economic history of Kenya and Southern Rhodesia 1900–1963*, Cambridge: Cambridge University Press.

Mukherjee, A. (2002) *Imperialism, nationalism and the making of the Indian capitalist class, 1920–1947*, New Delhi and Thousand Oaks: Sage Publications.

Musgrave, R. (1969) *Fiscal systems*, London: Yale University Press.

Naoroji, D. (1901) *Poverty and un-British rule in India*, London: S Sonnenschein.

Naseemullah, A. and Staniland, P. (2016) 'Indirect rule and varieties of governance', *Governance*, 29(1): 13–30.

Ndulu, B.J. (ed) (2007) *Political economy of economic growth in Africa*, Cambridge: Cambridge University Press.

Nkrumah, K. (1963) *Africa must unite*, New York: Frederick A. Praeger.

North, D.C. (1981) *Structure and Change in Economic History*, New York: Norton.

North, D.C. (1990) *Institutions, institutional change and economic performance*, Cambridge: Cambridge University Press.

North, D.C. and Thomas, R.P. (1973) *The rise of the western world: a new economic history*, New York: Cambridge University Press.

Nugent, P. (2004) *Africa since independence: a comparative history*, Basingstoke: Palgrave Macmillan.

Nunn, N. (2014) 'Gender and missionary influence in colonial Africa', in E. Akyeampong, R. H. Bates, N. Nunn and J.A. Robinson (eds), *Africa's development in historical perspective*, Cambridge: Cambridge University Press, pp 489–512.

Nyerere, J.K. (1974) *Man and Development*, Oxford: Oxford University Press.

O'Brien, P.K. (1988) 'The costs and benefits of British imperialism 1846–1914', *Past and Present*, 120(1): 163–200.

O'Brien, P.K. and Prados de la Escosura, L. (1999) 'Balance sheets for the acquisition, retention, and loss of European empires overseas', *Itinerario*, 23: 25–52.

Obstfeld, M. and Taylor, A.M. (2003) 'Sovereign risk, credibility and the gold standard: 1870–1913 versus 1925–31', *Economic Journal*, 113(487): 241–75.

Offer, A. (1993) 'The British Empire, 1870–1914: a waste of money?', *Economic History Review*, 46(2): 215–238.

Oonk, G. (2009) *The Karimjee Jivanjee family: merchant princes of East Africa 1800–2000*, Amsterdam: Pallas.

Osaghae, E.E. (1998) *Crippled giant: Nigeria since independence*, Bloomington: Indiana University Press.

Palen, M.-W. (2014) 'Adam Smith as advocate of empire, c. 1870–1932', *The Historical Journal*, 57(1): 179–98.

Pamuk, S. (1987) *The Ottoman Empire and European capitalism, 1820–1913: trade, investment and production*, Cambridge: Cambridge University Press.

Pearson, J.L. (2017) 'Defending empire at the United Nations: the politics of international colonial oversight in the end of decolonisation', *Journal of Imperial and Commonwealth History*, 45(3): 525–49.

Pearson, S.R. (1971) 'The economic imperialism of the Royal Niger Company', *Food Research Institute Studies,* 10(1): 1–20.

Peluso, N.L. (1991) 'The history of state forest management in colonial Java', *Forest and Conservation History*, 35(2): 65–75.

Peluso, N.L. and Vandergeest, P. (2011) 'Political ecologies of war and forests: Counterinsurgencies and the making of national natures', *Annals of the Association of American Geographers*, 101(3), 587–608.

Pepinsky, T.B. (2016) 'Colonial migration and the origins of governance: theory and evidence from Java', *Comparative Political Studies*, 49(9): 1201–37.

Perkins, W.T. (1981) *Constraint of empire: the United States and Caribbean interventions*, Westport, CT: Greenwood Press.

Pim, A. and Milligan, S. (1938) *Report of the Commission Appointed to Enquire into the Financial and Economic Position of Northern Rhodesia*, London: HMSO.

Po-yn Chung, S. (2003) 'Western law vs Asian customs: legal disputes on business practices in India, British Malaya and Hong Kong, 1850s–1930s', *Asia Europe Journal*, 1(4): 527–39.

Pollard, S. (1985) 'Capital exports, 1870–1914: harmful or beneficial?', *Economic History Review*, 38(4): 489–514.

la Porta, R., Lopez-de-Silanes, F. and Shleifer, A. (2008) 'The economic consequences of legal origins', *Journal of Economic Literature*, 46(2): 285–332.

Post, P. (2002) 'The Kwik Hoo Tong Trading Society of Samarang, Java: A Chinese business network in late colonial Asia', *Journal of Southeast Asian Studies*, 33(2): 279–96.

Prados de la Escosura, L. (2012) 'Output per head in pre-independence Africa: quantitative conjectures', *Economic History of Developing Regions* 27(2): 1–36.

Prados de la Escosura, L. (2015) 'World Human Development: 1870–2007', *Review of Income and Wealth*, 61(2): 220–47.

Rajan, S.R. (2006) *Modernizing nature: forestry and imperial eco-development, 1800–1950*, Oxford: Clarendon Press.

Rangarajan, M. and Sivaramakrishnan, K. (eds) (2012) *India's Environmental History*, Ranikhet: Permanent Black.

Rathbone, R. (1996) 'Defining Akyemfo: the construction of citizenship in Akyem Abuakwa, Ghana, 1700–1930', *Africa: Journal of the International African Institute* 66(4): 506–25.

Rathbone, R. (2008) 'Casting "the Kingdome into another mold": Ghana's troubled transition to independence', *The Round Table*, 97(398): 705–18.

Ravallion, M. (2018) 'Inequality and globalization: a review essay', *Journal of Economic Literature* 56(2): 620–42.

Ray, R. (1988) 'The Bazaar: changing structural characteristics of the indigenous section of the Indian economy before and after the Great Depression', *Indian Economic and Social History Review*, 25(3).

Ray, R. (1995) 'Asian capital in the age of European domination: the rise of the bazaar, 1800–1914', *Modern Asian Studies*, 29(3): 449–554.

Richens, P. (2009) 'The economic legacies of the "thin white line": indirect rule and the comparative development of sub-Saharan Africa', *African Economic History*, 37: 33–102.

Robbins, P. (1998) 'Nomadization in Rajasthan, India: migration, institutions, and economy', *Human Ecology*, 26(1): 87–112.

Rosenbaum, S. (1913) 'The trade of the British empire', *Journal of the Royal Statistical Society*, 76(8): 739–74.

Rothermund, D. (2006) *The Routledge Companion to Decolonization*, London: Routledge.

Roy, T. (2011) *The economic history of India, 1857–1947*, Oxford: Oxford University Press.

Roy, T. (2012) *Natural disasters and Indian history*, Delhi: Oxford University Press.

Roy, T. (2013) *An economic history of early modern India*, Abingdon: Routledge.

Roy, T. (2014) 'Geography or politics? Regional inequality in colonial India', *European Review of Economic History*, 18(3): 324–48.

Roy, T. (2016) 'The mutiny and the merchants', *Historical Journal*, 59(2): 393–416.

Roy, T. (2018*) A business history of India: Enterprise and the emergence of capitalism since 1700*, Cambridge: Cambridge University Press.

Roy, T. (2019) *How British Rule Changed India's Economy: The Paradox of the Raj*, London: Palgrave.

Roy, T. and Swamy, A.V. (2016) *Law and the economy in colonial India*, Chicago: University of Chicago Press.

Sahn, D.E. and Sarris, A. (1994) 'The evolution of states, markets and civil institutions in rural Africa', *Journal of Modern African Studies*, 32(2): 279–303.

Saravanan, V. (2001) 'Technological transformation and water conflicts in the Bhavani River Basin of Tamil Nadu, 1930–1970', *Environment and History*, 7(3): 289–334.

Schenk, C.R. (2008) 'Monetary institutions in newly independent countries: the experience of Malaya, Ghana and Nigeria in the 1950s', *Financial History Review*, 4(2): 181–98.

Schumpeter, J. (1954) 'The crisis of the tax state', in A.T. Peacock (ed), *International economic papers: translations prepared for the International Economic Association*, London, pp 5–38.

Seely, J. (1914) *The expansion of England: Two courses of lectures*, London: Macmillan.

Sen, A. (2001) *Development as Freedom*, Oxford: Oxford University Press.

Sengupta, N. (1980) 'The indigenous irrigation organisation in South Bihar', *Indian Economic and Social History Review*, 17(2): 157–87.

Sheriff, A. (1987) *Slaves, spices and ivory in Zanzibar*, London: James Currey.

Simson, R. (2019) 'Ethnic (in)equality in the public services of Kenya and Uganda', *African Affairs*, 118(470): 75–100.

Singh, C. (1998) *Natural premises: ecology and peasant life in the Western Hemalaya, 1800–1950*, Delhi: Oxford University Press.

Sivaramakrishnan, K. (2000) *Modern forests: statemaking and environmental change in colonial Eastern India*, Delhi: Oxford University Press.

Sivasubramonian, S. (2000) *The National Income of India in the Twentieth Century*, New Delhi: Oxford University Press.

Smith, W.D. (1974) 'The ideology of German colonialism, 1840–1906', *Journal of Modern History*, 46(4): 641–62.

Spear, T. (2003) 'Neo-traditionalism and the limits of invention in British colonial Africa', *Journal of African History*, 44(1): 3–27.

Stasavage, D. (2003) *The political economy of a common currency: the CFA franc zone since 1945*, Aldershot: Ashgate.

Stiansen, E. and Guyer, J.I. (eds) (1999) *Credit, currencies and culture: African financial institutions in historical perspective*, Stockholm: Nordiska Afrikainstitutet.

Stockwell, S. (2000) *The business of decolonization: British business strategies in the Gold Coast*, Oxford: Oxford University Press.

Stone, I. (1999) *The global export of British Capital: A statistical survey*, Houndmills: Macmillan.

Sunderland, D. (2013) *Financing the Raj: the City of London and colonial India, 1858–1940*, London: Boydell and Brewer.

Sunseri, T. (2003) 'Reinterpreting a colonial rebellion: forestry and social control in German East Africa, 1870–1915', *Environmental History*, 8(3): 430–51.

Swamy, A. (2015) 'Law and contract enforcement in colonial India', in B. Gupta, L. Chaudhary, T. Roy and A. Swamy (eds), *A new economic history of colonial India*, London: Routledge, pp 218–32.

Sweeney, S. (2009) 'Indian railroading: floating railway companies in the late nineteenth century', *Economic History Review*, 62(1): 57–79.

Szereszewski, R. (1965) *Structural changes in the economy of Ghana 1891–1911*, London: Weidenfeld and Nicolson.

Taylor, A.A. (2006) *An economic history of the Ashanti Goldfields Corporation, 1895–2004: Land, Labour, Capital and Enterprise*, London School of Economics.

Teera, J.M. and Hudson, J. (2004) 'Tax performance: a comparative study', *Journal of International Development*, 15: 785–802.

Thornton, A. P. (1999) 'The shaping of imperial history', in R. Winks, W. R. Louis and A. Low (eds), *The Oxford History of the British Empire, Volume V: Historiography*, Oxford: Oxford University Press, pp 612–34.

Tignor, R.L. (1976) *The colonial transformation of Kenya: the Kamba, Kikuyu and Maasai from 1900–1939*, Princeton: Princeton University Press.

Tignor, R.L. (1998) *Capitalism and nationalism and the end of empire: state and business in decolonizing Egypt, Nigeria and Kenya 1945–1963*, Princeton: Princeton University Press.

Tignor, R.L. (2007) 'The business firm in Africa', *Business History Review*, 81(1): 87–110.

Tomlinson, B.R. (1999) 'Economics and empire: the periphery and the imperial economy', in A. Porter and W.R. Louis (eds), *The Oxford History of the British Empire, Volume 3: The Nineteenth Century*, Oxford: Oxford University Press, pp 53–74.

Tooze, A. (2008) 'Trouble with numbers: statistics, politics, and history in the construction of Weimar's trade balance, 1918–1924', *American Historical Review*, 113(3): 678–700.

Tosh, J. (1980) 'The cash-crop revolution in tropical Africa: an agricultural reappraisal', *African Affairs*, 79(314): 79–94.

Toure, O. (1988) 'The pastoral environment of Northern Senegal', *Review of African Political Economy*, 42(32–39).

Treub, M.W.F. (1930) 'Dutch Rule in the East Indies', *Foreign Affairs*, 8(2): 248–59.

Trocki, C.A. (1999) *Opium, empire and the global political economy: a study of the Asian opium trade*, London: Routledge.

Trocki, C.A. (2002) 'Opium and the beginnings of Chinese capitalism in Southeast Asia', *Journal of Southeast Asian Studies*, 33(2): 297–314.

Uche, C.U. (1999) 'Foreign banks, Africans, and credit in colonial Nigeria, c. 1890–1912', *Economic History Review*, 52(4): 669–91.

United States Tariff Commission (1922) *Colonial Tariff Policies*. Washington DC: Government Publishing Office.

van der Eng, P. (1998) 'Exploring exploitation: the Netherlands and colonial Indonesia 1870–1940', *Revista de Historia Económica*, 16(1): 291–321.

van Leeuwen, B. and Földvári, P. (2017) 'The development of inequality and poverty in Indonesia, 1932–2008', *Bulletin of Indonesian Economic Studies*, 52(3): 379–402.

van Waijenburg, M. (2018) 'Financing the African colonial state: the revenue imperative and forced labor', *Journal of Economic History*, 78(1): 40–80.

Vandenbosch, A. (1930) 'A problem in Java: the Chinese in the Dutch East Indies', *Pacific Affairs*, 3(11): 1001–17.

Wallerstein, I. (1979) *The capitalist world economy*, Cambridge: Cambridge University Press.

Wantchekon, L. and Garcia-Ponce, O. (2013) 'Critical junctures: independence movements and democracy in Africa', CAGE Working Paper Series 173.

Wantchekon, L., Klašnja, M. and Novta, N. (2015) 'Education and human capital externalities: evidence from colonial Benin', *The Quarterly Journal of Economics*, 130(2): 703–57.

Wesseling, H.L. (1997) *Imperialism and colonialism: essays on the history of European expansion*, Westport, Conn: Greenwood.

White, N.J. (2011) 'Reconstructing Europe through rejuvenating Empire: the British, French and Dutch experiences compared', *Past and Present*, 210(S6): 211–236.

Winseck, D.R. and Pike, R.M. (2007) *Communication and empire: media, markets and globalization, 1860–1930*, Durham, NC: Duke University Press.

Woodberry, R.D. (2012) 'The missionary roots of liberal democracy', *American Political Science Review*, 106(2): 244–74.

Young, C. (1994) *The African colonial state in comparative perspective*, New Haven: Yale University Press.

Index

Printed and bound by CPI Group (UK) Ltd, Croydon, CR0 4YY

23/04/2025

14661025-0003